Eco-Networking for IoT

Designing Energy-Efficient Models to Enhance Network Performance

Dr. Divya Sharma
Dr. Bishwajeet Pandey

Apress®

Eco-Networking for IoT: Designing Energy-Efficient Models to Enhance Network Performance

Dr. Divya Sharma
Department of Computer Application,
Galgotias University,
Greater Noida, Uttar Pradesh, India

Dr. Bishwajeet Pandey
Department of Computer Application,
GL Bajaj Institute of Technology and Management,
Greater Noida, Uttar Pradesh, India

ISBN-13 (pbk): 979-8-8688-2316-9
ISBN-13 (electronic): 979-8-8688-2317-6
https://doi.org/10.1007/979-8-8688-2317-6

Managing Director, Apress Media LLC: Welmoed Spahr
Acquisitions Editor: Spandana Chatterjee
Development Editor: James Markham
Coordinating Editor: Gryffin Winkler
Copy Editor: Kezia Endsley

Cover designed by eStudioCalamar

Cover image by Freepik (www.freepik.com)

Distributed to the book trade worldwide by Springer Science+Business Media New York, 1 New York Plaza, New York, NY 10004. Phone 1-800-SPRINGER, fax (201) 348-4505, e-mail orders-ny@springer-sbm.com, or visit www.springeronline.com. Apress Media, LLC is a Delaware LLC and the sole member (owner) is Springer Science + Business Media Finance Inc (SSBM Finance Inc). SSBM Finance Inc is a **Delaware** corporation.

For information on translations, please e-mail booktranslations@springernature.com; for reprint, paperback, or audio rights, please e-mail bookpermissions@springernature.com.

Apress titles may be purchased in bulk for academic, corporate, or promotional use. eBook versions and licenses are also available for most titles. For more information, reference our Print and eBook Bulk Sales web page at http://www.apress.com/bulk-sales.

Any source code or other supplementary material referenced by the author in this book is available to readers on GitHub (https://github.com/Apress). For more detailed information, please visit https://www.apress.com/gp/services/source-code.

If disposing of this product, please recycle the paper

Table of Contents

About the Authors xv

About the Technical Reviewer xvii

Chapter 1: Introduction to IoT and Green Networking 1

Overview of IoT 5

Examples of IoT in Action 7

Cutting-edge Algorithms Used in IoT 8

The Importance of Networking in IoT 9

The Role of Networking in IoT 10

Network Challenges in IoT 11

Protocols in IoT 12

IoT Networking Technologies 13

Case Studies 14

Potential Future Directions 16

Zero Energy 16

Adaptive AI and ML 17

Wireless Charging 18

Intelligent Sleep Modes 18

Routing Schemes 19

Conclusion 20

Chapter 2: Foundational Concepts of Energy-Efficient Networking....21

Introduction....22

The Expanse of Networking Research....23

Increasing Energy Efficiency, Stability, and Dependability....26

Fog Computing....28

Fog Computing Characteristics....29

Literature Review....34

Virtual Network Embedding (VNE) in the Context of Energy-Efficient Networking....36

Energy-Efficient Approaches to Virtual Network Embedding....37

Power-Aware Node Mapping....38

Energy-Aware Link Mapping....38

Green Resource Allocation....38

Dynamic Network Adaptation....39

Network Function Virtualization (NFV) and Software-Defined Networking (SDN)....39

Energy-Efficient Routing Techniques in Wireless Networks....41

Minimum Energy Routing (MER)....42

Power-Aware Routing (PAR)....42

Energy-Aware Geographic Routing (EAGR)....42

Sleep-Wake Scheduling-Based Routing....43

Load-Balanced Energy Routing (LBER)....43

Opportunistic Routing (OR)....43

Multipath Energy-Efficient Routing....44

Cognitive Radio-Based Routing....44

AI-Driven Energy Optimization in Routing....45

Strategies for Achieving Energy-Efficient Networking....45

Adaptive Transmission....48

Network Virtualization....48

Energy-Aware Routing....49
Sleep and Wake Mechanisms....49
Green Cloud Computing....50
Cognitive Radio Networks (CRNs)....50
Device-to-Device (D2D) Communication....50
AI-Driven Energy Optimization....51
Distributed Artificial Intelligence in Green 6G Pervasive Edge Computing Communication Networks for Energy-Efficient IoT in Smart Industrial and Urban Environments....51
Challenges and Opportunities of Energy-Efficient Computing to Enable Sustainable Massive IoT Networks....53
IoT Network Proliferation....54
Battery Constraints of IoT Devices....54
Network Infrastructure Requirements....56
Computation and Data Processing Efficiency....57
Sustainable System Design....58
The Future of Energy-Efficient Wireless Networks....61
Discussion....63
Conclusion....64
Chapter 3: Energy Efficient IoT Architecture....67
IoT Energy Efficient Techniques....67
Energy Efficient IOT-Enabled Design and Implementation on FPGA....69
Energy Efficient IoT Design in Smart Cities....72
Energy Efficiency in IoT Agriculture....75
Energy Efficiency in Industrial IoT....76
Energy Efficient IoT in the 6G Era....78
Energy Efficiency in IoT Fog-Cloud Computing....79
Energy Efficiency in IoT Networks....81
Conclusion....82

Chapter 4: Hardware Optimization for IoT..83

Optimization of IoT Hardware Resources..84

Ultra Low Power Controllers..88

Power Optimized Communication Modules..90

Optimized AI on Edge..91

Memory and Storage Optimization..93

Security Optimization..94

IoT Middleware and OS..95

Future Scope..96

Conclusion..96

Chapter 5: Lower-Power Communication Protocols..99

Routing Requirements of Low-Power Networks and IoT Applications..100

Understanding Urban LLNs (U-LLNs)..101

Device Types in U-LLNs..102

Key Considerations for U-LLN Routing..104

LEACH (Low-Energy Adaptive Clustering Hierarchy) Protocol..106

Cluster-Based Communication vs. Traditional Routing..106

Working Mechanism of LEACH..107

Advantages of LEACH..109

Limitations of LEACH..111

Variants of LEACH..114

Applications of LEACH..115

Types of Low-Power Communication Protocols..116

Categorization Based on Range and Functionality..116

Applications of Low-Power Communication Protocols in the Real World..140

Advantages of Low-Power Communication Protocols..143

The Growing Importance of Low-Power Communication Protocols............147
Disadvantages of Low-Power Communication Protocols............147
Discussion............151
Conclusion............152
Chapter 6: Data Management Techniques in IoT Using API............153
Data Collection APIs............156
Data Filtering and Aggregation............158
Storage Management............159
Access Control and Security............160
Data Querying and Analytics............160
Interoperability and Integration............161
Conclusion............163
Chapter 7: AI-Based Power Management in IoT............167
The Need for Power Management in IoT............170
The Role of AI (ML&DL&FL) in Energy Optimization............172
Implementation in Real-World Applications............173
Conclusion............175
Chapter 8: Advanced IoT Network Design Using AMQP, MQTT, Ktor and Retrofit............177
AMQP in Advanced IoT Network Design............184
Role of MQTT in Advanced IoT Network Design............186
IoT Network Design for Water Supply System and NLP-Based Device Control............187
Conclusion............188
Future Scope............188

Chapter 9: Case Studies in Green IoT..189
Literature Review..191
Why Is Green IoT Important?...197
High-Energy Consumption in IoT Devices..198
E-Waste Generation from IoT Devices...199
Carbon Emissions from IoT Infrastructure..200
Finite Natural Resources and Raw Material Depletion.................................201
The Need for Sustainable Development in IoT 203
Core Concepts of Green IoT..204
Energy-Efficient IoT Architecture..205
Sustainable IoT Hardware 207
Renewable Energy Integration 208
Smart Energy Management..209
Low-Power Communication Protocols 210
Green Cloud Computing and Edge Computing..210
E-Waste Management 211
Applications of Green IoT 212
Smart Cities...213
Smart Agriculture 214
Healthcare 215
Smart Homes...216
Green Transportation 217
Industrial Automation and Manufacturing...218
Renewable Energy Management and Smart Grids.......................................219
Challenges and Future Trends of Green IoT 221
Challenges of Green IoT...221
Future Trends of Green IoT 224
Advantages of Green IoT 227

Energy Efficiency 227
Reduced Carbon Footprint 228
Cost Savings 228
Sustainable Manufacturing and Reduced E-Waste 229
Improved Environmental Monitoring and Conservation 229
Better Performance in Remote Areas 230
Regulatory Compliance and Corporate Responsibility 230
Disadvantages of Green IoT 230
High Initial Costs 231
Complexity in Implementation 232
Limited Power Supply in Certain Conditions 232
Security and Privacy Concerns 233
Limited Availability of Eco-Friendly Materials 233
Compatibility Issues with Legacy Systems 234
Potential Reduction in Performance 234
Case Studies on Modular and Recyclable IoT Devices 235
Case Study 1: Fairphone – A Modular Smartphone with IoT Capabilities 235
Case Study 2: Google's Project Ara – A Vision for Modular IoT Devices 236
Case Study 3: Circular Economy in Industrial IoT (IIoT) – Siemens' Sustainable Sensors 237
Case Study 4: Modular Smart Home Devices – IKEA's TRÅDFRI Smart Lighting 238
Reducing Energy Waste in IoT Supply Chains with Smart Contracts 239
How Smart Contracts Reduce Energy Waste in IoT Supply Chains 240
Case Studies on Smart Contracts in Energy-Efficient IoT Supply Chains 241
Challenges and Future Outlook 244
Green IoT for Disaster Management 244
The Role of Green IoT in Disaster Management 245
Case Studies on Green IoT in Disaster Management 247

Future Trends in Green IoT for Disaster Management 250

Quantum Computing and Green IoT: A Sustainable Technological Synergy 252

The Role of Quantum Computing in Green IoT 253

Applications of Quantum Computing in Green IoT 254

Challenges in Implementing Quantum Computing for Green IoT 257

Future Trends and Prospects 258

Future Opportunities in Green IoT 260

The Way Forward 263

Chapter 10: Future Trends in Energy Efficient IOT Networking 265

Introduction 266

Literature Review 267

Energy-Efficient and Sustainable IoT Solutions 272

Low-Power Wide-Area Networks (LPWANs) 275

Energy-Harvesting Technologies 276

Edge Computing for IoT 277

AI-Driven Power Management 279

Sleep Mode and Duty Cycling Mechanisms 281

Energy-Efficient Communication Protocols 282

Blockchain for Energy-Efficient IoT Security 284

Challenges Faced with Future Trends in Energy-Efficient IoT Networking 286

Power Consumption and Battery Life 288

Scalability and Network Management 289

Data Transmission and Processing Overhead 290

Standardization and Interoperability 291

Environmental Impact and Sustainable Energy Sources 292

Latency and Real-Time Processing 293

Advantages of Future Trends in Energy-Efficient IoT Networking 294

Extended Device Lifespan 296
Improved Network Efficiency 297
Enhanced Reliability and Stability 298
Reduced Environmental Impact 298
Increased Scalability of IoT Deployments 299
Better Performance in Remote and Harsh Environments 299
Optimized Resource Utilization 300
Secure and Low-Power Communication 300
Disadvantages of the Future Trends in Energy-Efficient IoT Networking 301
Limited Data Transmission and Processing Capabilities 304
High Initial Deployment Costs 305
Complexity in Network Management and Maintenance 305
Security Risks Due to Low-Power Constraints 306
Scalability Challenges in Large-Scale Deployments 306
Dependence on Environmental Conditions for Energy Harvesting 307
Limited Standardization and Compatibility Issues 308
Applications of Future Trends in Energy-Efficient IoT Networking 309
Smart Cities 310
Healthcare and Remote Patient Monitoring 310
Industrial Automation and Smart Manufacturing 311
Smart Agriculture and Precision Farming 311
Smart Energy Management and Power Grids 312
Environmental Monitoring and Disaster Management 313
Smart Transportation and Logistics 313
Home Automation and Smart Buildings 314
Wearable Technology and Personal IoT 314
Water Management and Smart Irrigation 315
Conclusion 316

Chapter 11: Security and Privacy in Green IoT Systems 317
Literature Review...321
Understanding Green IoT Systems...324
Key Applications of Green IoT..325
Notable Case Studies and Real-World Implementations.........................336
Case Study 1: Smart City Lighting Systems...336
Case Study 2: Renewable Energy-Powered Environmental Monitoring Sensors...338
Research Opportunities..340
Security in Green IoT Systems...343
Key Security Challenges...344
Security Requirements for Green IoT Systems.......................................348
Security Solutions for Green IoT Systems..350
Case Study: Smart Grids and Green IoT Security....................................354
Future Trends and Research Directions..354
Security Challenges in Green IoT Systems...355
Privacy in Green IoT Systems..356
Privacy Challenges in Green IoT Systems...358
Privacy Requirements for Green IoT Systems...360
Privacy-Preserving Techniques in Green IoT Systems..............................362
Privacy in Specific Green IoT Applications..363
Privacy Regulation Compliance...364
Future Directions and Research...365
Privacy Concerns in Green IoT Systems...366
Mitigation Strategies..367
Future Directions..375
Conclusion...378

Chapter 12: Scalable Solutions for Large-Scale IoT Networks.........381

Distributed Computing and Network Architectures..385

Scalable Data Handling and Analytics..386

Security, Privacy, and Trust...387

Conclusion 388

Future Scope...389

References...391

Index...425

About the Authors

Dr. Divya Sharma is an assistant professor of Computer Science & Engineering at the Galgotias University, Greater Noida, India.

Dr. Sharma has several research publications in reputed Scopus-indexed journals and international conferences in areas such as IoT, artificial intelligence, machine learning, and cybersecurity. She has also contributed book chapters in emerging technologies including AI and renewable energy prediction models. With experience in teaching, software development, and mentoring, she is passionate about integrating modern technologies into education and guiding students in research and innovation.

Aside from her academic duties, Dr. Sharma partners with industry professionals to translate theoretical research into practical solutions and advances IoT applications in the real world. Her publications have appeared in top journals, and she has presented her research at national and international conferences.

Dr. Sharma is keen to contribute to IoT and play a part in positively impacting the future of technology.

Dr. Bishwajeet Pandey is a professor at GL Bajaj Institute of Technology and Management, India. He has been a senior member of IEEE since 2019. He holds an MTech in computer science from IIIT, Gwalior, India, and a PhD in computer science from the Gran Sasso Science Institute, Italy. He has taught at esteemed institutions such as Chitkara University, Chandigarh; Jain University, Bangalore; Astana IT University, Kazakhstan; Eurasian National University, Kazakhstan (QS World Rank 321); Walsh College, USA; and UCSI University, Malaysia (QS World Rank 265). Dr. Pandey is a prolific researcher with over 30 published books and more than 240 research papers indexed in Scopus. He has garnered over 4,800 citations. His leadership roles include serving as the research head of the school of CSE at Jain University, Bangalore, from 2021 to 2023, and as the head of the International Global Academic Partnership Committee at Birla Institute of Applied Science, Bhimtal, from 2020 to 2021. In 2023, Dr. Pandey was honored with the prestigious Professor of the Year Award at Lord's Cricket Ground by the London Organization of Skills Development. Beyond his outstanding research output, his greatest strength lies in his global academic network. He has visited 49 countries, participated in 105 international conferences, and co-authored papers with 218 professors from 93 universities across 42 nations.

About the Technical Reviewer

Sultana Begum is a semiconductor product management expert and AI technology enthusiast with over 12 years of experience at Intel and Accenture. She is a quantum computing enthusiast with deep understanding of quantum mechanics and physics principles of Qubits. She is the lead author of the book *Competitive Semiconductor Product Management*. Sultana has held critical roles in technical product marketing and hardware and software product management and gained a broad and deep-rooted expertise in the semiconductor technology industry. With deep technical expertise and a keen eye for strategic thinking, her expertise spreads widely across semiconductor design development to define and execute a competitive product strategy, with hands-on experience launching multiple software and hardware products.

Sultana holds bachelor's and master's degrees in electronics, an MBA in product management, and a Stanford LEAD Executive Management Education from Stanford University.

CHAPTER 1

Introduction to IoT and Green Networking

The advancement of Internet of Things (IoT) technologies has transformed how devices talk to one another and has formed interlinked environments that permeate every facet of contemporary existence, spanning areas like healthcare, connected homes, automated industries, and modern farming. Nevertheless, the burgeoning expansion of IoT devices has also raised significant concerns regarding energy consumption, environmental sustainability, and the long-term viability of the actual systems.[2] This chapter examines the intersection of IoT and green networking, highlighting the importance of networking energy-efficient design in today's connected world.

It presents the idea of IoT, along with its components, architecture, and the significance of networking for inter-device communication. Green networking is a paradigm that attempts to use networking systems with the smallest environmental impact by optimizing energy consumption in network processes in order to reach this goal, thus setting the stage for a deep investigation of its paper.[1] This chapter illustrates how these domains can work together harmoniously, permitting IoT and green networking to address the urgent issues of the digital age.

The chapter also reveals the core concepts and methods for creating energy-efficient IoT solutions, from novel low-power communication techniques to adaptive protocols and sustainable hardware designs. It

Dr. D. Sharma and Dr. B. Pandey, *Eco-Networking for IoT*,
https://doi.org/10.1007/979-8-8688-2317-6_1

examines available case studies and real-world applications that show how green networking principles can be practically incorporated into IoT design and implementation, offering concrete illustrations of their possible effects on different industry sectors.

There is a blend of technical detail and broader context, and by the end of this chapter, you will have a sense of high-level benefits of both IoT and green networking. This journey is meaningful in and of itself, but also because it highlights the urgency of aligning these technological advances with environmental stewardship—a theme that runs through every topic in the digital transformation story.

IoT is not merely a technical development but a transformative concept; it is a domain-altering system of industries, societies, and human interactions. IoT allows everyday devices to connect effortlessly to the Internet, blending the physical and digital worlds to build smart systems that serve people more effectively. Be it wearables, autonomous vehicles, or industrial automation systems, these IoT applications have emerged as a foundation for contemporary innovation, enabling unmatched comfort, proficiency, and perspectives. An unprecedented, explosive growth of IoT devices has also led to important challenges, especially related to energy consumption and environment sustainability.

The globe is focusing more on environmental conservation and sustainable practices than ever, but coupled with that is the rise of the IoT. Globally, the use of IoT devices is on track to cross 29 billion by the year 2030, which has further highlighted concerns over the energy footprint of these systems. Because they are built for responsiveness, IoT devices often run around the clock, using power 24-7 to collect, send, and prepare data. To add to that, their energy demand compounds and continues to grow, emitting greenhouse gases and contributing to climate change when you consider the billions of devices around the globe. As such, energy efficiency is another top requirement for IoT development, both as a matter of cost and for global sustainability.

The Internet is generally described as a global system of interconnected computer networks that use TCP/IP communication protocols to link devices together.[1] Many of the technologies that make up the Internet have accumulated from decades of research and development in computer networking, communication systems, and information technology. This has allowed more and more devices to be connected and to talk using a local network, creating a much more connected world. Smart devices and intelligent objects, increasingly integrated into our daily lives, have given rise to this new networking paradigm. Over the past 50 years, the Internet has evolved from a small-scale system that initially linked just two computers into a global infrastructure that now connects millions, even billions, of physical smart devices.

One potential solution to the energy concern is green networking, which involves a set of technologies aimed at minimizing the environmental damage caused by communication and data networks. Green networking lessens power consumption without compromising performance—and sometimes it even enhances network performance—by adopting energy-efficient protocols, hardware, and algorithms. The integration of IoT with principles of green networking can give rise to smart and eco-friendly systems.

Significant progress in energy-aware routing protocols, for instance, can reduce power consumption in IoT networks, and the latest advancements in low-power wireless communication can also prolong device life and lower overall energy consumption in the IoT ecosystem.

The impact of IoT and green networking goes beyond technology, shaping all aspects of society and economy. In healthcare, IoT-enabled solutions like remote patient monitoring and telemedicine are transforming access to medical care, especially in underprivileged regions. Urban areas can optimize energy use, limit waste, and create healthier, more efficient living environments. Implementing green networking principles in such applications ensures that IoT benefits are not attained at the expense of environmental harm. See Figure 1-1.

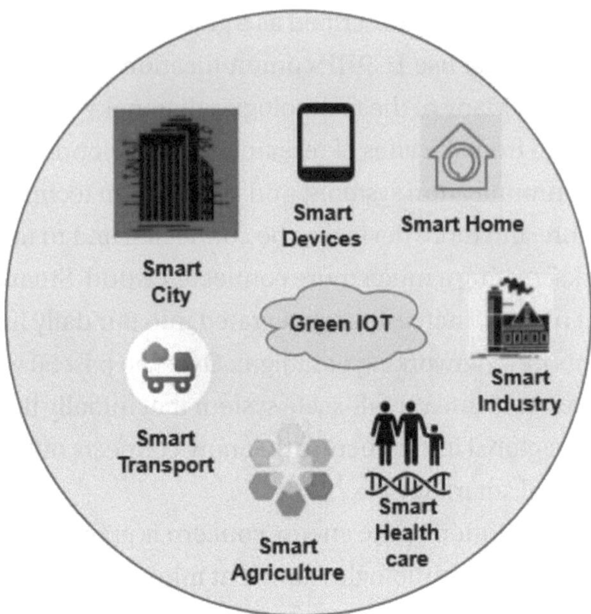

Figure 1-1. *Green IoT applications*

This chapter discusses the confluence of IoT and green networking, whereby energy-efficient architectures lead to sustainable networked systems. It starts with an in-depth introduction to IoT, along with its architecture, components, and applications. The chapter then discusses green networking principles for reducing energy consumption in IoT deployments. By combining real-life case studies, emerging technologies, and novel algorithms, this chapter presents a holistic perspective of the intersection of IoT and green networking.

This chapter sets the stage by explaining why energy-harvesting is vital to the future of IoT systems, the technologies enabling this transformative power, and what this signifies for the industry and the environment. Choosing a technology based on its effects on the environment is the larger theme of this book.

Note Implementing green networking in IoT systems will enable sustainability and will help the world achieve its environmental goals while addressing technological challenges. This chapter introduces the importance of this synergy, together with the potential of energy-efficient designs in facilitating a sustainable digital age.

Overview of IoT

IoT is a vast and ever-evolving ecosystem that thrives on connectivity, data sharing, and smart decision-making. IoT is defined by the integration of the physical and digital worlds to allow devices to sense, communicate, and act independently or semi-independently. Advancements in key technologies—including edge computing, artificial intelligence (AI), machine learning (ML), and 5G networking—have made this a reality.

Key components of IoT are illustrated in Figure 1-2 and listed here:

- **Devices and sensors:** The first step of IoT consists of embedded devices and sensors that extract real-time data from the environment. For example, temperature sensors within a smart thermostat detect environmental conditions and relay that information back to control heat or air conditioning accordingly.[3]
- **Connectivity:** To transfer data, IoT devices use a variety of communication protocols and networks, including Wi-Fi, Zigbee, Bluetooth Low Energy (BLE), and LoRaWAN. SoftBank and other Japanese telcos have launched 1Q15 Warlord5 as a commercial service, following up on the first commercial uses of this technology in IoT, including 5G.

- **Edge and cloud computing:** With edge computing, the ability to have devices process data near the source cuts down on latency and bandwidth requirements. In industrial IoT (IIoT), for example, edge devices process machine performance data on site, and only those insights that require action are transmitted to the cloud.
- **Data analytics and AI:** Advanced AI and ML algorithms are employed to analyze the vast amounts of data generated by IoT. This allows for predictive maintenance, anomaly detection, and decision-making. In smart agriculture, for instance, AI algorithmic models can help forecast weather trends, optimize irrigation schedules, and minimize resource waste.
- **Actuators and automation:** IoT devices have actuators that perform actions based on processed data. In a smart home, for instance, a motion detector can trigger lights or alerts as movement is detected.

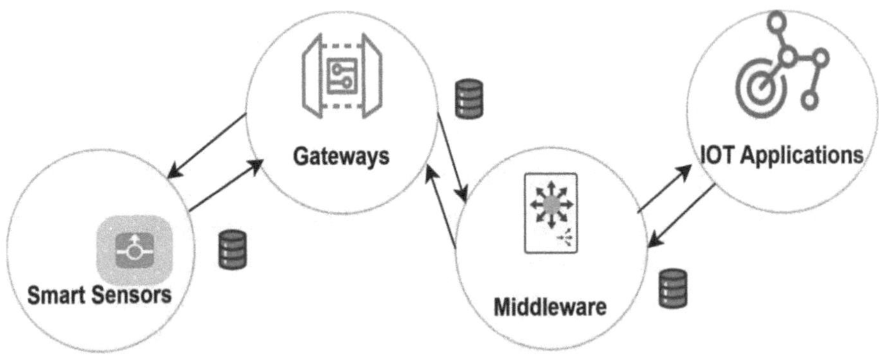

Figure 1-2. *Key components of IoT*

Examples of IoT in Action

- **Healthcare:** Wearable devices such as smartwatches and health trackers monitor real-time biometric parameters, including heart rate, blood pressure, and oxygen saturation. Such data may be analyzed and give tailored health suggestions, or alert medical professionals to emergencies.
- **Smart cities:** IoT is being used by cities to streamline traffic flow, manage waste, and create safer environments in cities across the globe. For example, Barcelona uses IoT sensors to track air quality, and smart parking systems help motorists find empty spaces.
- **Industry:** For example, in manufacturing, IoT-enabled predictive maintenance systems monitor data from machinery sensors to forecast potential failures. Random Forests or Support Vector Machines algorithms use pattern analysis to predictively schedule repairs with an aim reduce downtime.
- **Agriculture:** Precision farming combines IoT sensors, drones, and AI to monitor soil conditions, optimize water use, and boost crop yields. For instance, a combination of IoT soil sensors and reinforcement learning algorithms can analyze and determine optimal irrigation schedules, reducing excess water use while maintaining productivity.

Cutting-edge Algorithms Used in IoT

- **Federated learning:** Federated learning allows multiple IoT devices to build AI models in a peered manner, which compels devices to train the AI models without exposing raw data to the cloud. This helps with privacy conservation and lowers the volume of data that organizations transfer. It's becoming a common approach for applications such as personalized healthcare and home automation organizations.
- **TinyML:** TinyML refers to using machine learning models on constrained IoT devices. TinyML optimizes the algorithms for low power and for lower memory. It is changing the landscape of wearable devices, smart sensors, and remote monitoring.
- **Blockchain for IoT:** Blockchain offers secure and decentralized data management for IoT networks, satisfying the need to protect data integrity and privacy. This is especially powerful in supply chain management, where IoT sensors and blockchain have increased transparency and traceability.
- **Digital twins:** A digital twin is a digital replica of a physical asset that can be monitored and simulated in real time. Such technology is common in smart manufacturing, where IoT sensors respond to incoming data to digital twins to assess operations and forecast maintenance needs.

Connected devices continue to represent the future of technology, but the IoT ecosystem remains in a constant process of evolution, with innovations that combine connectivity, intelligence, and automation.[8]

As this synopsis shows, IoT is not just connecting machines; it's all about making intelligent sustainable systems that change sectors and improve lives. The subsequent sections of this chapter explore the role of green networking in reducing the environmental impact of IoT, presenting a comprehensive view of how we can construct a sustainable digital future.

The Importance of Networking in IoT

Networking lies at the heart of IoT—it is the point that allows communication between devices, data centers, and end users (see Figure 1-3). The interrelated nature of IoT depends on extremely strong and efficient networking in order to operate. Networking enables data transfer, serves as a unique interoperability platform connecting disparate equipment, and supports real-time decision-making processes. This section touches on the importance of networking in IoT and the technologies, protocols, and innovations that make it possible.

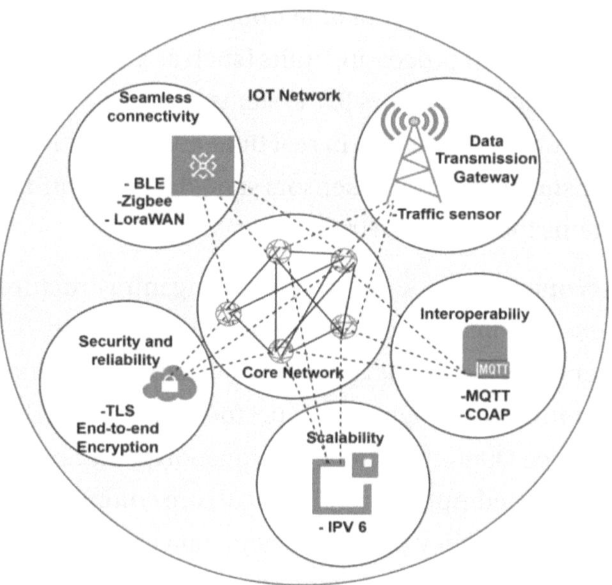

Figure 1-3. *The importance of IOT networking*

The Role of Networking in IoT

The network that forms part of an IoT architecture must allow necessary communication between the devices so that they can collect, process, and transfer data. We need this communication in order to develop intelligent systems that can automate work, optimize systems, and generate actionable insights.

- **Seamless connectivity:** Networking enables diverse protocols and standards such as Wi-Fi, Bluetooth Low Energy (BLE), Zigbee, LoRaWAN, and 5G to communicate between IoT devices, each designed for an individual use-case. A case in point is BLE, which is best suited for short-range interactions in the context of wearable technology, versus LoRaWAN, which is suitable for long-range, low-power conditions such as smart farming.
- **Data transmission:** Specifically, networking enables the real-time transfer of data from connected sensors and devices to processing units (such as gateways) and back again. This allows IoT systems to process and respond to information in real time. In smart cities, for instance, IoT traffic sensors send data to control systems that optimize traffic flow.
- **Interoperability**: A robust networking infrastructure is essential for ensuring seamless interoperability among diverse IoT devices and platforms. To facilitate communication, lightweight protocols such as MQTT (Message Queuing Telemetry Transport) and CoAP (Constrained Application Protocol) are commonly employed, as they enable efficient data exchange, even in devices with limited computational and energy resources.

- **Scalability:** Different networking architectures cater to this fast-growing segment of the IoT ecosystems. IPv6 and similar technologies provide for the connectivity of nearly limitless quantities of devices, meeting the scalability requirements of IoT.
- **Security and reliability:** Networking in IoT encompasses protocols that protect data integrity and maintain communication reliability. Communication in IoT involves sending and receiving data between devices, as well as to and from the cloud. Secure protocols such as TLS (Transport Layer Security) and end-to-end encryption are crucial for safeguarding sensitive information, including healthcare, financial, and industrial IoT information.[4]

Network Challenges in IoT

Table 1-1 explains some of the challenges with IoT and includes examples.

Table 1-1. *Network Challenges in IOT*

Challenge	Description	Example
Energy efficiency	IoT devices generally run on comparatively lower power sources, so low-energy networking protocols are required.	Integrating BLE or Zigbee with smart home sensors using battery power.
Scalability	Processing billions of devices and their data traffic can outscale traditional networking systems.	Expansion of IoT networks in smart cities to support thousands of sensors.

(continued)

Table 1-1. *(continued)*

Challenge	Description	Example
Interoperability	Diverse manufacturers and standards result in compatibility challenges in IoT ecosystems.	Devices with multiple protocols: Zigbee, Wi-Fi, and LoRaWAN.
Latency	Ultra-low latency for real-time application operation.	In the connective technology of autonomous vehicles through the use of 5G for immediate decision-making on the road.
Security	For user privacy and system security, secure communication and data transmission is necessary.	Advanced encryptions mechanism protecting IoT medical devices from cyberattacks.

Protocols in IoT

IoT data transfer relies on unique networking protocols. These protocols define how data is sent, routed, and interpreted between devices, as explained in Table 1-2.

Table 1-2. *Networking Protocols in IOT*

Protocol	Purpose	Example Use Case
Message Queuing Telemetry Transport (MQTT)	Lightweight messaging protocol for small devices.	Home automation and wearables.
Constrained Application Protocol (CoAP)	Optimized for low-powered devices.	Sensors for environmental monitoring.

(continued)

Table 1-2. (*continued*)

Protocol	Purpose	Example Use Case
HTTP/HTTPS	The Web of Things (WoT) is a standard web protocol for IoT applications.	Cloud-based applications and smart TVs.
Z-Wave	Secure communication of smart home devices.	Locks on doors, cameras, and lights.

IoT Networking Technologies

Networks of IoT devices use a variety of technologies customized to the use case. These technologies provide fast communication over different distances and data needs, as shown in Table 1-3.

Table 1-3. Networking Technologies in IOT

Technology	Description	Applications
Wi-Fi	Local Area Network (LAN): high-speed connectivity for devices in a local area.	Smart homes, video surveillance, personal devices.
Bluetooth Low Energy (BLE)	Low power, short-range network.	Wearable devices, medical tracking, and proximity-based systems.
LoRaWAN	Low-power, long-range communication for sparse networks.	Agriculture, environmental monitoring, and smart cities.

(*continued*)

Table 1-3. (*continued*)

Technology	Description	Applications
Zigbee	Ideal for IoT networks with many connected devices using low-power, short-range communication.	Smart meters, lighting controls, and home automation.
5G	Promises ultra-low latency and high-speed communication, allowing for real-time data sharing.	Self-driving cars, remote surgery, and factory automation.

Case Studies

- **LoRaWAN: The Future of Smart Agriculture**

  In the Netherlands, a large-scale farming operation mounted IoT-enabled soil moisture sensors connected using LoRaWAN to minimize irrigation. Because of the low-power, long-range capabilities of LoRaWAN, the sensors could be deployed in remote fields and transmit data to a centralized system. This system helped save water by 25%, improved crop yield, and reduced operational cost significantly.

- **Singapore: Smart Traffic Management**

  In Singapore, the Land Transport Authority has implemented a 5G-enabled IoT traffic management system, where real-time traffic data is gathered through road-embedded sensors and transmitted to cloud servers for analysis. AI algorithms are employed to process real-time data from a multitude of sources in order to help validate the changing traffic patterns and adjust the traffic signals in real time, thus minimizing congestion and travel time.

- **Healthcare Monitoring Using BLE:**

  A California hospital deployed Bluetooth Low Energy (BLE) devices for patient monitoring. Wearable devices continuously assess vital signs like heart rate and oxygen levels and send that information to a shared dashboard. (This has also added to patient comfort and care efficiency, as the low-power BLE protocol means that the devices last for days before requiring recharging.)

- **Industrial IoT in Smart Manufacturing:**

  A German automotive company leveraged IoT-enabled sensors and actuators in its conventional assembly lines for real-time data processing using edge computing and an industrial ethernet. The networking system promised low latency by calculating the robots and machinery to work in perfect time. As a result, it led to a 30% decrease in production downtime, enhanced quality control, and improved operational efficiency.

- **IoT Network Design for Wildlife Conservation:**

  An African wildlife conservation project used low-power IoT sensors and GPS trackers linked through a mesh network to monitor endangered species. It tracked animal movements and detected threats such as poaching with solar-powered devices. Satellite links transmitted data to conservationists, allowing them to intervene in real time. Even remote areas without robust networking infrastructures were continuously monitored.[7]

Potential Future Directions

Zero Energy

Another fundamental area of research are self-powering IoT devices via self-sustained power sources like solar, wind, and kinetic energy. This would use autonomous and sustainable IoT networks. One of the critical problems with IoT systems is how to replace or recharge the batteries. This method eliminates the problem entirely, due to self-sustaining energy. In the design of self-sustained IoT devices, an important aspect is choosing the suitable energy generation systems. The design of IoT devices should allow them to run independently, using straightforward energy-harvesting techniques that tap into resources from their environment, and then transform this into electrical energy that can directly power the IoT device. These include solar cells for harvesting sunlight, piezoelectric elements for turning vibrations into electricity, and miniature wind turbines for collecting wind energy. Apart from energy-harvesting methods, the design of IoT devices powered by self-sustaining sources must also account for the device's own energy consumption devices. These are generally energy-efficient ones to prolong the battery life. Power use is less of an issue when devices are supported by self-sufficient energy sources.

Conversely, investigating the benefits of energy storage approaches (battery/supercapacitor) or similar solutions whereby IoT devices do not require a continuous power supply has also been an active research avenue.[5] There are options in the market—batteries being one and supercapacitors being the other—to power IoT devices using energy storage solutions. Commonly used in many IoT devices because they are widely available, inexpensive, and have a high energy density, batteries store energy chemically. Unlike batteries, which store energy via ion exchange and have a lower energy density than their supercapacitor counterparts, supercapacitors store energy electrostatically, allowing for higher power densities and faster charge and discharge rates. One such consideration of using energy storage systems for an IoT device is the selection of an energy storage technology.

Adaptive AI and ML

The adoption of AI-enabled energy-management solutions, guided by machine learning, is opening new possibilities for improving how efficiently and sustainably IoT networks operate. With ongoing changes in usage, network conditions, and energy supply, algorithms can dynamically fine-tune and optimize how power is consumed. For example, AI-powered energy-management systems utilize machine learning algorithms to process and analyze data generated by IoT devices, such as usage patterns and energy consumption, to discover opportunities for energy optimization. External data, including weather conditions, energy prices, and so on, can also be fed into these systems to further optimize energy usage. The algorithms learn from the previous data and any future power use can be predicted so that energy use can be adjusted in real time.

AI-based energy-management systems can be used to optimize energy consumption in a smart home. These systems rely on data from sensors, smart devices, and energy storage units to monitor and optimize energy use in real time. They can, for example, regulate the temperature of a room depending on occupancy patterns, weather conditions, and the availability of energy. They can also help optimize energy storage charging to take advantage of low energy prices or greater availability of renewable energy. In addition to building energy management systems, AI-based energy management systems are also broadly used to optimize energy utilization in smart cities. These systems are capable of analyzing data from traffic patterns, sensors, and energy consumption to optimize energy usage as it happens. An example of how this can be done is fine-tuning traffic lights timing according to traffic flow, which will ultimately help ease traffic. They can also leverage energy storage assets to capture firm supplies of renewable energy whenever they are available.

Wireless Charging

Wireless charging is gaining popularity as it enables users to charge their devices without ports and cables. But conventional wireless charging methods do have certain limitations, foremost among which is that they are not very energy efficient. Experts are researching ways to increase wireless charging efficiency. Optimizing the power transfer between the charger and the device being charged is one way to improve the efficiency of wireless charging. By creating a specialized set of circuits with adjustable power transfer, we can scale up the charging process within the limits. One way to enhance the wireless-charging efficiency is by increasing the distance of the charge transfer. Resonant wireless charging technologies that can transfer power over a longer distance using magnetic resonance make this possible. This can charge all devices at once, which is perfect for charging in public places like airports and coffee shops. However, the adoption of such systems has been relatively slower due to the lower power transfer efficiency as the distance between transmitter and receiver increases.

Intelligent Sleep Modes

Intelligent sleep modes are a promising area for developing more efficient IoT devices. Intelligent sleep mode algorithms can make IoT devices more energy-saving without compromising their functionality. The principle of conserving power during sleep is based on substituting functions and parameters. A power-saving mode is a mode in which the operating voltage of the part decreases, the transmission frequency on the bus slows down, the power of the display decreases, and other parameters change. Intelligent sleep modes can use machine learning for predictions and optimize network use. For example, if it learns that the user uses the device during the day, it turns it off at night. Moreover, in the case of idle time, it uses deeper modes of falling asleep to maintain the charge for a long time. If the machine becomes denser, it will send fewer packets over the network, and if the machine becomes viable, in contrast, it can be off at idle in this way.[9] Some manufacturers aim to reduce energy consumption and develop intelligent sleep mode algorithms. For example, if the user's machine is running low on battery, the algorithm can block power-consuming functions and reduce the brightness of the screen. These algorithms can help balance energy saving and performance, thus ensuring longer operation on a single charge and increasing energy capacity.

Routing Schemes

The future of IoT networks is an important area of research. To be "smart," routing schemes must adaptively adjust routes based on actual network conditions, such as traffic patterns, delivery times, and energy availability. Traditional routing schemes commonly utilized in IoT networks tend to be static and do not adjust to the changing conditions of the network or energy resources, resulting in non-optimal network resource allocation as well as higher energy consumption.[6]

Routing schemes that dynamically adjust the way the packets travel (taking into account real-time data) to accommodate for factors such as network conditions, traffic patterns, and energy availability, are called "smart" routing schemes. Such mechanisms can be applied at different points of the network, from the sensor nodes to the edge devices and the gateways. When we consider energy at the sensor-node level, the energy usage of individual nodes can be adjusted dynamically, with “smart” routing schemes that take the energy availability or network conditions or both into account in determining the node's transmission power and, in some cases, frequency.

As an illustration, low-energy nodes may scale down their transmission power and frequency, and high-energy nodes may enhance their transmission power and frequency to improve the quality of network services. Smart routing schemes at the edge device and gateway level can be used to route data packets based on the network conditions and traffic patterns. Nodes with high energy levels or stronger connectivity help route the packet, thus avoiding packet loss and enhancing network efficiency.

Conclusion

IoT is no longer just a futuristic concept—it has become an integral part of how we live, work, and interact with the world around us. Yet, with this rapid adoption comes an undeniable responsibility: ensuring that the growth of IoT does not compromise the planet we depend on. This chapter has highlighted how the convergence of IoT and green networking is not only possible but essential. By embedding energy-efficient, sustainable, and environmentally-conscious practices into IoT systems, we move closer to building a digital ecosystem that serves people and the planet.

The case studies and emerging solutions discussed here illustrate a simple but powerful truth: innovation and sustainability are not opposing forces. Instead, they can be partners in shaping a future where technology empowers human progress without exhausting natural resources. From smart cities to healthcare, and agriculture to industry, every application of IoT can—and should—carry the imprint of environmental stewardship.

As we look ahead, the call is clear: researchers, engineers, policymakers, and end users must collaborate to make IoT not just smarter, but greener. The path forward lies in adaptive algorithms, renewable energy integration, and thoughtful network design that respect ecological limits while unlocking new possibilities. By doing this, we are not merely deploying connected devices; we are shaping a sustainable digital age where connectivity fuels progress responsibly.

CHAPTER 2

Foundational Concepts of Energy-Efficient Networking

The significance of energy-efficient networking extends far beyond economic and technical benefits—it is a critical component of green computing and a key factor in reducing the global carbon footprint of digital operations. By decreasing the energy demands of networking infrastructure, organizations can contribute to worldwide efforts aimed at mitigating climate change, promoting sustainable technological development, and creating a more energy-conscious digital future.

This chapter provides a comprehensive and in-depth exploration of the core concepts, challenges, and future directions of energy-efficient networking. It serves as an essential resource for researchers, engineers, IT professionals, and policymakers who are working to design and implement sustainable networking solutions that align with the increasing demand for high-performance, scalable, and environmentally responsible digital ecosystems.

Through detailed discussions, real-world applications, and insights into cutting-edge research, this chapter aims to bridge the gap between theoretical principles and practical implementations, empowering stakeholders to build the next generation of energy-efficient networks.

Dr. D. Sharma and Dr. B. Pandey, *Eco-Networking for IoT*,
https://doi.org/10.1007/979-8-8688-2317-6_2

Introduction

Energy-efficient networking plays a pivotal role in achieving sustainable digital transformation. Beyond its economic and technical advantages, it stands as a vital component of green computing and a key contributor to reducing the global carbon footprint of digital infrastructure. By optimizing energy use across networking systems, organizations can actively support global efforts to mitigate climate change and promote sustainable technological development.

This chapter explores the fundamental concepts, current challenges, and emerging trends in energy-efficient networking. It provides researchers, engineers, and policymakers with practical insights for designing scalable, high-performance, and environmentally responsible digital ecosystems.

The discussion is structured into the following key sections:

- **Foundations of energy-efficient networking:** Introduces the principles and driving factors behind energy-aware network design.
- **Technological approaches and architectures:** Examines the models, algorithms, and tools developed to improve network energy performance.
- **Applications and case studies:** Presents real-world examples of sustainable networking implementations.
- **Future directions and research opportunities:** Highlights ongoing innovations and potential pathways for greener networking infrastructure.

Through this structure, the chapter bridges the gap between theoretical understanding and practical implementation, empowering stakeholders to build the next generation of energy-efficient networks.

The Expanse of Networking Research

The field of networking research has started examining important issues about communication networks' energy efficiency. The TREND Network of Excellence was created by the European Commission as part of the FP7 initiative to unite the EU research community and bolster Europe's leadership in green networking. In order to produce energy-efficient, scalable, and sustainable networks, TREND brings together key European stakeholders, such as manufacturers, operators, and research centers, to objectively evaluate the energy consumption of present and future telecom infrastructures. The TREND initiative's main conclusions are presented in this article, which also ends with a roadmap detailing the next stages for business and academic research, regulatory bodies, and standardization. Specifically, quicker interfaces use less energy per bit than slower interfaces, but slower interfaces use less energy per throughput than faster interfaces when using ALR. Additionally, we observe that the energy/bit for existing technologies is the same at 1 Gbps and 10 Gbps, indicating that a smaller decrease in energy usage has not kept pace with the link rate rise.[1]

With wireless devices proliferating, wireless networks have become a worldwide information infrastructure and ubiquitous part of life. Nevertheless, this explosive growth has also resulted in a dramatic increase in data traffic and power consumption.

Therefore energy-efficient wireless networks have become an urgent and daunting problem in the big data era.[2] The task-processing capabilities of mobile edge and cloud computing were analyzed in the context of decentralized network control and power grid system monitoring.

Energy-efficient networking has emerged as a fundamental pillar of modern communication systems, addressing the pressing need to reduce power consumption, optimize resource allocation, and ensure the long-term sustainability of digital infrastructure. With the rapid expansion of global data traffic, fueled by the proliferation of cloud computing, IoT devices, 5G networks, and data-intensive applications, traditional networking architectures are struggling to keep pace. These legacy systems often suffer from inefficiencies that lead to excessive energy consumption, increased operational costs, and a growing environmental impact. The ever-increasing demand for faster, more reliable, and scalable networks has created an urgent need for innovative solutions that balance high-performance connectivity with energy conservation.

This chapter explores the foundational principles that drive energy-efficient networking and examines various techniques and strategies designed to enhance efficiency while maintaining robust network performance. Key concepts such as network virtualization, traffic-aware routing, dynamic resource allocation, and low-power hardware design are at the core of energy-efficient networking. By leveraging these approaches, network operators can reduce unnecessary energy consumption, improve system reliability, and ensure that network resources are utilized in the most efficient manner possible.

At the heart of energy-efficient networking lies a series of foundational concepts and strategies that optimize resource usage while maintaining the required levels of network performance, reliability, and scalability. One of the key components of energy-efficient networks is network virtualization, which enables the abstraction of physical network resources, allowing them to be dynamically allocated and managed based on demand. Virtualization technologies not only enhance resource management but also reduce the need for redundant infrastructure, making networks more flexible and efficient. By abstracting hardware functions, network virtualization allows multiple applications and services to coexist on shared resources, thus improving network utilization and reducing unnecessary energy consumption.

Another foundational principle is traffic-aware routing, which focuses on optimizing the flow of data across the network to minimize energy consumption. In traditional networks, data is often transmitted along fixed routes, regardless of the network's current load or efficiency. Traffic-aware routing, on the other hand, dynamically adjusts data paths in real time, based on factors such as network congestion, power consumption, and available bandwidth. This ensures that data is routed along the most energy-efficient paths, reducing the need for energy-intensive data transfers over long distances and preventing unnecessary strain on the network.

The concept of dynamic resource allocation plays an equally important role in energy-efficient networking. By monitoring real-time network demand and adjusting resource allocation accordingly, networks can avoid running excess infrastructure during periods of low traffic. Dynamic resource allocation uses algorithms that adjust computing and storage resources on the fly, ensuring that power is consumed only when and where it is needed. For example, when network traffic decreases, unnecessary servers can be powered down or put into low energy states, and when demand peaks, additional resources can be brought online to handle the load efficiently.

The design of low-power hardware is another key element of energy-efficient networks. Hardware components such as routers, switches, and data storage systems are often energy-intensive, contributing significantly to the overall energy footprint of a network. With advancements in hardware design, however, there is a growing emphasis on creating energy-efficient devices that consume less power while delivering the necessary performance. Innovations in low-power semiconductor technologies, energy-efficient processors, and power-saving protocols have made it possible to reduce the power consumption of these devices without compromising their functionality.

In addition to these core principles, this chapter highlights the transformative impact of emerging technologies that are redefining energy efficiency in networking. Software-defined networking (SDN) introduces centralized network management, enabling intelligent traffic control, automated resource provisioning, and enhanced energy-aware decision-making. Fog computing and edge computing play a crucial role in minimizing long-distance data transmissions by processing data closer to its source, significantly reducing bandwidth requirements and lowering overall power consumption. Energy-aware networking protocols and algorithms have also been developed to optimize power usage across both wired and wireless networks, allowing for dynamic adjustments in energy allocation based on real-time network demands.

Beyond technological innovations, the chapter discusses the importance of best practices in designing, implementing, and maintaining energy-efficient network architectures. Strategies such as intelligent data processing, power-aware infrastructure design, adaptive energy management, and network traffic optimization contribute to a more sustainable networking ecosystem. Organizations, data centers, and service providers are increasingly recognizing the value of integrating these energy-efficient solutions to not only reduce operational costs but also to meet regulatory standards for environmental sustainability and corporate social responsibility.

Increasing Energy Efficiency, Stability, and Dependability

From an academic experiment to a basic infrastructure for information access, knowledge sharing, e-commerce, and entertainment, telecommunication, and computer networks have grown to be an essential component of contemporary civilization. The way we live and work has changed dramatically since broadband Internet became widely available.

For example, before the Internet era, students could not find as much material online as they can now from trusted sources like the *Encyclopedia Britannica*. Online trip planning has grown so easy that many traditional travel businesses have found it difficult to remain in business. Furthermore, a far greater selection of films and TV shows is now readily available online than in conventional movie theatres or on television. As a result, many people around the world now consider having access to the Internet to be essential, to the extent that some organizations support adding it to the list of human rights and that addictions are starting to appear.[1]

Due to the quick spread of wireless devices, such as smartphones, smart meters, wireless sensors, unmanned vehicles, and drones, wireless networks have developed into a worldwide information infrastructure that can support a variety of applications in many different industries. *Big data* is the term used to describe the enormous increase in data volume brought about by this trend. The foundation of contemporary digital communication is provided by wireless networks, which facilitate smooth data interchange and enable real-time applications that propel technical and economic progress.[2]

Modern smartphones, for example, are no longer just communication tools but have evolved into powerful computing devices equipped with an array of advanced sensors. These include high-resolution cameras, microphones, accelerometers, GPS modules, gyroscopes, compasses, and ambient light sensors, making each smartphone a significant data generation point. As a result, vast amounts of data are continuously being produced, collected, and transmitted through wireless networks.

The exponential growth in data traffic is largely driven by various online and digital activities, including high-speed multimedia downloads, social media interactions, content sharing, e-commerce transactions, online gaming, entertainment streaming, behavioral tracking, health monitoring, distributed data storage, cloud computing services, and cloud-based radio access networks (C-RAN). This rapid expansion of data-intensive applications places an immense burden on wireless networks, demanding more bandwidth, lower latency, and higher processing power. As wireless communication infrastructure continues to evolve, there is a growing need for energy-efficient networking solutions that can support the increasing data demands while minimizing power consumption and reducing environmental impact.[3] Energy-efficient networking aims to optimize power consumption in communication systems while ensuring seamless data transmission, high performance, and reliability. To optimize the advantages of current hardware, virtual resources are dynamically mapped into actual hardware.[4] In 6G networks, energy-efficient methods are essential for storage and computing services based on fog nodes and IoT devices.[6] These networks optimize power consumption, resource usage, and energy efficiency while enabling the use of fog and edge devices to carry out computational activities. Smart automated devices and autonomous linked cars can use energy-saving strategies in 6G IoT networks based on fog computing to sustain ubiquitous connectivity in extended reality settings. The Internet of Energy cyber-physical systems are configured through the integration of physical energy resources, software-driven power networks, and distributed renewable energy resources. [7] The components of these systems, which include data processing infrastructure, intelligent measuring systems, energy transmission lines, software network nodes, real-time communication technologies, power grids, and control mechanisms, are dependent on power management. They facilitate distributed network intelligence, optimum power currents, and flexible energy control by utilizing smart meters, distributed energy sources, and sensors. Managing data processing energy, balancing energy production and consumption, and employing wireless communication technologies for distributed supply systems can all lead to increased energy efficiency, stability, and dependability.[8]

Fog Computing

The term *fog computing* was primarily coined by Cisco to describe and illustrate various IoT-related supporting applications.[9] An expansion of cloud computing, fog computing allows for a new class of applications and services by bringing cloud services closer to the ground. In addition to helping with traditional cloud computing, fog processing is offered to provide cloud-like services to nearby network edge devices.[10] IoT frameworks offer a wealth of useful data in a particular field that may be used in a variety of ways. In the various idleness-based services, the delay caused by transferring data to the cloud for processing and then back to the application is insufficient.[11] Sending large amounts of data to the cloud for processing, storage, and management would limit adaptability and slow down the system. Fog computing, on the other hand, is a decentralized computing model that delivers cloud-like services closer to network-edge devices. It complements the cloud by utilizing both edge resources and its infrastructure. At a fundamental level, this innovation processes IoT data locally using proximate clients or devices. This assists in overcoming major capacity, management, communication, coordination, and organization limitations.[12]

Fog Computing Characteristics

Fog computing adds capabilities to the cloud by making computation, storage, and network capacity closer to end devices at the edge of the network. It is particularly suitable for IoT environments, as it accommodates latency-sensitive and real-time applications. The following sections cover some of the key features of fog computing.

Low Latency

Fog nodes are strategically deployed near IoT devices and sensors at the network edge. This proximity allows data to be processed locally without the need to transmit it to distant cloud servers, which greatly reduces the communication delay. As a result, fog computing supports real-time processing and immediate responses, making it ideal for latency-sensitive applications like autonomous vehicles, industrial automation, smart healthcare systems, and augmented reality services.[12]

Enhanced Scalability

A scalable distributed infrastructure that can adapt dynamically to varying workloads and user needs is offered by fog computing. Multiple strategically located edge nodes enable this scalability through deployment. By performing processing and storage responsibilities locally, these edge nodes offload the burden from centralized cloud servers.

Fog computing efficiently manages the growing number of devices connected and the vast volumes of data generated by them as IoT networks continue to spread. Fog computing facilitates the seamless delivery of service and prevents system saturation by dynamically dividing up resources at the edge based on real-time conditions. Fog networks are a future-proof solution for IoT environmental settings due to their decentralized nature, which also allows them to scale without the need for significant changes to the existing infrastructure. This capacity to grow and evolve makes fog computing a vital building block for creating robust, large-scale networks.

Localized Data Processing

The capacity of fog computing to analyze data closer to its source is one of its main benefits. Fog nodes manage calculations locally at the network's edge rather than forwarding all data to remote cloud servers for analysis. Applications that need to make decisions in real time can respond more quickly as a result of the decreased bandwidth consumption and stress on central servers. For instance, traffic lights in a smart city can instantaneously adjust to changes in traffic conditions that are picked up by sensors. Similar to this, fog computing supports effective operations in industrial control systems by making decisions instantly based on sensor data.

Reduced Network Bandwidth

Fog computing moves computation and storage to the network's edge, enabling data processing and storage between endpoints and the traditional cloud. Some computational functions are carried out locally within fog computing, including redundancy elimination, data cleansing, processing, filtration, and extracting relevant information. Rather than sending all data via the Internet, only useful and critical information is relayed to the cloud. This strategy also saves network bandwidth and substantially eliminates the amount of data exchanged. Moreover, decisions are taken on fog nodes in place of conventional cloud for myriad applications, leading to an additional improvement in the efficiency of networks.[12]

Context Awareness

Fog nodes are context-aware, meaning they can interpret and respond to their physical and environmental surroundings. This includes factors such as geographic location, network conditions, and the operational status of connected devices. Context-awareness allows fog computing to deliver personalized and location-specific services. For example, in smart agriculture, fog nodes can adjust irrigation schedules based on soil moisture levels and weather forecasts. This adaptability improves service quality and system efficiency.

Data Security and Privacy

With major advantages in terms of data security and privacy, fog computing places host services close to end users. It uses encryption and isolation methods to instantly secure data. To protect sensitive information, fog nodes employ access control techniques, encryption policies, integrity checking, and isolation techniques.

Fog nodes also assist in minimizing the risks involved with system upgrades. Fog computing removes the need for *over-the-air technology* (OTA) firmware updates, which is different from standard remote updates, which are sometimes beset by inefficiencies and issues including firmware updates that result in lost connections. Only apps and algorithms require upgrades. Fog nodes decrease the attack surfaces as well as the data transmission distance. Fog nodes are able to offer more robust crypto processing than many smart devices that are internally supported since they are typically larger in terms of cost, power capacity, and physical size than scattered IoT devices. Compared to abnormally pressured IoT devices, fog nodes may be mechanically more resilient to destruction, illegal alterations, or outright burglary, making them more dependable.[12]

Energy Efficiency

Decentralized data processing in fog computing reduces the need for continuous data transmission to cloud data centers, which can be energy-intensive. By processing data locally, fog nodes consume less power and contribute to a more energy-efficient system architecture. This is particularly advantageous for battery-operated IoT devices, which benefit from reduced communication demands. In industrial environments, energy-efficient fog computing solutions help lower operational costs while maintaining productivity.

Mobility

Fog computing consists of an assortment of mobile devices, including vehicles, smartwatches, and smartphones, which continuously change positions in the end layer. However, other end devices such as traffic cameras do not move. Likewise, a fog node can be either mobile or act as a fixed platform for computing resources. Seamless interaction between fog computing and mobile nodes is required in fog environments. Further, mobile nodes directly communicate with each other without relaying data via the cloud or a base station. Rather, the enormous quantities of data coming from IoT are computed within intermediate or terminal devices, promoting effective mobile data analysis. Service delivery to an increased number of nodes is accelerated by this procedure.[12]

Interoperability and Flexibility

Fog computing environments are designed to be interoperable, supporting a wide range of hardware and software components. This ensures that various IoT devices, sensors, and network systems can work together seamlessly. The flexibility of fog computing allows it to accommodate various communication protocols and data formats, clarifying the integration of new devices and applications. This interoperability is complex for industries like smart manufacturing, where machines from several vendors need to communicate effectively.

Support for Latency-Critical Applications

Fog computing is ideal for applications that need immediate data processing and low latency. By computing locally, fog nodes provide instantaneous responses, which is essential to sustain the operational effectiveness in latency-sensitive applications. Fog computing is making our cities smarter, healthcare systems more responsive, and digital experiences smoother. In smart cities, it behaves as an intelligent security system by processing real-time video streams from surveillance cameras. Rather than simply capturing video, it can automatically recognize suspicious behavior and notify authorities, preventing things from occurring in the first place. In medicine, fog computing is a vigilant protector, always keeping an eye on patients' vital signs. If a person's heart rate accelerates or oxygen levels decrease, it can immediately notify physicians, providing prompt medical care when seconds count.

Even in entertainment, fog computing enhances AR and VR experiences by reducing lag and keeping interactions seamless. Whether you're exploring a virtual world or using augmented reality in real time, it processes data close to the user, making everything feel smooth and immersive. By bringing intelligence closer to where it's needed, fog computing is shaping a future where technology responds instantly, making our lives safer, healthier, and more connected.

Literature Review

Meo Michela, Esther Le Rouzic, Ruben Cuevas, and Carmen Guerrero (2014)[1] explored the challenges of designing energy-efficient networks. They emphasized the urgent need for power optimization strategies and introduced adaptive approaches to better manage energy consumption in communication networks. Fischer M.T., De Meer H., Beck M.T., and Hesselbach X. (2013)[2] conducted an in-depth study on virtual network embedding, analyzing ways to improve resource allocation and enhance the efficiency of network infrastructure. They examined resource-allocation techniques and presented novel methods to optimize network efficiency, highlighting dynamic resource mapping as a critical solution for energy conservation. Nonde, Leonard, Taisir El-Gorashi, and Jaafar Elmirghani (2014)[3] focused on energy-efficient cloud networks. Their research provided insights into the optimization of virtual network resources and proposed intelligent solutions for enhancing the energy efficiency of cloud infrastructures. Bi, S., Zhang, R., Ding, Z., and Cui, S. (2015)[4] addressed wireless communication challenges in the era of big data. They proposed data-driven frameworks and innovative communication techniques to minimize energy consumption while ensuring high network efficiency. Cao, Xianghui, et al. (2017)[5] surveyed energy-efficient solutions for wireless networks in the big data era. They analyzed scalable traffic management systems and discussed adaptive routing techniques to reduce energy use while enhancing data flow management. Malik, U.M., Javed, M.A., Zeadally, S., and ul Islam, S. (2022) [6] examined fog computing as a potential solution for achieving energy efficiency in 6G-enabled IoT systems. They identified trends and strategies for optimizing bandwidth usage and reducing energy consumption in large-scale IoT environments. Ghiasi, M., Wang, Z., Mehrandezh, M., Jalilian, S., and Ghadimi, N. (2023)[7] explored smart grids' evolution toward the Internet of Energy. They introduced a framework for leveraging fog computing and decentralized systems to support deep decarbonization and optimize energy management. Fernando, Xavier, and George Lăzăroiu (2024)[8] investigated energy-efficient solutions for industrial IoT systems in the context of green 6G networks. They proposed sustainable data communication techniques that reduce energy usage while maintaining industrial performance standards. Mahmud, R., Kotagiri, R., and Buyya, R. (2018)[9] provided a comprehensive taxonomy of fog computing. They highlighted its key applications and challenges, focusing on the potential to optimize latency, energy efficiency, and resource utilization in digital environments. Bonomi, F., Milito, R., Zhu, J., and Addepalli, S. (2012)[10] introduced the concept of fog computing, highlighting its significance in improving IoT operations. They emphasized the benefits of decentralized data processing, which helps minimize latency and enhance energy efficiency, making IoT systems more responsive and effective. Dastjerdi, A.V., and Buyya, R. (2016)[11] expanded on this idea by exploring practical ways to implement fog computing in IoT environments. They emphasized the importance of fog nodes, which enable local data processing and reduce the dependence on centralized cloud systems, leading to lower energy consumption and improved system performance. Kaur, Loveleen, and Rajbir Kaur (2021)[12] conducted a comprehensive survey on energy-efficient routing techniques in wireless sensor networks (WSNs). Their study focused on various routing strategies that incorporate fog computing to enhance resource management and optimize energy use in IoT applications. Alsharif, Mohammed H., et al. (2024)[13] carried out an extensive study on energy-efficient computing for large-scale IoT networks. Their research tackled key challenges such as communication bottlenecks and battery constraints while proposing innovative solutions to create more sustainable and energy-efficient IoT ecosystems.

Virtual Network Embedding (VNE) in the Context of Energy-Efficient Networking

The Virtual Network Embedding (VNE) problem involves mapping virtualized network resources onto a physical or substrate network in an efficient and optimal manner. This process is crucial for network virtualization, where multiple virtual networks (VNs) coexist over a shared physical infrastructure. In energy-efficient networking, VNE plays a key role in optimizing resource allocation to minimize energy consumption while maintaining high performance.

As described in "Virtual Network Embedding: A Survey," by Fischer, M. et al.[4], (VNRs) represent the requirements of virtual networks in terms of computational and communication resources. These requests specify node and link demands, such as processing power, memory, bandwidth, and latency requirements. Similarly, the substrate network, which provides the underlying infrastructure, is characterized by its available node and link resources (e.g., CPU capacity, bandwidth, and power consumption capabilities).[5]

To efficiently embed virtual networks onto the substrate network, demand-resource matching must be performed. This means ensuring that virtual network nodes and links are allocated to physical resources that can meet their requirements while optimizing for energy efficiency. The goal is to achieve complete embeddings, where all virtual nodes and links are successfully placed onto the physical network without exceeding capacity constraints or causing inefficient resource utilization.

Energy-Efficient Approaches to Virtual Network Embedding

In traditional VNE solutions, the primary focus is on maximizing resource utilization and network performance. However, in energy-efficient networking, VNE strategies must also minimize power consumption. Figure 2-1 represents various energy-efficient approaches to virtual network embedding. Several approaches can be used to achieve this, as discussed in the following sections.

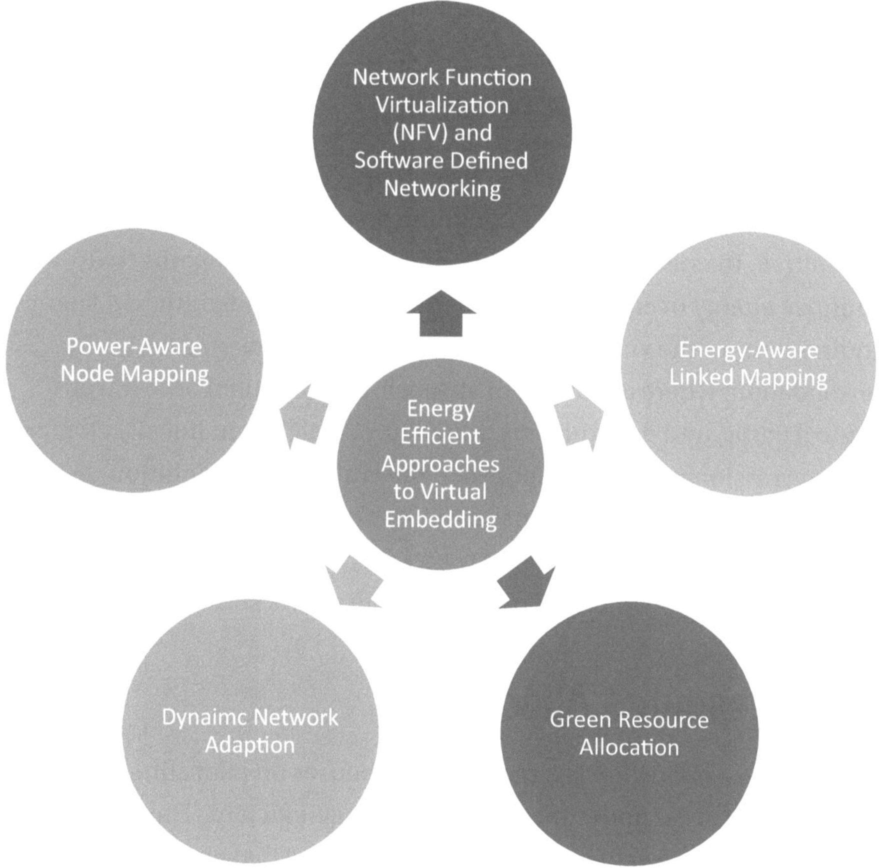

Figure 2-1. *Various energy-efficient approaches to virtual embedding*

Power-Aware Node Mapping

Power-aware node mapping is a fundamental approach to reducing energy consumption in VNE. Instead of distributing virtual nodes across a large number of physical nodes, energy-efficient VNE prioritizes consolidating virtual network resources (VNRs) onto fewer, more energy-efficient physical nodes. This consolidation allows unused network components to be put into low-power or sleep modes, significantly reducing the overall power consumption of the network. By optimizing the placement of virtual nodes and minimizing the activation of physical nodes, this technique ensures that energy is only used when and where it is necessary.

Energy-Aware Link Mapping

Network links, which are responsible for data transmission, consume a significant amount of power depending on the volume of data being transmitted. In energy-efficient VNE, the goal is to select paths that minimize energy overhead while still meeting the bandwidth and latency requirements of the virtual network requests. Methods such as traffic consolidation, where a number of virtual links are routed onto fewer physical paths, and dynamic link adaptation, which dynamically changes the transmission power in response to the current load condition, minimize energy-intensive transmissions. Through optimizing virtual link routing and using energy-efficient routes, VNE can minimize the network's energy consumption, particularly under high-traffic conditions.

Green Resource Allocation

Green resource allocation is a method that focuses on allocating virtual network requests to nodes that are more energy-efficient. These are nodes that use renewable energy sources or nodes that are fitted with low-power hardware. By taking real-time energy information, including power consumption statistics and environmental conditions, into account, virtual resources can be dynamically mapped to the most energy-efficient part of the network. This practice not only saves energy expenses but also promotes green practices by making sure that virtual networks are operating on cleaner, greener inputs.

Dynamic Network Adaptation

Dynamic network adaptation leverages machine learning and AI methods to forecast network traffic behaviors and dynamically respond by allocating resources. Using historical information and trends, AI-based systems can look ahead and forecast times of high and low demand and dynamically reallocate the activation and deactivation of network elements accordingly. This involves on-demand resource allocation, in which elements are activated only when needed, and powering down idle network components during low-demand hours. Through the adjustment of the network's configuration to suit usage patterns, dynamic network adaptation balances performance and energy usage so that energy is saved during low-demand hours but high performance is achieved during peak hours.

Network Function Virtualization (NFV) and Software-Defined Networking (SDN)

The combination of *network function virtualization* (NFV) and *software-defined networking* (SDN) provides a boost in energy efficiency to VNE through the decoupling of network functions from hardware devices and centralized network resource control.

- NFV allows network functions to be instantiated virtually and run on general-purpose servers instead of specialized hardware. This decoupling allows for efficient scaling and resource optimization since network functions can be dynamically assigned to resources depending on demand, eliminating the need for underutilized hardware and conserving energy.
- SDN, however, provides for centralized management of network traffic, allowing for smart rerouting of data across energy-efficient paths. By dynamically adapting routing decisions in accordance with real-time energy measurements, SDN optimizes the use of resources so that data travels through the most energy-efficient paths. Additionally, the capacity of SDN to quickly change network configurations in reaction to shifting traffic patterns guarantees that energy is being used efficiently at all times.

Energy-efficient VNE solutions provide a comprehensive framework for minimizing power consumption in contemporary networks. With methods such as power-aware node mapping, energy-aware link mapping, green resource allocation, dynamic network adaptation, and NFV-SDN integration, VNE can play a significant role in the sustainability of networks. These practices, aside from reducing energy expenses, also serve to minimize the carbon footprint of network infrastructures. With data and connectivity demands escalating, these energy-efficient measures will be paramount in ensuring network performance while being environmentally responsible.

Energy-Efficient Routing Techniques in Wireless Networks

Energy-efficient routing is one of the central features of modern networking, and especially in wireless networks, the power usage translates directly into how battery-powered equipment, network lifetimes, and system sustainability improve. Conventional routing protocols target throughput and latency maximization, but energy-aware routing intends to minimize energy usage while maintaining connectivity and responsiveness.

Figure 2-2 represents various energy-efficient routing techniques, as discussed in the following sections.

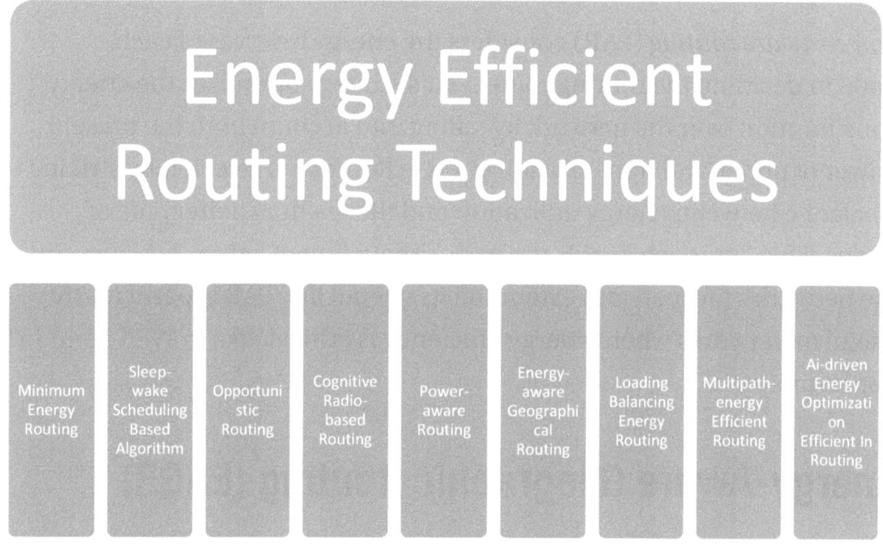

Figure 2-2. *Energy-efficient routing techniques*

Minimum Energy Routing (MER)

Minimum energy routing (MER) is a method aimed at minimizing the overall energy expenditure in data transmission. This method chooses paths that use the minimum amount of energy by taking into account factors like transmission power, relay nodes, and node-to-node interference levels. Through the optimization of these parameters, MER makes data packets travel through the most energy-efficient path, thus minimizing the power used for communication. MER is especially suited for wireless sensor networks (WSNs) and mobile ad hoc networks (MANETs), where the nodes tend to run on batteries.

Power-Aware Routing (PAR)

Power-aware routing (PAR) considers the energy reserves of each node in deciding the routing routes. This strategy optimizes the energy consumption over the network by taking into account both the present power of nodes and transmission energy. Routes are selected by striking a balance between energy utilization and the residual battery life of nodes. This approach avoids the early exhaustion of key nodes, ensuring the network's lifespan and extending its overall life. PAR is particularly useful in networks where energy efficiency is critical, like in WSNs and IoT deployments.

Energy-Aware Geographic Routing (EAGR)

Energy-aware geographic routing (EAGR) applies geographic location information to make routing decisions that are energy-efficient. In EAGR, the nodes decide on the next hop by considering their distance from the destination as well as their residual energy. This is done such that packets of data are relayed by nodes that are not only near the destination but also have enough energy to carry out the task. EAGR works very well in situations where location awareness is important, such as in WSNs and IoT networks, where devices tend to be mobile or geographically dispersed over a wide area.

Sleep-Wake Scheduling-Based Routing

Sleep-wake scheduling-based routing conserves energy by enabling idle nodes to go into low-power or sleep states when not engaged in data transmission. Nodes wake up periodically to monitor for incoming data before going back to sleep mode if no data is found. This method is especially useful in wireless sensor networks with periodic data transmission, like environmental monitoring systems.

By limiting the duration of active mode, sleep-wake scheduling reduces unnecessary energy consumption and improves the energy efficiency of the network.

Load-Balanced Energy Routing (LBER)

Load-balanced energy routing (LBER) emphasizes the distribution of data packets equally across more than one path available instead of depending on a single path. This avoids overloading any node to spend huge amounts of energy, causing bottlenecks and premature exhaustion of resources. By distributing the load of traffic across several paths, LBER assists in prolonging the lifetime of the network and promoting fairer energy consumption. This method is particularly beneficial in high-scale wireless sensor networks (WSNs) and IoT infrastructures, where effective resource allocation is very important in ensuring performance.

Opportunistic Routing (OR)

Opportunistic routing (OR) is a dynamic routing technique that doesn't pre-assign a fixed route for data transport. Rather, OR selects the most energy-efficient forwarding node in real time based on current network conditions (e.g., traffic loading, node energies, and channel qualities). This results in less retransmission and sensitivity to changing network topologies and greater overall energy efficiency. By opportunistically making routing decisions, OR ensures that energy is conserved, particularly in networks where nodes keep changing positions or the topology of the network keeps changing, as in the case of mobile ad hoc networks (MANETs).

Multipath Energy-Efficient Routing

Multipath energy-efficient routing leverages multiple paths of transmission to share the energy load more evenly throughout the network. Through redundant paths, this method decreases power consumption per node and increases network reliability since it offers backup paths in the event of node failure or congestion. In situations where nodes are subject to power drain, such as in MANETs and mesh networks, multipath routing provides a compromise between energy efficiency and fault tolerance, making the network more sustainable and resilient.

Cognitive Radio-Based Routing

Cognitive radio networks (CRNs) adjust available spectrum resources in real time to maximize transmission and minimize interference. *Cognitive radio-based routing* optimizes energy utilization by picking the best frequency bands for transmission, thus reducing congestion and interference. Through crowded channel avoidance, cognitive radio systems ensure that data is sent with as little energy as possible. This method is especially valuable in next-generation wireless communications, including 5G and 6G, where the effective utilization of the spectrum is paramount in terms of supporting high data rates without excessive power consumption.

AI-Driven Energy Optimization in Routing

Machine learning (ML) and AI algorithms can potentially transform energy-efficient routing by analyzing traffic patterns, network status, and battery levels to make optimal routing decisions. These AI-based methods rely on real-time data to modify the routes dynamically based on multiple parameters, such as energy usage, network load, and environmental factors. This adaptive, energy-conscious routing is especially useful in intricate, large-scale systems like smart cities, industrial IoT networks, and autonomous vehicles, where continuous optimization is required to guarantee energy savings without compromising performance.

Energy-efficient routing methods are of prime importance in diminishing the energy used by wireless networks without compromising performance, reliability, and scalability. Wireless networks can be made more sustainable and increase the operational life of battery-operated devices with the help of strategies like minimum energy routing, power-aware routing, energy-aware geographic routing, and sleep-wake scheduling. In addition, methods such as multipath routing, opportunistic routing, and AI-driven optimization help networks become more adaptive, robust, and energy-efficient. With wireless technology advancing, these routing techniques will remain integral in solving the energy issues of contemporary communication systems.

Strategies for Achieving Energy-Efficient Networking

Energy-efficient networking calls for a multi-faceted solution comprising hardware-level optimizations, smart network management, and sophisticated protocols. Energy-aware routing methods, wherein network routes are selected according to energy expenditure factors instead of performance or reliability, are one key strategy (see Figure 2-3). Dynamic voltage and frequency scaling can reduce power consumption by adjusting the operating frequencies of devices according to changing loads within the network. Low-power routers and switches are instances of power-saving hardware that must be implemented.

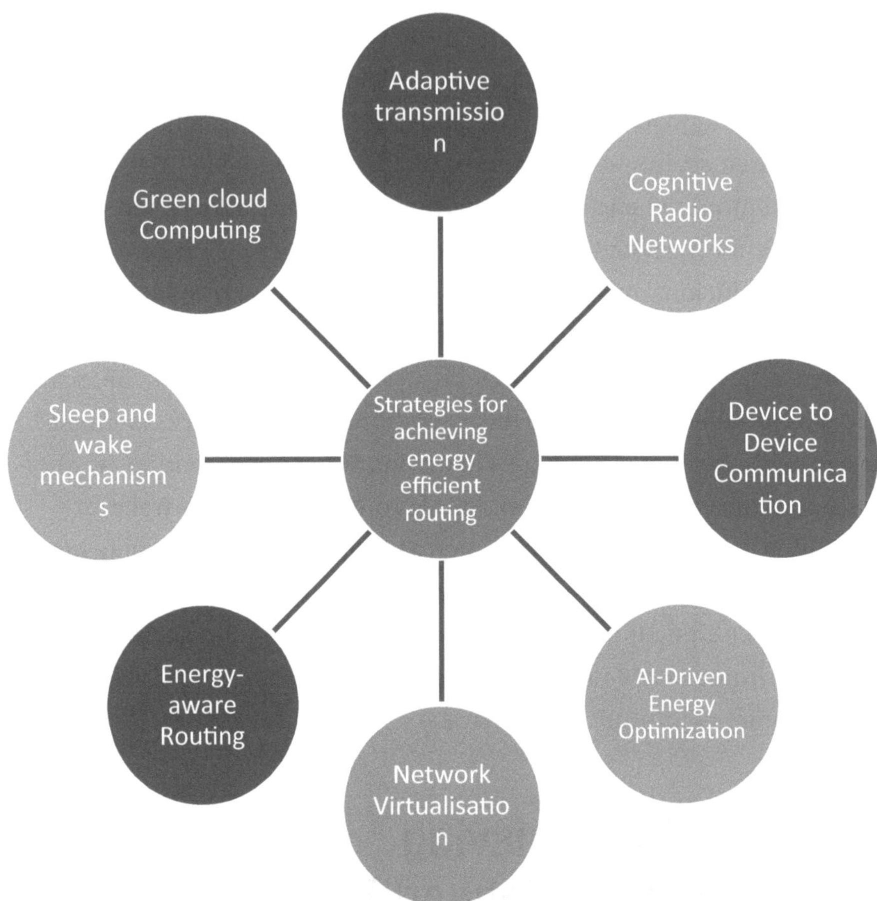

Figure 2-3. *Strategies for achieving energy-efficient routing*

Sleep modes for idle devices also help in cutting down energy use when there is minimal network usage. Virtualization technologies, which consolidate many network operations into fewer physical devices, also help save energy. By using machine learning methods on the software side, traffic patterns can be predicted and resources may be dynamically allocated to maximize energy efficiency without sacrificing performance. To promote sustainability, network infrastructure can be powered by renewable energy sources. When combined, these tactics provide a well-rounded strategy for lowering networking's carbon footprint without sacrificing operational effectiveness.

SDN and NFV are two technologies that network operators can investigate to further improve energy-efficient networking. By separating network control from the underlying hardware, these technologies allow for centralized management and dynamic reconfiguration of network resources in response to real-time demand.

This allows for more granular control over energy usage, as resources can be dynamically scaled up or down depending on network traffic.

Another emerging approach is the deployment of edge computing, which brings data processing closer to the data source. By reducing the need to transmit large volumes of data over long distances to centralized data centers, edge computing not only reduces latency but also conserves energy by minimizing the power consumed in data transmission.

As communication networks continue to evolve and expand, the demand for energy-efficient solutions has become increasingly critical to ensure sustainability and reduce operational costs. Achieving energy efficiency in these networks requires a multipronged approach that involves a combination of innovative techniques and technologies. From adaptive transmission techniques that dynamically optimize important parameters such as transmission power and data rates, to network virtualization, energy-aware routing, and sleep-wake strategies that maximize resource utilization, there are a number of approaches geared towards enhancing energy efficiency. Also, newer technologies like green cloud computing, cognitive radio networks, device-to-device communication, and AI-based energy optimization are further revolutionizing the scene. These strategies not only minimize energy consumption but also contribute to building more sustainable and efficient communication environments, ensuring that networks can support the growing demands of modern users while reducing their environmental impact.

Adaptive Transmission

Adaptive transmission is a powerful technique that helps communication networks operate more efficiently by intelligently adjusting key parameters like transmission power, bandwidth allocation, and data rates. It continuously responds to real-time network conditions and user demands, ensuring optimal performance while conserving energy. By fine-tuning transmission power based on actual communication needs, networks can avoid unnecessary energy waste and reduce operational costs. Similarly, smart bandwidth allocation ensures that resources are used effectively, providing seamless connectivity for various services. Adjusting data rates to match current network conditions not only improves communication performance but also cuts down on energy consumption. Overall, adaptive transmission enhances system efficiency, supports sustainable operations, and plays a vital role in creating a more energy-conscious and eco-friendly communication environment.

Network Virtualization

The use of virtualization in networking, powered by technologies like SDN and NFV, has caused a major shift in how communication resources are managed. By separating physical hardware from network operations, virtualization enables more flexible and efficient resource sharing, making networks more scalable and adaptable. This approach reduces dependence on traditional hardware, allowing virtual network functions to be easily deployed, updated, and adjusted as needed. With the ability to dynamically reconfigure networks, resources are used more efficiently, redundancies are minimized, and energy consumption is reduced. As a result, virtualization not only boosts network performance but also supports more sustainable and eco-friendly operations.

Energy-Aware Routing

Traditional routing methods are mainly focused on improving network performance by minimizing delays and maximizing data transfer speeds. However, energy-aware routing takes a more sustainable approach by using smart algorithms that prioritize energy efficiency while ensuring reliable connectivity. These algorithms analyze different routing options and choose the most energy-efficient paths, helping to extend the battery life of connected devices and reduce overall power consumption across the network. By optimizing energy usage, this approach not only enhances the longevity of network infrastructure but also contributes to building greener and more sustainable communication systems.

Sleep and Wake Mechanisms

One of the biggest sources of energy waste in communication networks comes from networking components running at full capacity even when they aren't actively transmitting data. To tackle this issue, energy-efficient sleep and wake mechanisms have been introduced. These techniques allow nodes, routers, and base stations to switch to low-power or idle modes during periods of inactivity and then resume full operation when needed. By reducing unnecessary energy consumption, sleep and wake mechanisms significantly enhance energy efficiency, especially in wireless sensor networks and mobile communication systems. This not only conserves power but also extends the lifespan of network infrastructure while maintaining smooth and reliable performance.

Green Cloud Computing

With the growing reliance on cloud computing and distributed storage systems, the need for energy-efficient data center operations has become more important than ever. Green cloud computing focuses on minimizing energy waste while still delivering high performance. This is achieved by incorporating renewable energy sources, enhancing cooling systems, and implementing smart workload-balancing techniques. These efforts not only reduce the carbon footprint of data centers but also make cloud services more sustainable and cost-effective. By striking a balance between environmental responsibility and operational efficiency, green cloud computing paves the way for a more eco-friendly and efficient digital future.

Cognitive Radio Networks (CRNs)

Cognitive radio technology represents a major leap forward in wireless communication, allowing networks to intelligently sense and adapt to available spectrum in real time. By detecting and utilizing unused frequency bands, *cognitive radio networks* (CRNs) help improve spectrum efficiency, ease network congestion, and optimize power usage. This smart adaptability not only enhances the overall performance of wireless networks, but also contributes to building more sustainable and energy-efficient communication systems.

Device-to-Device (D2D) Communication

Device-to-device (D2D) communication is revolutionizing how data is exchanged within networks. By enabling direct communication between nearby devices without relying on central base stations, D2D significantly cuts down transmission distance and conserves energy. This approach not only enhances network efficiency but also ensures faster, more reliable connections. As a vital component of modern network architectures like 5G and beyond, D2D communication plays a key role in optimizing resources and supporting energy-efficient, high-performance communication systems.

AI-Driven Energy Optimization

The integration of AI and ML into wireless networks is transforming the way energy consumption is managed. With the ability to analyze network conditions in real time and predict traffic patterns, AI-powered algorithms can intelligently allocate resources where they are needed most. This smart decision-making helps reduce power consumption without sacrificing performance. By making networks more adaptive and efficient, AI-driven energy optimization is paving the way for a future of smarter, more sustainable communication systems.

Distributed Artificial Intelligence in Green 6G Pervasive Edge Computing Communication Networks for Energy-Efficient IoT in Smart Industrial and Urban Environments

The arrival of sixth-generation (6G) networks is transforming communication by integrating advanced technologies like pervasive edge computing and distributed AI.[6] These innovations are especially important for improving energy efficiency in smart cities and industrial IoT environments, where massive amounts of data need to be processed efficiently. One of the biggest challenges with these settings is managing resources effectively while keeping energy consumption low.

To tackle this, intelligent energy-aware resource management plays a key role. By strategically distributing computing and storage tasks across IoT, fog, and edge nodes, networks can minimize energy use and reduce delays. A major technique in this approach is task offloading, where complex operations are shifted from small, energy-limited devices to more powerful fog and edge nodes. This not only lightens the energy load on individual devices but also enhances overall system performance, making networks faster and more efficient.

The integration of distributed AI with 6G networks further enhances energy efficiency by enabling intelligent, real-time resource management. AI-driven algorithms can predict network conditions, optimize task allocation, and determine the most energy-efficient data processing paths. This distributed approach, wherein decision-making occurs at the edge of the network rather than relying on distant cloud systems, reduces energy-intensive communication and latency, contributing to a more sustainable network operation. By processing data closer to the source, edge computing not only minimizes energy consumption associated with long-range data transmission but also enables faster decision-making, which is crucial for real-time applications.

Within the realm of smart industrial environments, this blend of AI, edge computing, and 6G technology yields revolutionary advancements in operational effectiveness. AI-powered predictive maintenance can identify faults ahead of time, reducing downtime and excess energy consumption. Process optimization through edge intelligence helps ensure that energy-draining processes are conducted with reduced waste, supporting more efficient manufacturing processes. Real-time monitoring also enhances operational control, enabling constant optimization of energy use throughout the system. In urban areas, the integration of the same technology is also significant. Intelligent transportation systems (ITS) gain from optimizing traffic flow in real time, minimizing fuel use and emissions. Smart grids fueled by AI and edge computing have the capacity to dynamically balance energy supply and demand, making the grid more efficient. AI-based urban planning systems are also able to assist cities in optimizing energy consumption in different areas, ranging from streetlights to garbage collection, leading to a cleaner and more sustainable urban experience.

Ultimately, the synergy among distributed AI, pervasive edge computing, and energy-efficient 6G technologies is a powerful catalyst for building smarter, more sustainable industrial and urban ecosystems. As 6G networks continue to evolve, they will pave the way for greener communication infrastructures, where energy efficiency is seamlessly integrated into every layer of the network. This will not only drive innovation in IoT applications but also create more sustainable and intelligent communication networks capable of supporting the increasingly complex and energy-conscious needs of tomorrow's smart cities and industries.

Challenges and Opportunities of Energy-Efficient Computing to Enable Sustainable Massive IoT Networks

The rapid proliferation of IoT networks has transformed various industries, including smart cities, healthcare, and industrial automation. However, achieving energy-efficient computing for sustainable massive IoT networks presents both challenges and opportunities across several critical dimensions. The scalability and complexity of IoT deployments require innovations in energy management to ensure that the systems remain efficient while supporting growing demands.

IoT Network Proliferation

Challenges

The rapid growth of IoT devices has played a major role in network congestion. The added traffic overloads communication channels, resulting in increased energy consumption. With more devices constantly sending data, it becomes difficult to maintain efficient network performance. Energy-efficient technologies and optimized network management are needed to address this problem.[13]

Opportunities

To manage the growing number of networked devices, embracing energy-efficient computing technologies is crucial. They optimize resource consumption, lowering the power requirements throughout networks. By improving operational effectiveness, they ensure efficient, long-term management of large-scale IoT deployments. Best practices in computing are the basis for responsibly facilitating future IoT growth.[13]

Battery Constraints of IoT Devices

Challenges

IoT devices are usually equipped with batteries of limited capacity, which need to be replaced or recharged frequently.[13] Ongoing data communication and sensor activities drain battery life rapidly, necessitating frequent maintenance and replacement of devices. This is especially problematic for large-scale IoT networks, where battery maintenance and replacement across thousands of devices can be logistically infeasible and expensive. There is a requirement for energy-efficient technology that maximizes battery life and minimizes the need for device replacement.

- Limited battery capacity of most IoT devices, leading to frequent replacements or recharging.[13]
- Continuous data communication and sensor operations rapidly deplete battery life, increasing maintenance efforts.
- Battery replacements are not feasible on a large scale, especially in remote or inaccessible locations.

Opportunities

Energy-harvesting methods that utilize energy from the ambient environment, including solar, vibration, or radio frequency (RF) energy, have the potential to increase the operational lifetime of IoT devices. Energy-saving measures, such as sleep mode, can also enable devices to enter low-power states when they are idle, thereby saving battery life. These strategies will greatly lower maintenance expenses and improve the long-term sustainability of IoT networks.

- Energy harvesting techniques (solar, vibration, RF) can extend IoT device operational lifespans.
- Implementing sleep mode strategies can conserve battery life during idle periods.
- Efficient battery management practices will reduce maintenance costs and increase operational sustainability.

Network Infrastructure Requirements

Challenges

Massive IoT networks require a significant amount of energy to support their communication needs. Traditional network infrastructure, including routers, base stations, and data centers, often consumes large amounts of power, which can result in high operating costs and increased carbon footprints. As IoT deployments scale, the cost and environmental impact of keeping these infrastructures permanently powered becomes a serious concern.

- High energy consumption of traditional network infrastructure, including routers, base stations, and data centers.
- Significant operating costs and increased carbon footprints due to the permanent powering of network infrastructure.
- Difficulty in scaling existing infrastructure to meet the needs of massive IoT deployments.

Opportunities

The use of green networking technologies, like *energy-efficient ethernet* (EEE), can make network operations more efficient and decrease power usage considerably. SDN also allows for dynamic management of resources so that energy usage can be improved. Virtualization methods also contribute by network workload consolidation and reducing idle resource utilization, resulting in more efficient network infrastructures capable of supporting large-scale IoT networks in a sustainable manner.

- Green networking technologies, such as EEE, can optimize energy use across the network.
- SDN offers dynamic resource management and reduces power consumption by allocating resources as needed.
- Virtualization techniques can consolidate workloads, minimizing idle resource consumption and improving infrastructure efficiency.

Computation and Data Processing Efficiency

Challenges

The huge amounts of data produced by IoT devices need large amounts of computational power, resulting in high energy usage in cloud and edge setups. Use cases such as autonomous cars, medical monitoring, and smart manufacturing, that need real-time processing of data put even more strain on the system's energy needs. As IoT networks grow, it will be important to manage these computational loads while keeping energy usage to a minimum.

- Large-scale data processing requirements lead to increased energy consumption in cloud and edge environments.
- Real-time applications like autonomous vehicles and healthcare monitoring require significant computational resources, further intensifying energy demand.
- Cloud systems must balance processing power and energy use while ensuring real-time data handling.

Opportunities

AI-powered energy management systems present a promising solution for forecasting data processing burdens and optimizing computing resources in a dynamic manner. Through machine learning models, the system can dynamically allocate tasks, making sure energy is utilized optimally without a performance trade-off. Distributed systems like fog and edge computing push computation to the vicinity of the data source, minimizing the necessity for distant data communication and considerably reducing energy expenditure. This localized strategy decreases latency and facilitates quicker response rates for mission-critical applications.

- AI-driven energy management systems can predict processing loads and optimize computing resource allocation in real time.
- Distributed architectures like fog and edge computing bring computation closer to the data source, minimizing energy spent on data transmission.
- Optimizing resource allocation based on network traffic patterns can reduce latency and conserve energy.

Sustainable System Design

Challenges

To balance performance with energy efficiency in enormous IoT networks, companies must have deep system redesigns. They need to rethink the classical networking and computation architectures to incorporate power-saving concepts right from inception. This means designing hardware and software solutions in concert that optimize power reduction without compromising on performance.

- Balancing performance and energy efficiency in large IoT networks requires redesigning network and computational architectures.
- Traditional designs may not integrate energy-saving features, hindering long-term sustainability.
- Achieving eco-friendly IoT solutions requires holistic approaches that span across hardware, software, and operational strategies.

Opportunities

Low-power chip innovation and energy-efficient protocols create new avenues for sustainable IoT networks. Hybrid power solutions blending conventional power supply and renewable energy can offer an environmentally friendly, more robust alternative for IoT device power. Also, cross-industry, academia, and government partnerships can advance standardized frameworks and green technologies to enable sustainable IoT system design. By incorporating energy-efficient architecture right from the design stage, IoT networks can be made more sustainable as well as capable of future-proofing technological upgrades.

- Low-power chip designs and energy-efficient communication protocols can significantly reduce power consumption.
- Hybrid energy systems, combining renewable and traditional power sources, offer more sustainable solutions.
- Cross-industry collaborations can drive the development of green technologies and regulatory frameworks for IoT systems.

Figure 2-4 illustrates these challenges and opportunities.

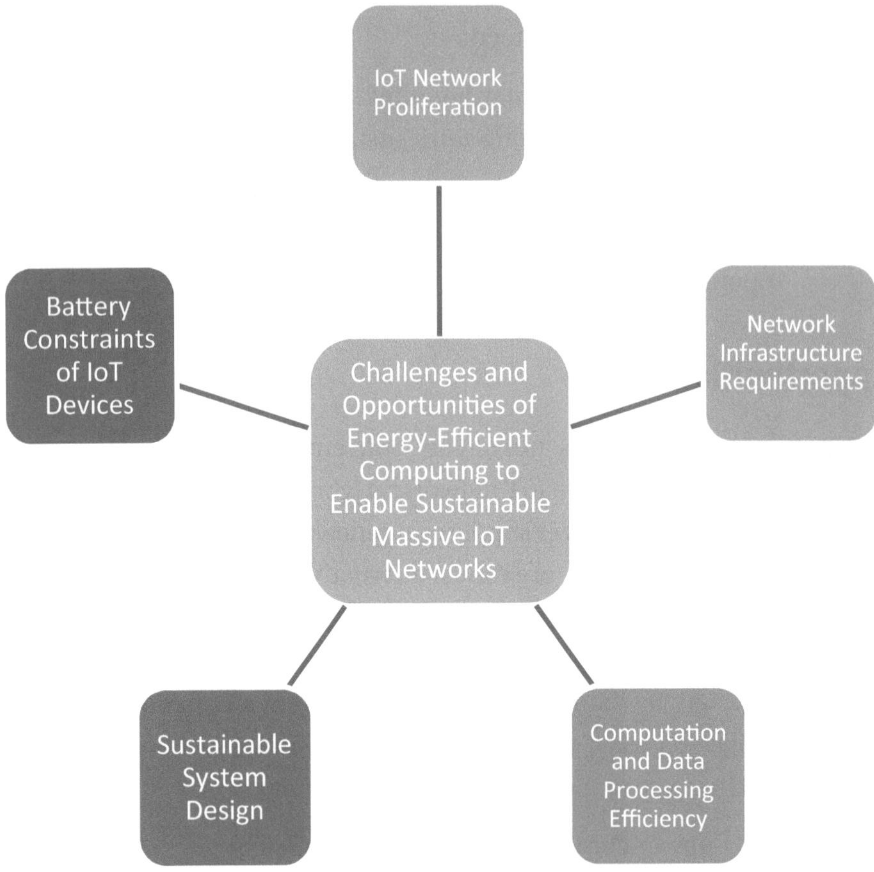

Figure 2-4. *Challenges and opportunities of energy-efficient computing to enable sustainable massive IoT networks*

Finally, the future of massive IoT networks with sustainability is in the integration of energy-efficient technologies, smart management approaches, and collaborative innovation. By solving the challenges and seizing the opportunities of energy-efficient computing, we can build IoT ecosystems that are not only scalable and high performance but also green and long-term sustainable.

The Future of Energy-Efficient Wireless Networks

The future of efficient wireless networks holds the promise to be shaped by a thrilling combination of innovative new technologies, savvy innovations, and increasing attention on sustainability. As the need for ubiquitous connectivity keeps growing, fueled by the growth of IoT-connected devices and the deployment of 5G and ultimately 6G networks, energy efficiency will be an essential metric to enable such extensive and dynamic networks. To manage the huge data streams and the explosive growth in connected devices, the wireless communication infrastructure of the future must not only be high-performance but also energy-aware to prevent unsustainable energy usage and its related environmental effects.

One of the most important methods of achieving energy-efficient wireless networks will be the incorporation of renewable energy sources such as solar, wind, and even energy-harvesting technologies into network infrastructure. By depending less on conventional power grids, wireless networks will be able to decrease their carbon footprint and help with more sustainable operations. Moreover, technologies such as AI and ML will have a revolutionary impact on maximizing energy usage in networks. With predictive analytics, AI will be capable of predicting network traffic patterns, dynamically allocating resources according to real-time information and optimizing network performance while reducing energy consumption

SDN and NFV will also improve energy efficiency by separating network control and management from hardware. This decoupling enables finer-grained, dynamic control over the resources in the network, allowing the system to respond to varying demand without over-provisioning and energy wastage. In addition, the technologies will make it simpler to manage resources because they will permit more flexible and efficient scaling, minimizing unnecessary energy usage.

As the evolution toward higher energy-efficient networks, the use of edge and fog computing will be a mainstay. Through keeping the computation near the source of data, these paradigms cut down on the necessity of transporting data over long distances, thus lowering energy requirements. Not only does this enhance network performance by lessening latency, but it also lowers the overall burden on central data centers where energy is usually required in higher capacity. Communication protocols will also come into play by embracing energy-conscious methods, like adaptive transmission, which varies transmission power and data rates based on actual network conditions, minimizing even more energy waste.

The advent of 5G and 6G networks will necessitate revolutionary breakthroughs in wireless technologies to keep up with the continually increasing demand for high-speed connections while controlling power usage. Low-power radio access technologies, smart beamforming, and non-terrestrial networks (NTNs) are some of the technologies that will lead the way to energy-efficient communication. These technologies will assist in countering the rising energy requirements of contemporary networks by offering more efficient means of transmitting data, thereby reducing power consumption. Besides this, advancements in more efficient hardware components, like base stations, antennas, and routers, will decrease network infrastructure's energy needs and make it possible to power the network over long stretches in a sustainable way.

As for devices, the future of efficient wireless networks also relies in part on improved capability to efficiently control power use. With advances in battery technology and energy management systems, mobile phones and IoT devices will last longer with fewer recharges. Technologies that harvest energy from ambient light, vibrations, or even radio frequency energy will offer backup power, maximizing battery life and minimizing external charging requirements.

With these innovations combined, the future of energy-efficient wireless networks will be a vision of sustainable high-performance systems that support billions of connected devices while keeping energy use in check.

Discussion

Through the reduction of transmission emissions, routing delays, and network traffic, clustered wireless sensor networks enhance energy-efficient communication.[6] In 6G IoT energy-efficient fog computing networks, the process of resource allocation, which includes heterogeneous distributed devices, relies on accurate network data and sophisticated ML algorithms to maximize transmission energy efficiency. Several aspects, including computational workloads, networking limitations, and latency restrictions, must be thoroughly examined for smooth resource allocation in order to accomplish effective workload distribution without overtaxing computer devices. Low-carbon sustainable energy in green spaces is advanced by the Internet of Energy, smart control systems, distributed energy generation through smart grids, and zero-carbon technologies.[7] Network efficiency in energy usage and distribution management is improved by automated consumption, optimization made possible by the interoperability of intelligent energy systems and electric mobility. Large-scale renewable electricity generation, power, grid, and data networks all have an impact on greenhouse gas emissions, as do waste and electric energy use.[8] The minimization of waste and the maximization of energy distribution are key strategies to reduce environmental effects and ensure sustainable energy consumption.

Fog computing is critical in contemporary networking through the offering of computational power nearer-to-end devices, hence lowering latency and bandwidth consumption. Some of the major features of fog computing are its decentralized structure, which positions data processing nearer to end users, lowering dependence on remote cloud centers. This approach dramatically improves energy efficiency and guarantees response times to be quicker, making it especially worthy for use in applications that require real-time processing of data (i.e., industrial automation and smart city applications). Moreover, its mobility support feature ensures smooth data management across dynamic environments.

The other key component of contemporary networking is energy-efficient routing, particularly vital in wireless networks where power consumption has a significant influence on power-hungry battery-operated devices, network lifespan, and system sustainability as a whole. Traditional routing protocols concentrate mainly on achieving maximum throughput and minimum latency, whereas energy-efficient routing methods do the opposite by prioritizing lower power usage while ensuring good connectivity and robust network performance.

By combining fog computing with energy-efficient routing protocols, today's IoT networks and smart spaces can become more sustainable. These technologies not only minimize their environmental footprint but also optimize operations, opening the door to intelligent, energy-aware communication systems that can handle the increasing needs of connected technologies.

Conclusion

Sixth-generation network-based energy-efficient systems integrate fog and edge device computational resources, energy harvesting and efficient computing techniques, and low-power communications[6] through precise sensing and localization, device data sharing, and optimization of connectivity and computational capabilities. Fog computing utilization is a vital function in edge proximity computation, where real-time computation is made possible and unwanted energy waste related to data communication is centralized to cloud servers.

One of the fundamental pillars of energy-efficient networking in 6G systems is the incorporation of energy-harvesting technologies. These methods harvest ambient energy from natural sources like solar, vibration, and radio frequency (RF) signals to energize devices and network elements, lowering the reliance on traditional, energy-hungry power supplies. By tapping into energy from the environment, these systems offer a greener energy solution, prolonging the life of devices and lowering the carbon footprint of the network infrastructure.

In addition, effective computing strategies are also crucial in controlling energy consumption effectively. Using fog and edge computing capabilities, the consumption of energy is drastically decreased through the processing of data closer to where it is created instead of depending on cloud servers in a centralized way that may involve huge amounts of energy for transferring data over large distances. Fog computing enables such decentralized systems to become more energy-efficient and provides the benefit of low-latency real-time processing. Such performance is necessary in applications across areas such as industrial automation, smart cities, healthcare, and autonomous systems, where responses need to be almost instantaneous.

Energy-efficient communication protocols are another principal element that enforces energy savings in 6G networks. These protocols optimize power consumption by sending data in the most energy-efficient way, with little wasted energy on non-essential transmission. Moreover, improvements in sensing technologies and accuracy in localization enable improved resource management, which minimizes the energy consumption of the network as well.

The capacity to maximize connectivity and computing power through localized processing and more effective data-sharing devices guarantees that these networks can sustain strong performance while at the same time reduce their energy needs. By reducing the energy needed for communication, storage, and processing, these technologies help make the network ecosystem more sustainable. This becomes more crucial as IoT devices, sensors, and other connected systems keep growing, and the environmental footprint of global network infrastructures becomes an important issue.

The contribution of edge computing and fog computing to this environment cannot be overemphasized. These systems not only assist in reducing the energy expenses of long-distance communication but also improve network reliability and flexibility by facilitating distributed resource management. This decentralized process lightens the burden on centralized data centers, which are normally accountable for high energy consumption, and ensures that network tasks are executed by the most suitable resources according to real-time requirements.

Finally, the incorporation of energy-efficient networking principles is essential for the development of future-proof, eco-friendly communication systems that can keep pace with the increasingly mounting demands of an extremely interconnected world. Through the use of energy harvesting, green computing, and low-power communications protocols, we are setting the stage for a future where network infrastructure is both green and capable of accommodating the dynamic requirements of contemporary technology. As we continue to advance toward 6G and beyond, the integration of these energy-efficient strategies will play a key role in achieving a more sustainable, resilient, and intelligent network ecosystem, ensuring that communication networks are not only more powerful and efficient but also environmentally responsible.

CHAPTER 3

Energy Efficient IoT Architecture

This chapter reviews more principles of energy-efficient IoT-enabled design on FPGA platforms, machinery architecture considerations, optimization methods and steps, and implementation processes. It also investigates power estimation through the Vivado ISE Simulator and develops an HDL-oriented IoT architecture.

IoT Energy Efficient Techniques

In IoT, everything interconnects through different communication protocols in a different topology. The term "things" includes actuators, firmware, hardware, middleware, sensors, and storage related to various critical infrastructures, such as smart homes, smart cities, agriculture, manufacturing, 5G/6G telecommunication, healthcare, transportation, and so on. Hardware, middleware, and presentation are the three components of IoT. Battery operated sensors, actuators, and communication systems are the hardware components of IoT. The sensor reads information, which is stored as data, and the communication system transmits that data to the middleware. The middleware processes the sensor readings and initiates a command for actuators. The middleware also analyzes the data using data analysis tools and extracts meaningful

Dr. D. Sharma and Dr. B. Pandey, *Eco-Networking for IoT*,
https://doi.org/10.1007/979-8-8688-2317-6_3

information. The user interface of IoT is responsible not only for the visualization of extracted information in a legible manner but also for accepting user commands and instructions and feeding them to the middleware element to initiate sensors or actuators. The battery power of things in IoT is dissipated during the collection and transmission of data. The amount of collected and transmitted data is directly proportional to the battery power consumption. The lifetime of IoT devices is one of the deciding factors of the energy efficiency of IoT infrastructure.[1] Energy efficiency is essential to achieve the goal of sustainability and scalability of IoT systems. The goals of sustainability is achieved through the wise usage of green computing technologies, energy efficient IoT-enabled design, and renewable energy sources. In order to develop an energy-efficient IoT architecture, we need to create environment-friendly IoT devices. The power dissipation of any architecture is the sum total of the power dissipation of all IoT devices working on every layer of the IoT architecture. Clock gating, process scaling, voltage scaling, ambient temperature scaling, frequency scaling, and IO standards are the main energy-efficient processes used to design IoT-enabled devices, as shown in Figure 3-1.

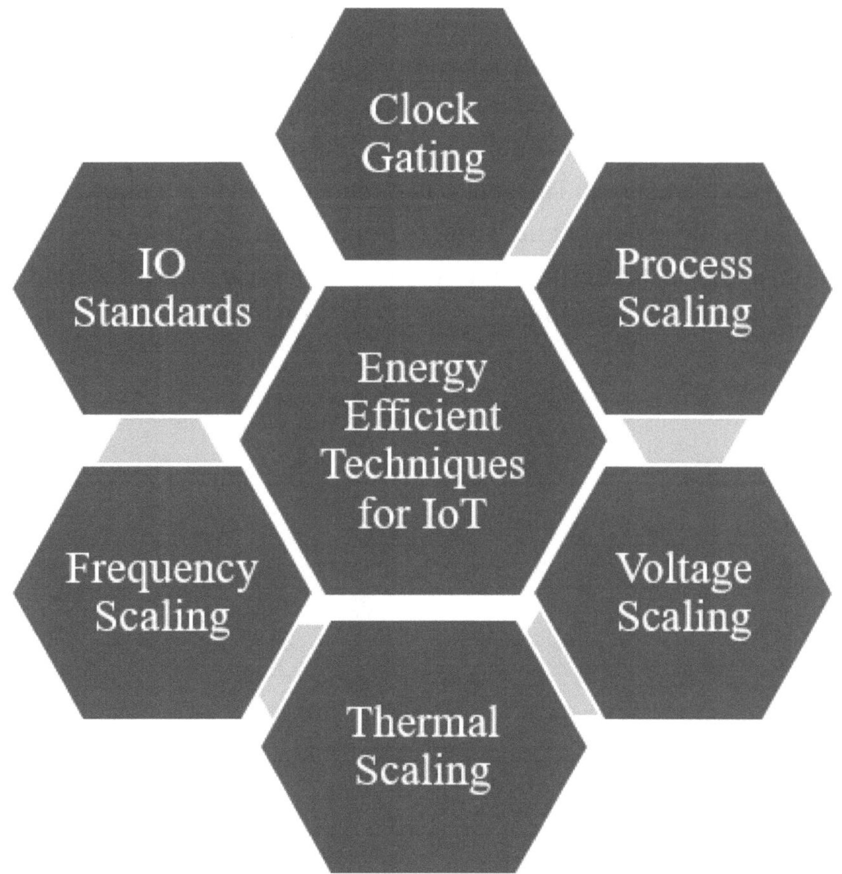

Figure 3-1. *Energy efficient techniques used in IoT design*

Energy Efficient IOT-Enabled Design and Implementation on FPGA

To track an object, the object-tracking mechanism processes image frames, locking onto a target and keeping track of how that target moves in relation to the other participants. Many methods have been proposed for tracking objects, one of which is called the Active Contour Model (ACM) or "snakes" (see Figure 3-2). Active contours, or snakes, are a common method used in image processing and computer vision to define object boundaries by separating object contours from a noisy 2D image. Researchers delved robust object-tracking systems capable of adapting to changes in visual features while managing occlusions and shape deformations. The goal is to enhance ACM by making it more computationally efficient and easier to implement. For an open-source solution, a camera takes snapshots at intervals while a robot processes the data through ACM algorithms.

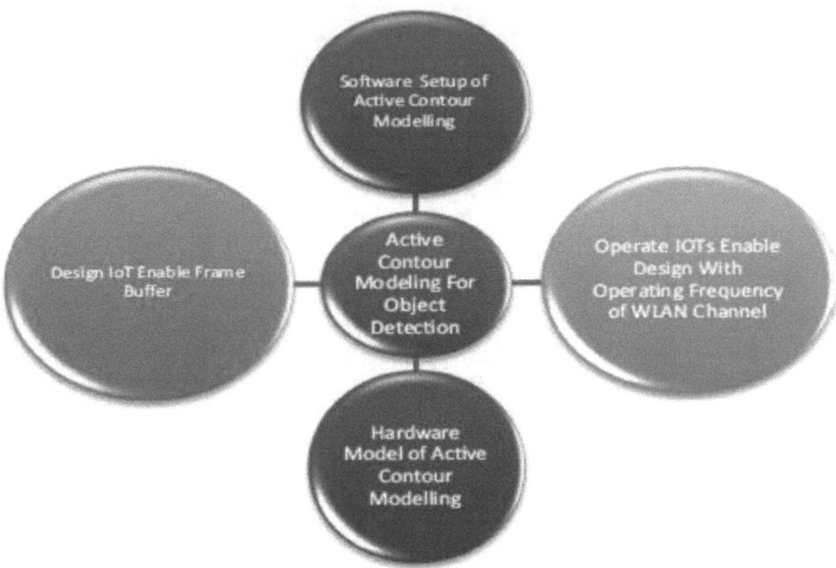

Figure 3-2. *Process of active contour modelling[3]*

ACMs are primarily used to detect objects and features in grayscale images. These models use parametric curves and progressively morph from the initial onto the target shape, and therefore are adaptive to changes in lighting. Applying smoothness constraints to the contour's curvature and the object's motion in ACM yields accurate results over a range of conditions.[3]

One of the critical concerns is energy efficiency. Conventional IoT architecture involves huge amounts of power consumption, as there is constant data collection, processing, and communication. One way to address these energy issues is through *Field Programmable Gate Arrays* (FPGAs), which can provide a customizable solution for IoT devices on low power designs, as shown in Figure 3-2. In addition to the IoT-enabled frame buffer, researchers also developed IoT-enabled RAM design using Verilog hardware description language and implemented that design on FPGA, as shown in Figure 3-3. The hardware frontend designers added a 128-bit IPv6 address in the RAM memory design. An Internet Protocol (IP) address is distinct for each system connected to the Internet. Therefore, researchers access their proposed IoT-enabled RAM chip from across the globe by using their IP address.[4]

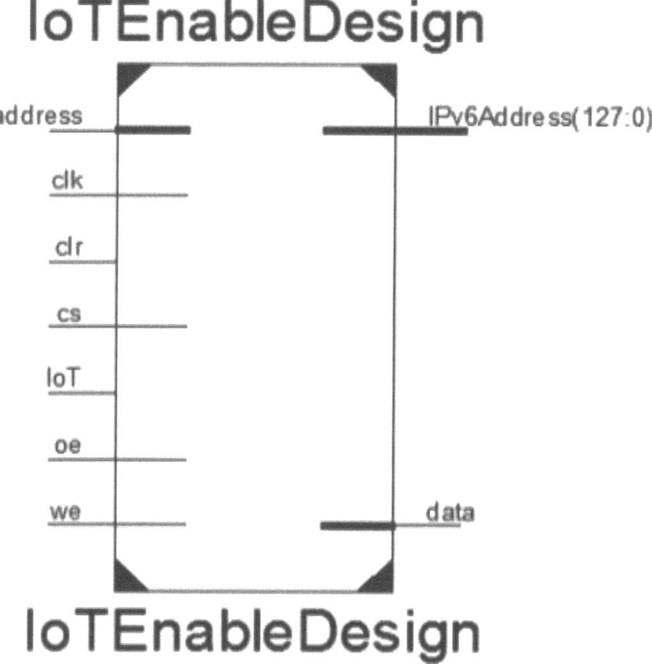

Figure 3-3. *IoT-enabled RAM memory design[4]*

This IoT-enabled RAM is designed exclusively for the IoT-based computer processor. Therefore, this design facilitates access from any geographic coordinate.[4]

Energy Efficient IoT Design in Smart Cities

In [5], researchers developed a natural language-based IoT system control using the QuickScript integrated development environment (QS IDE). The QS IDE is not a proprietary tool and has user-friendly interfaces that make it easy to learn. Researchers proposed some improvements in the implementation of QS IDE and developed a simple architecture that is used to create an English-based IoT design, as illustrated in Figure 3-4.[5]

>> TURN ON THE FAN PLEASE
{ON} <fan_id>
>> TURN OFF THE FAN PLEASE
{OFF} <fan_id>
>> WILL YOU SWITCH OFF THE LED
{OFF} <led_light_id>

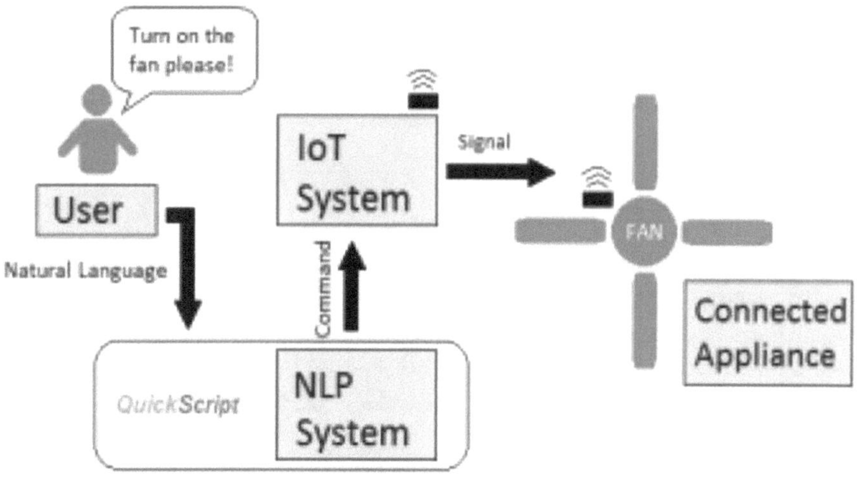

Figure 3-4. *QuickScript-based natural language-enabled IoT architecture[5]*

In Pandey, B. K., et al. (2020)[6], researchers discussed many possibilities of IoT-enabled design, including IoT-enabled bicycles, coffee makers, ATMs, image sensors, grocery carts, smart homes, light bulbs, water faucets, vehicles, frame buffers, key generators for encryption, Wi-Fi encoders, and more, as shown in Figure 3-5. In addition to these IoT devices, there are many other possibilities for IoT integration in ur day-to-day lives.

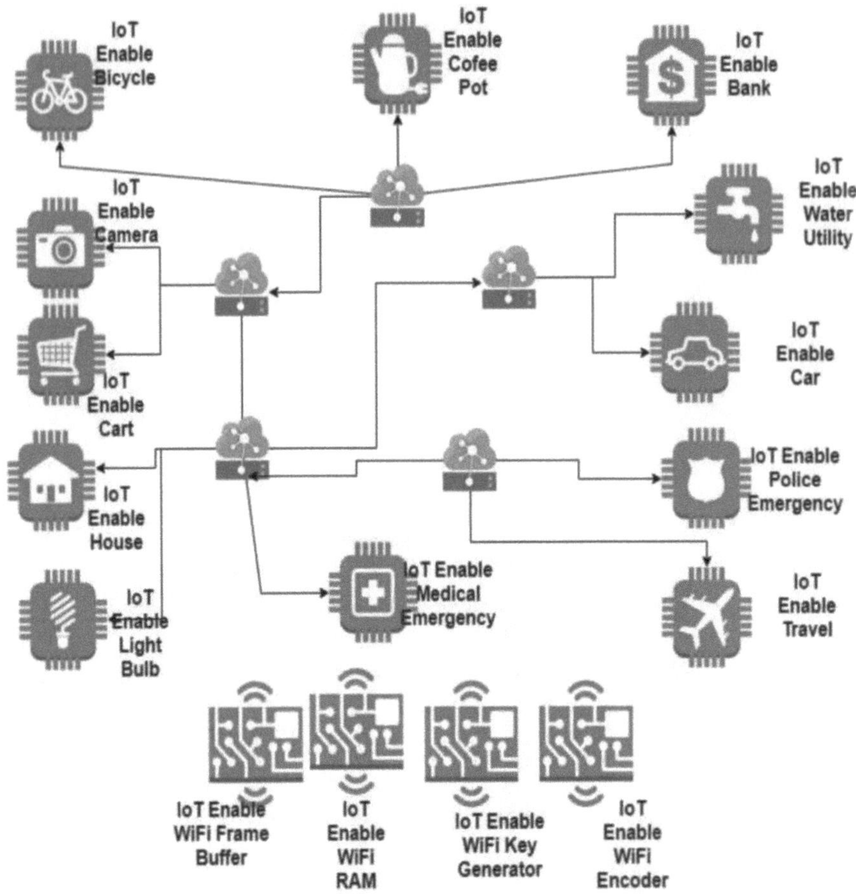

Figure 3-5. *IoT-enabled architecture of Smart City[6]*

With the application of ever-changing IoT technologies, researchers developed an energy-efficient IoT architecture.[8] Every device is assigned a unique address, and for communication among these devices, the Constrained Application Protocol (CoAP) is used. To get efficiency in terms of energy, researchers proposed a smart construction architecture. They achieved about 30.86% in power dissipation using CoAP in intelligent building in comparison to Message Queuing Telemetry Transport (MQTT)-based smart building.[8] In Yashwant, A., et al. (2024)[11], researchers tried to solve the novel problem of water crisis in Indian cities with the help of IoT sensors and actuators.

Energy Efficiency in IoT Agriculture

The architecture of IoT-enabled irrigation system design uses sensors for soil moisture, environmental temperature, and humidity.[7] The irrigation system is tested with Arduino and FPGA. The soil moisture sensor takes capacitance to measure the dielectric permittivity of the soil. dielectric permittivity is proportional to the moisture. With the help of the agriculture farmland, the sensor generates a voltage corresponding to the dielectric permittivity, as shown in Figure 3-6, and therefore the moisture of the soil is measured and used to initiate irrigation system.[7]

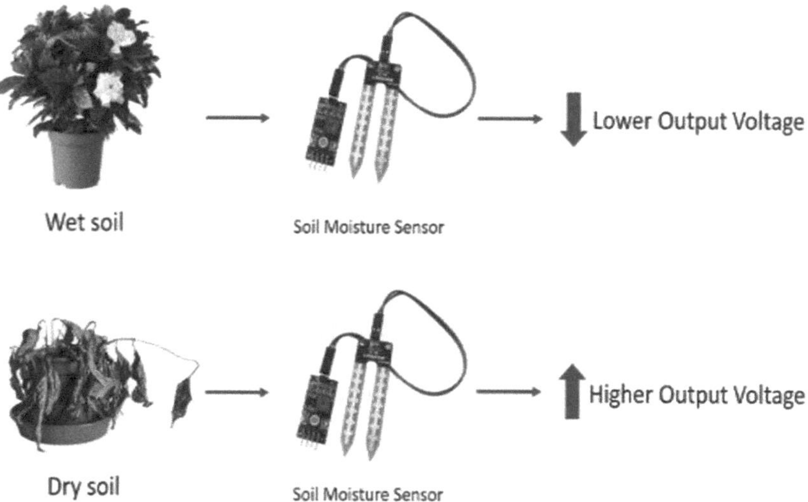

Figure 3-6. *Working soil moisture sensor[7]*

The IoT architecture proposed in Alharbi, H. A., & Aldossary, M. (2021) [9] reads data from various sensors, as shown in Table 3-1. The proposed architecture is well equipped for processing sensor data that demands real-time execution (for example, environmental temperature, humidity, soil moisture, etc.) in three layers (edge, fog, and cloud). Therefore, the immediate data processing by sensors is done by both edge and fog layers. This reduces the burden of the cloud layer and decreases power dissipation. According to the results of various agriculture sensors, the proposed architecture in Alharbi, H. A., & Aldossary, M. (2021)[9] provides 36% better results in comparison to the traditional cloud architecture.

Table 3-1. *Parameters at IoT Sensor Layer[9]*

Parameter	Value
Number of sensor (single farm)	0.1 million sensors in each farm (sensing 60,000, processing 30,000, and heavy workload 10,000)
Number of lora gateway (single farm)	3 in each farm
Power consumption of gateway	30 watts
Power consumption of IoT sensor	0.44 watts

Energy Efficiency in Industrial IoT

We are witnessing a rapid expansion of the IoT systems. When IoT is integrated in the industries, especially in manufacturing, it is called Industrial IoT (IIoT). IIoT is a trending research area nowadays, especially energy-efficient IIoT. The limited resources of IIoT devices greatly impacts the lifespan of IIoT systems. These heavy and large sensors, devices, and machines dissipate significant power. In Mao, W., et al. (2021)[10], researchers presented a survey on energy-efficient IIoT systems (for example, smart grids and smart manufacturing). The major distinctions between IoT and IIoT are summarized in Table 3-2.

Table 3-2. *Comparison of IoT and IIoT[10]*

		IoT	**Industrial IoT (IIoT)**
Characteristics Features		Consumer based	Production based
Target To		Upgrade quality of life	Decrease manufacturing expenses and enhance productivity
Communication	Gadgets	Intelligent gadgets	Industrial systems
	Network scaling	Small to moderate	Larger to largest
	Delay tolerance	Moderate to high	Low
	Networking	Wireless LAN, mobile network	WPN, wireless LAN, cellular network, low power WAN
	Technologies	Wi-Fi, Bluetooth, 5G, etc.	IEEE 802.15.4, RFID, 5G, LoRa, etc.
Computation	Data volume	Moderate to large	Larger to largest
	Tolerance of delay	Moderate to high	Much less
	Requirements of data security	Moderate	High
	Complexity of tasks	Moderate to high	Higher to highest
	Resource allocation	Dynamic	Stable

Energy Efficient IoT in the 6G Era

In Plastras, S., et al. (2024)[12], Internet of Remote Things (IoRT) architecture is discussed. This is the collaboration of various allied architecture, such as Internet of Arctic Things (IoAT), Internet of Agricultural Things (IoAT), Internet of Battle Things (IoBT), Internet of Maritime Things (IoMT), Internet of Satellite/Space Things (IoST), Internet of Underground Things (IoUT), and Internet of Underwater Things (IoUwT), and as shown in Figure 3-7.

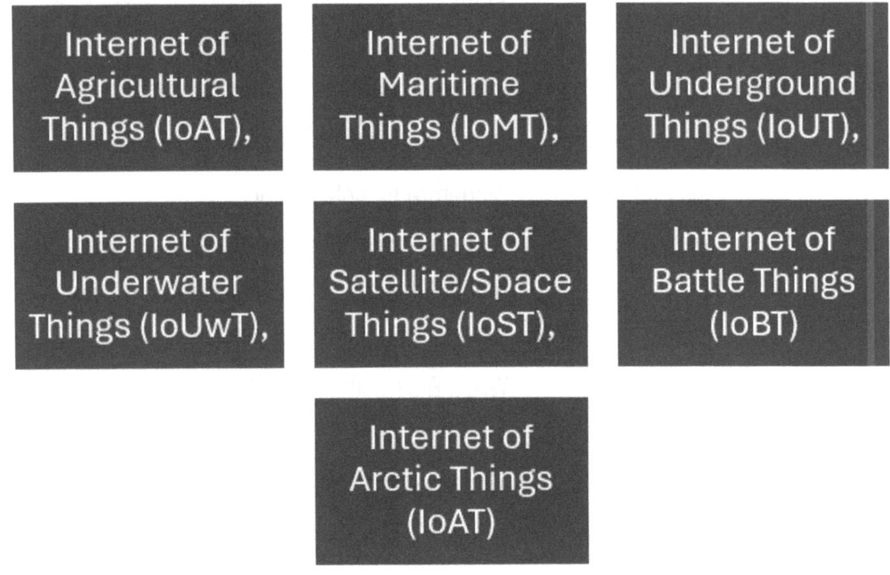

Figure 3-7. *Internet of Remote Things (IoRT) using NTN*

Elevated, above ground, positioning of IoT devices improves the quality of the radio link, deducing signal loss and minimizing interference from ground-based obstacles. The combination of terrestrial and satellite networks in IoT provides a 3D strategy for network coverage, which leads to trustworthy services in thick wilderness, uncharted ground, varied topography, high-altitude locations, challenging terrain, and deep-sea environments, as shown in Figure 3-8.

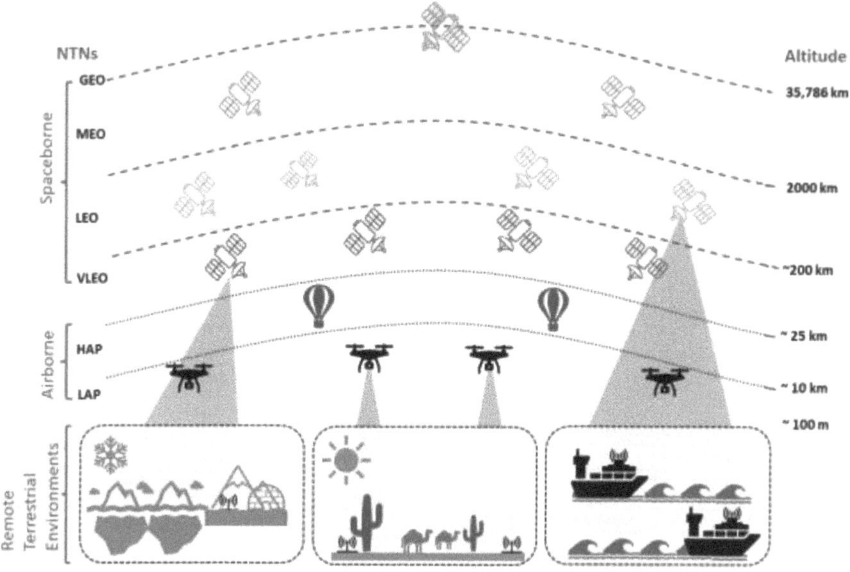

Figure 3-8. *Non-terrestrial network[12]*

As you have read, IoT-enabled devices have limited energy resources. This limitation creates hurdles in processing, validating, and storing data. To address this issue, computing devices like actuators provide an efficient method for conserving energy in IoT devices through high-performance low-power computing. Therefore, energy-efficient IoT, or "green IoT," has emerged as a key area of research for researchers developing large-scale IoT networks. In Alsharif, M. H., et al. (2024)[13], researchers provide a detailed survey of recent research done in areas of energy-efficient IoT and green IoT systems.

Energy Efficiency in IoT Fog-Cloud Computing

The architecture of the energy-efficient Internet of Healthcare Things (IoHT) is demonstrated in Figure 3-9. The proposed architecture of IoHT consists of three layers: the medical devices layer, the fog layer (a collector layer with an edge layer), and the cloud layer. The edge layer deals with a multi-sensor monitoring network that collects the dynamic readings of a patient's vitals, such as during intakes and physical actions like pulses, blood pressure, and so on. Fog devices in the fog layer process the data gathered by sensors, transform it into meaningful information, and transmit to the last layer, known as the cloud layer. The cloud layer is the last stop, where the data is gathered, collected, and analyzed.

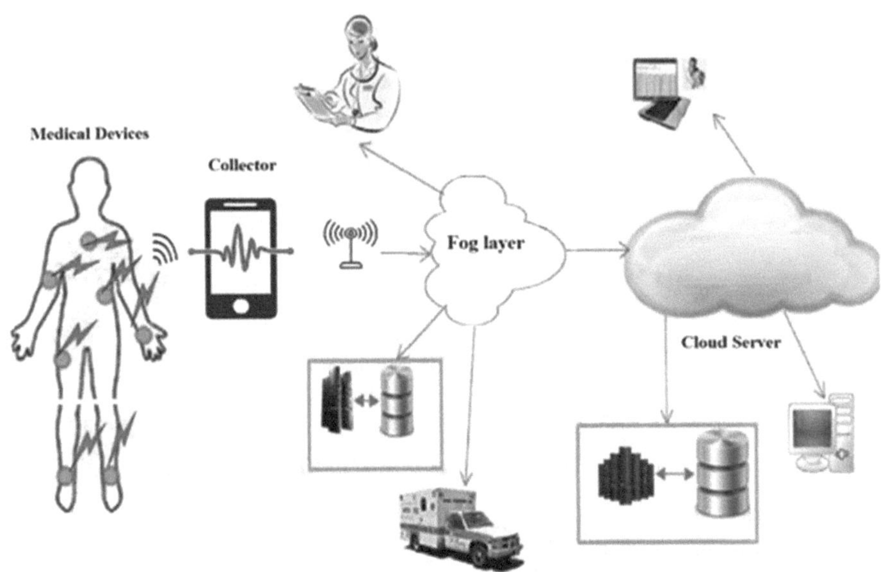

Figure 3-9. *Fog computing based, energy efficient Internet of Healthcare Things[14]*

Wildlife trafficking is a significant global issue that endangers wildlife and ecology. There are some unsubstantiated medical claims about the use of animal remains and trends to use wildlife remains as souvenirs or decorative items. There are many IoT-driven solutions to enhance the accuracy and reach of wildlife monitoring. However, these solutions have some limitations. For example, Unmanned Aerial Vehicles (UAVs) cover vast areas but cannot detect poaching instantly if UAV power is drained. The application of RFID collars on animals is not a practical idea. Researchers proposed a fog computing-based wildlife monitoring framework without any animal contact.[15] The framework in Siyanwal, R., et al. (2025)[15] consists of Motion Sensing Units (MSUs), a camera, a processor, and intelligent hub-based Actuating and Processing Units (APUs). MQTT is used for communication between MSUs and APUs.[15]

Energy Efficiency in IoT Networks

In Almudayni, Z., et al. (2025)[16], researchers highlight eleven prevalent technical challenges that affect energy consumption in IoT environments, as illustrated in Figure 3-10.

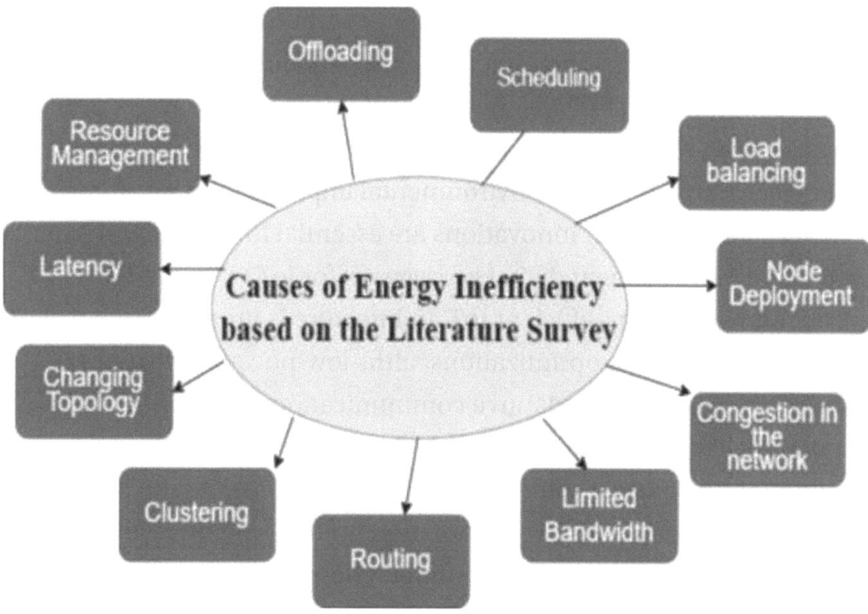

Figure 3-10. *Eleven issues decide the energy requirement of IoT devices[16]*

Researchers formulate the IoT-based system and integrate a multi-objective optimization approach in it to achieve energy efficiency and extend the battery life of IoT systems.[17] The PSK method is most energy efficient, as its computational cost is only around 1% of PKI-based and blockchain-based methods.[18]

Conclusion

Energy-efficient IoT architecture is crucial for sustainable development in terms of the United Nation Sustainable Development Goals (UN SDG) across various critical infrastructures, including smart cities, agriculture, industry, 6G networks, and fog-edge-cloud computing. This chapter highlighted key strategies, architectures, and technologies that optimize power consumption in IoT systems. By implementing energy-efficient designs, IoT can significantly reduce operational costs, extend the lifespan of IoT devices, and minimize environmental impact. As IoT continues to evolve, energy-efficient innovations are essential for creating smarter, greener, and more resilient digital ecosystems for IoT.

The future of energy-efficient IoT architecture is promising if it will integrate with AI-driven optimizations, ultra-low-power hardware, 6G, quantum computing, and adaptive communication protocols. Emerging technologies like energy harvesting, blockchain for resource management, and quantum computing could revolutionize IoT sustainability. Additionally, standardized frameworks and policies will drive global adoption, ensuring scalable, secure, and intelligent energy-efficient IoT solutions for smart cities, industries, and connected environments. Energy-efficient IoT architectures will also play a crucial role in tackling global warming by reducing energy consumption, minimizing carbon footprint, and optimizing resource utilization.

CHAPTER 4

Hardware Optimization for IoT

IoT demands highly optimized hardware to ensure efficient, low-power, and cost-effective data processing and connectivity. Hardware optimization is instrumental in enhancing energy efficiency, performance, and reliability while simultaneously reducing latency, cost, and resource consumption. Traditional RAM architectures were not IoT-compatible without specific modifications, such as IPv6 input ports. Innovations in AI-powered hardware for IoT delivered low-power processors, task-offloading techniques, and real-time processing units.

Additionally, advancements in trust-region algorithms, TinyML, and energy-autonomous sensor nodes reflect the industry's growing emphasis on sustainable and intelligent IoT systems. Key aspects like ultra-low power controllers, communication modules, edge AI optimization, memory management, energy harvesting, and security are vital for scalable and long-term IoT deployment. Through detailed analysis and review, this chapter presents the latest strategies and technologies driving IoT hardware optimization, fostering the development of next-generation, intelligent, and energy-efficient IoT infrastructures.

It covers the key strategies for hardware optimization in IoT and discusses ultra-low power controllers, power-optimized communication modules, and different optimizations of AI on the edge. Later, you'll look at memory and space optimization for IoT devices and processing elements

Dr. D. Sharma and Dr. B. Pandey, *Eco-Networking for IoT*,
https://doi.org/10.1007/979-8-8688-2317-6_4

and then survey different energy-harvesting techniques for increasing the lifetime of IoT devices. Finally, the security optimization of IoT hardware is discussed in detail, along with the different uses of IoT middleware in the perfect execution of IoT hardware.

Optimization of IoT Hardware Resources

The world of IoT relies on efficient, low-power, and cost-effective hardware to enable seamless connectivity and data processing. The primary objective of hardware optimization for IoT is to increase performance, energy efficiency, and reliability. The secondary aim of hardware optimization is to decrease the cost, latency, and resource consumption. Hardware optimization is crucial to enhance performance, energy efficiency, and reliability while minimizing latency and resource consumption. In HDL Coding of Traditional RAM, there is no input port like IPv6(127:0).[1] Traditional RAM has only input ports such as 32-bit data input din(31:0), 16-bit read address raddr(15:0), 16-bit write address waddr(15:0), clock (clk), read enable (re), and write enable (we).[1] Insertion of input port IPv6(127:0) in any traditional hardware transforms that hardware into an IoT device, as shown in Figure 4-1.[2]

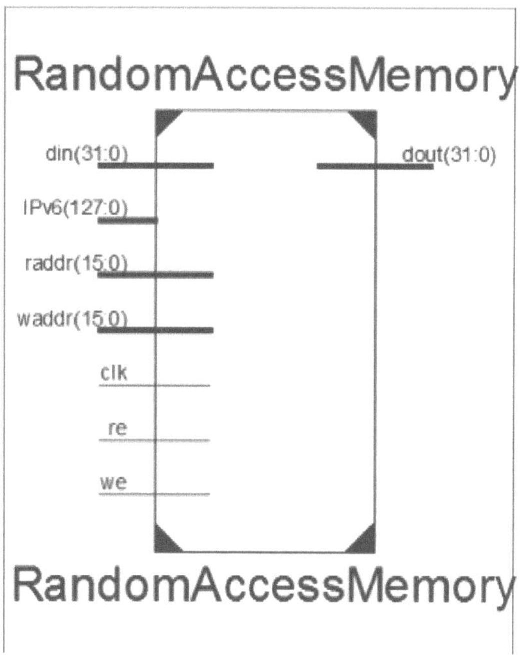

Figure 4-1. *IoT-enabled RAM design[2]*

Researchers have shifted their focus to designing energy-efficient, high-performance hardware for AI-powered IoT applications.[3] They proposed an AI-optimized architecture featuring low-power processors, specialized accelerators, and memory hierarchies. Their design addresses IoT constraints like limited power, small size, and real-time processing needs. It also incorporates advanced task offloading and distributed processing for collaborative AI execution. Simulations and experiments show enhanced energy efficiency, speed, and scalability, supporting next-gen AI-enabled IoT solutions.[3] In Bekasiewicz, A. (2023)[4], researchers introduced an automated framework for optimizing finite difference (FD) step sizes in trust-region (TR) algorithms used for IoT microwave and antenna design. The method dynamically adjusts FD perturbations via numerical optimization to improve model accuracy without increasing computational cost. Tested on 12 design problems, it shows up to 50%

improvement over traditional TR methods with fixed perturbations. Its effectiveness is validated through integration in a real-time IoT localization system. In Dutta, L., & Bharali, S. (2021)[5], researchers explored TinyML, which enables on-device machine learning in IoT systems, emphasizing low latency, improved privacy, and reduced reliance on cloud connectivity. A key focus is on hardware-software co-design for efficient, low-power execution of ML algorithms within constrained IoT devices. The integration of 5G further enhances TinyML's potential for real-time, on-premise analytics. Their review highlights current advancements and outlines future research directions, especially in hardware optimization for scalable TinyML deployment. ARM developed a high-performance ML processor called Ethos-U55, which is specially designed for IoT devices limited to very few areas. ARM is a market leader in designing IoT-based MCU architecture and in optimizing tooling for Cortex-M hardware, Keil MDK, and the IoT-based Mbed Operating System. 5G and its future, 6G, are going to shift us into a hyper-connected world—a world where everybody and everything is connected. The union of ML, 5G, and TinyML is depicted in Figure 4-2.

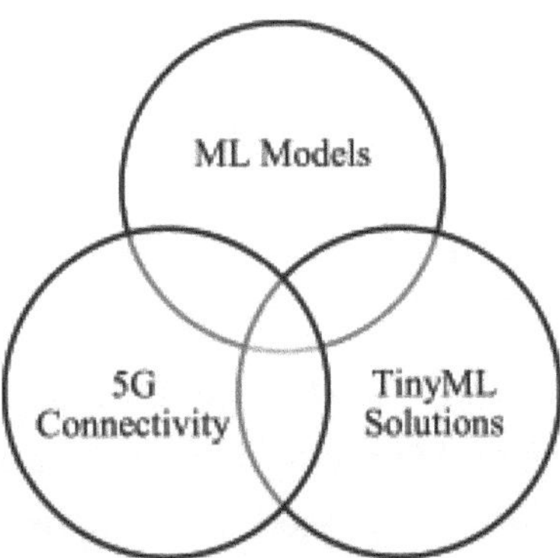

Figure 4-2. *Union of 5G, ML, and IoT [5]*

In Raval, M., et al. (2021)[6], researchers used hardware-optimization techniques such as miniaturized IoT sensor nodes at the millimeter scale with power-efficient wireless transmission. In their research, they demonstrated a management system for energy requirements of IoT devices, addressing energy challenges through hardware and software optimization. This system models energy usage in sensing, processing, and communication, emphasizing energy transparency and efficiency. Hardware-focused optimization is achieved via a multi-agent system enhanced by genetic algorithms, showing significant energy savings in simulations.

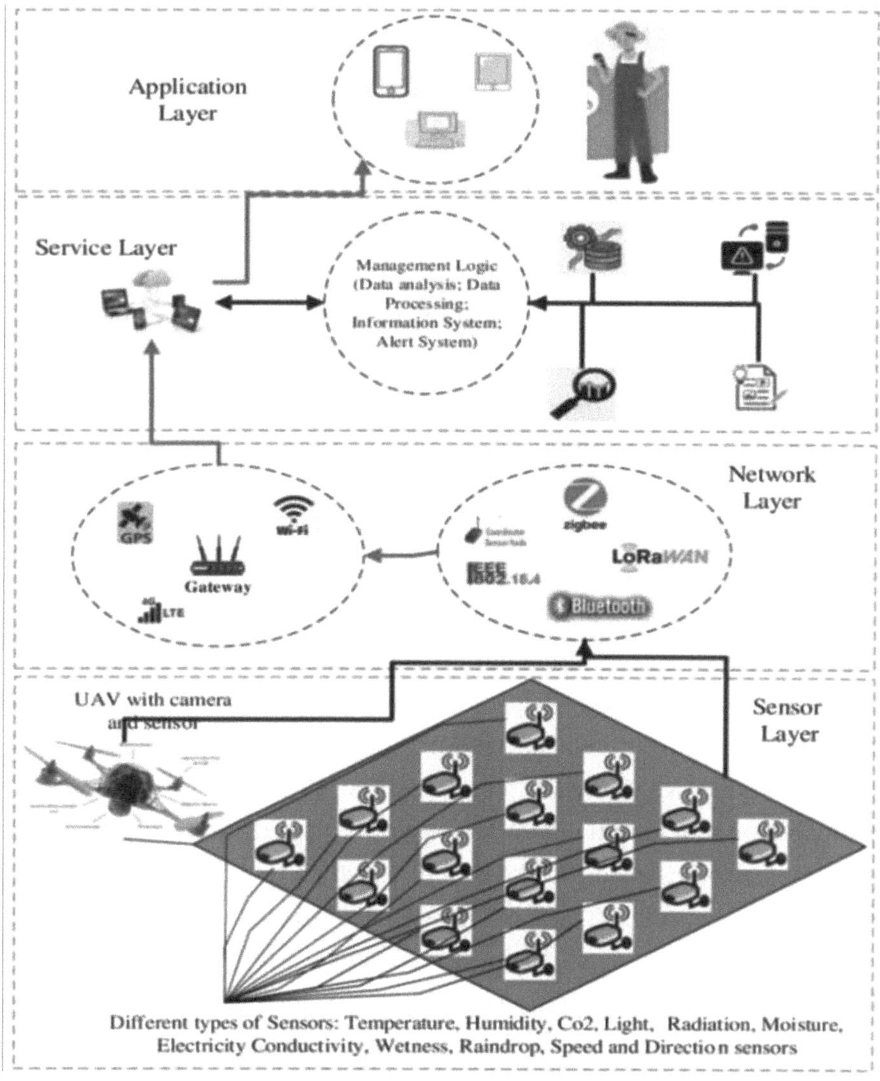

Figure 4-3. *Sensor, network, service and application layer[7]*

In Prakash, C., et al. (2023)[7], researchers performed an in-depth study of farming-associated technology-based constituents like IoT, wireless networking protocols, and sensors and actuators, as shown in Figure 4-3.

Ultra Low Power Controllers

Low-power microcontrollers and processors use ultra-low-power microcontroller units (MCUs) (such as RISC-V, ARM Cortex-M) designed for IoT applications. These controllers implement dynamic voltage scaling and dynamic frequency scaling (DVFS) to manage energy consumption based on workload. These controllers are also equipped to leverage hardware acceleration for cryptographic operations and AI inference to reduce CPU load. In Loo, M. H. W., et al. (2022)[8], researchers categorize ultra-low-power timers into open-loop and closed-loop types. The open-loop timers offer faster settling but poorer temperature compensation (TC), while closed-loop timers provide better TC at similar power levels. They gave designers the freedom to prioritize design goals and choose the appropriate architecture, as both types are vital for energy-efficient IoT applications. Deep Learning (DL) is driving a range of applications in IoT edge devices like mobile phones, effectively transforming them into intelligent microcontrollers—for example, Apple's Siri enables seamless human-computer interaction. Platforms such as TensorFlow Lite by Google, EdgeML by Microsoft, and CMSIS-NN by ARM support the deployment of neural network models on these devices. Additionally, STMicroelectronics introduced X-Cube-AI, which is using STM 32-bit MCU to run DL models. These MCUs are customized for TinyML due to their compact size (~1 cm^3), energy efficiency (1 milliWatt), and affordability (1 USD), integrating a CPU, digital/analog components, embedded flash memory (eFlash) for program storage, and SRAM for temporary data handling.[9]

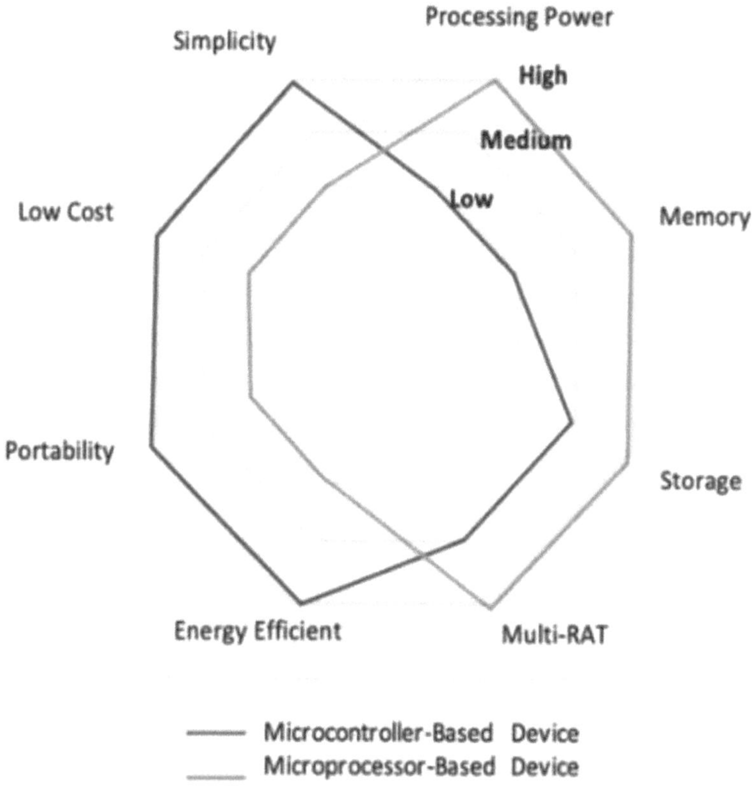

Figure 4-4. *Microcontroller or microprocessor-based IoT devices[9]*

Figure 4-4 highlights the differences in features between microprocessor-based and microcontroller-based IoT devices. Microprocessors are the most popular control units in IoT domains involving deep learning due to their high processing power, memory, and storage capabilities. Still, they come with higher costs, greater memory consumption, and limited portability compared to microcontrollers.

Power Optimized Communication Modules

Energy-efficient communication modules optimize communication protocols (e.g., LoRaWAN, NB-IoT, Zigbee) based on application needs. You can use wake-up radios or duty cycling to minimize active transmission time and implement edge processing to reduce data transmission and save energy. In Raval, M., et al. (2021)[10], researchers address energy management in IoT systems, focusing on hardware and software perspectives. They model energy consumption during sensing, processing, and communication to ensure energy transparency. They propose a multi-agent system to represent IoT devices, with parameters optimized using a genetic algorithm. Simulations using MATLAB Simulink and OpenModelica showed significant energy savings through decentralized intelligence. In Sathish Kumar, L., et al. (2022) [11], researchers present an energy-efficient technique for mobile WSNs (wireless sensor networks) and IoT, considering factors such as node location, region radius, and network probability. A mathematical model based on probability theory is used to analyze node behavior relative to the detection region. The proposed method enhances connectivity and significantly reduces energy consumption. Simulation results show an average of 40% lower energy usage compared to popular methods like LEACH, ZTR, and DSR at a 100-radius. The radius is shown in Figure 4-5.

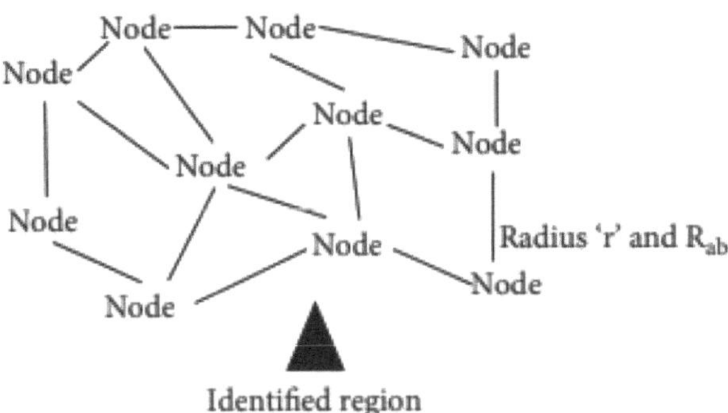

Figure 4-5. *Node-based IoT region [11]*

NB-IoT is more costly and power-demanding than LoRaWAN, consuming two mAh more per network joining and 1.7 milliampere per hour extra for uplink messages.[12] However, it offers better reliability, security, and network capacity by using the available cellular infrastructure. By delivering a throughput of 264 bits per second and 837 milliseconds latency, NB-IoT outperforms LoRaWAN in IoT communications.[12]

Optimized AI on Edge

The most promising integration of edge computing and AI in IoT is making the space to use specialized AI-enabled chips (e.g., NVIDIA Jetson, Google Edge TPU, and Intel Movidius) for on-device inference. These chips reduce data transfer to cloud services by processing sensor data locally and delivering optimized AI models for embedded hardware using model quantization and pruning. In Pooyandeh, M., & Sohn, I. (2021)[13], the network edge shifts computational needs near the network edge, not far from the IoT equipment. The fastest and most intelligent network edge, as shown in Figure 4-6, typically makes informed decisions in a shorter response time and utilizes AI for intelligent processing. AI is now acting as a key component in almost all edge devices. This edge hardware includes cars, UAVs, drones, sensors, robots, humanoid robots, autonomous vehicles, smart home appliances, and smart IoT devices.

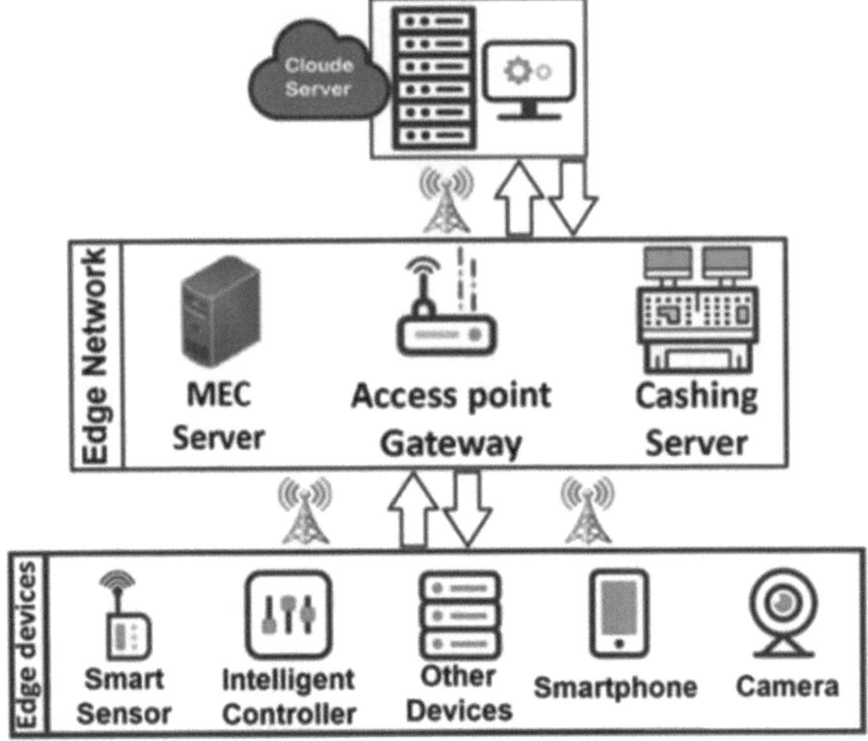

Figure 4-6. *IoT Edge network[13]*

In Surianarayanan, C., et al. (2023)[14], researchers categorize energy-efficient optimization methods for machine learning into three distinct layers—training, platform, and hardware—as shown in Figure 4-7.

The two main subphases of the training layer are federated learning and knowledge distillation. Federated learning distributes model training across multiple devices, reducing the need for data transfer and improving energy efficiency. Knowledge distillation refers to the technique of conveying knowledge from a large-scale model to a smaller one while maintaining performance with less resource utilization.

The platform layer deals with model optimization methods and hyperparameter tuning. Model optimization methods are techniques to simplify models (e.g., pruning and quantization) to reduce computational load. Hyperparameter tuning is an efficient search strategy to optimize performance with less computation.

The hardware layer takes care of hardware optimization. This involves designing or utilizing energy-efficient hardware (e.g., edge devices and AI accelerators) to run ML models more efficiently. All these components collectively contribute to achieving energy-efficient optimization in machine learning systems.

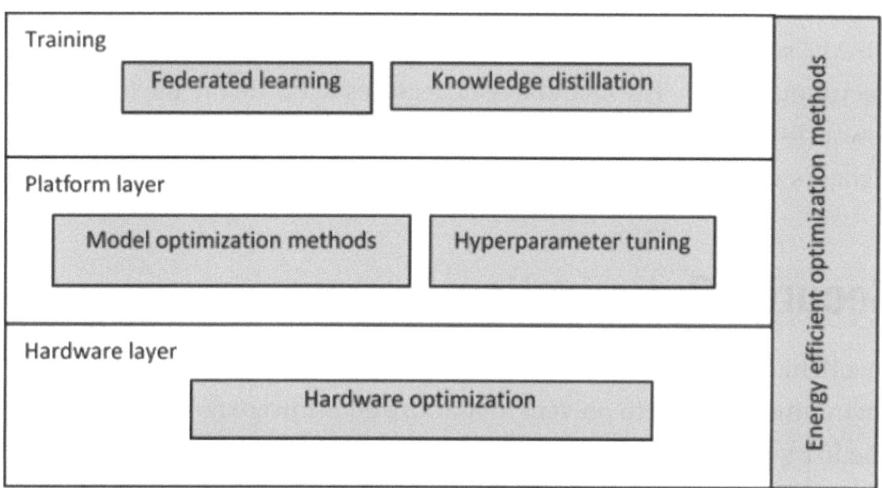

Figure 4-7. *Energy-Efficient Optimization for AI-Enabled IoT Systems[14]*

Memory and Storage Optimization

PCM, STT-MRAM, and Flash memory represent recent advancements in non-volatile memories (NVMs). These NVMs are gaining space in main memory, CPU cache, and secondary storage. These NVMs are improving performance, reducing power consumption, and increasing the memory/storage capacity of cyber-physical systems (CPS) for novel CPS and IoT applications.[15] You can use FRAM (Ferroelectric RAM) and MRAM for non-volatile memory with low power consumption. They optimize data storage with lightweight file systems (e.g., LittleFS, SPIFFS) for embedded devices. Compress sensor data before storage to extend the device's lifespan. Ferroelectric random-access memory (FRAM) and other NVMs, such as resistive random access memory (ReRAM), phase-change random access memory (PRAM), and magneto resistive random access memory (MRAM), are used in IoT devices. Still, FRAM is the first commercially available NVM. Recently, a few MB of extremely dependable FRAM have become very popular. Its superior electric features make FRAM a smart choice in sophisticated smartcards, RFID tags, and other electronic devices. The characteristic features of FRAM are the lowest power dissipation, faster read/write speeds of around 50ns, and the highest switching durability of approximately 10^{13}.[16]

Security Optimization

Secure hardware design implement secure boot and trusted execution environments (TEE) to prevent unauthorized firmware modifications. The IoT uses hardware security modules (HSMs) for cryptographic key management and integrates Physically Unclonable Functions (PUFs) for device authentication. In Xie, H., et al. (2023)[17], researchers proposed a trusted execution environment and a blockchain-supported data sharing (TEBDS) architecture. The TEBDS architecture consists of both on-chain and off-chain methods to deliver a secure IoT data-sharing framework. Hardware security modules (HSMs) provide physical security in IoT systems by utilizing a hardware-based root of trust. When HSM is combined with blockchain, it offers robustness, reliability, authenticity, authorization and integrity in industrial IoT systems.[18] The PUFs approach is a very good alternative to traditional cryptography.

Traditional cryptography is useless for IoT due to the high computational requirements. The high computational requirement in conventional cryptography drains the battery of lightweight IoT devices. Also, traditional cryptography uses hardness to solve mathematical problems. However, advances in quantum computers make this requirement irrelevant.[19] Also, cryptography requires a third party to access the keys. This is not feasible for IoT applications, which leads to high overhead on the network. Meanwhile, PUF is suitable for IoT networks. PUF uses a universal truth, such as no two identical chips having the exact characterization, regardless of whether both are going through the same manufacturing process. The identical chips will not share the exact physical properties caused by process-induced variations during chip fabrication. PUF circuits use these feature variations. The PUF utilizes such variations to create a secret key to authenticate IoT equipment.[19]

IoT Middleware and OS

Lightweight IoT operating systems and middleware use optimized OS (e.g., FreeRTOS, Zephyr, TinyOS) for low-power embedded systems and use optimized middleware for efficient resource management and real-time performance. FreeRTOS is a lightweight real-time operating system designed to run efficiently on microcontrollers, although it's not limited to them.[20] Zephyr and TinyOS are modular RTOS options tailored for resource-constrained IoT devices and wireless sensor networks, respectively.[20] IoT middleware and OS are implementing modular firmware updates to reduce memory footprint.[21] There are three ways to extract firmware—bus sniffing, firmware dumping, and reverse engineering. IoT vendors do not publish their firmware to safeguard their Internet Protocol (IP) or limit access to it. That's why researchers used debug ports (e.g., Joint Test Action Group (JTAG)) and Universal Serial Bus (USB) ports manually to extract or dump firmware from IoT devices.[21]

Future Scope

The future of IoT hardware optimization lies in the deeper integration of AI, 6G-ready communication modules, and intelligent energy management systems. Research can explore the deployment of neuromorphic and quantum-inspired processors to enhance edge intelligence while maintaining ultra-low power consumption. As IoT applications become more data-intensive, there is a need for dynamic memory architectures that adapt to varying workloads with minimal energy overhead. Furthermore, security hardware co-design must evolve to counteract emerging cyber threats in IoT environments. Future hardware frameworks should enable plug-and-play modularity, allowing seamless interoperability between diverse IoT devices. Optimization of real-time analytics using federated learning and decentralized AI models will further reduce cloud dependency and enhance privacy. Energy harvesting from non-traditional sources such as ambient light, vibrations, and thermal gradients should be refined to support perpetual operation. Finally, open-source ecosystems for hardware-software co-design will be crucial for accelerating innovation and adoption across verticals, such as healthcare, smart cities, and precision agriculture.

Conclusion

Hardware optimization in IoT is much needed to improve the efficiency, security, and battery life of devices. By leveraging power-efficient microcontrollers, optimized communication modules, AI at the edge, and advanced power management strategies, IoT hardware achieved significant performance gains while reducing costs. Hardware optimization is fundamental to the widespread adoption and scalability of the IoT. This chapter has explored various innovative strategies that collectively enhance the performance, reliability, and energy efficiency of IoT devices while reducing their latency, power usage, and operational costs.

Traditional RAM architectures, when augmented with IPv6 ports, exemplify the transformation of conventional hardware into IoT-compatible components. Modern developments, such as AI-driven low-power architectures, automated optimization frameworks, and TinyML, significantly push the boundaries of real-time data analytics on edge devices with constrained resources. We also observed that IoT systems increasingly benefit from 5G integration, enabling low-latency communication and fostering seamless AI deployment. Advanced energy-management techniques, including genetic algorithm-based hardware optimization and energy harvesting, further extend the operational life of IoT systems. Sections of this chapter have emphasized the importance of ultra-low-power controllers, optimized communication protocols, memory and space efficiency, and robust security mechanisms. Collectively, these advancements lay the foundation for more resilient and scalable IoT ecosystems. As IoT use cases expand from smart homes to industrial automation and smart agriculture, ensuring that the hardware stack becomes not just beneficial but essential. These efforts will determine how effectively we harness IoT's full potential while ensuring environmental sustainability and operational efficiency.

CHAPTER 5

Lower-Power Communication Protocols

The number of Internet-connected devices is growing as a result of developments in various technological fields, including embedded systems, sensors, microelectronic circuits, communication technologies, and mobile operating systems. Nowadays, smart gadgets and objects fuel the majority of Internet traffic. The *Internet of Things* (IoT), as you have learned, is a global network of devices that can connect with each other through certain communication protocols that are object detecting and data processable.[1] Smart cities, smart buildings, security, traffic, remote monitoring, health, energy, disaster detection, agriculture, and industry are just a few of the many uses for IoT.

Wireless Sensor Networks (WSN) are a fundamental part of IoT since they allow for the creation of applications with the ability to sense multiple variables concerning the environment into which the devices are inserted.[3] WSN is a particular type of LoWPAN (*low-power wireless personal area network*) made up of nodes with various types of sensors (e.g., temperature, humidity, and luminosity).[2]

Dr. D. Sharma and Dr. B. Pandey, *Eco-Networking for IoT*,
https://doi.org/10.1007/979-8-8688-2317-6_5

IoT devices gather environmental information, exchange information with other devices using network technologies, and can be accessed via the Internet. Due to their limited hardware capabilities, important performance parameters like throughput, delay, and energy usage are important. Cloud computing technologies enable efficient data processing, collection, and analysis of IoT networks within acceptable timeframes.

Several IoT application-layer communication protocols have been created to solve various issues, with an emphasis on reducing latency, maximizing throughput, and minimizing energy expenditure. Since IoT applications entail a large number of devices, data volume transmitted and security measures in place have significant effects on overall system performance.

WSNs have thrilled the world with their ability to make human life better. WSNs have extensive uses in applications, including agricultural monitoring, industrial monitoring, smart homes, in the automobile sector, and in military use. WSNs are composed of a multitude of tiny sensors that sense, process, and transmit data. These sensors exchange data with other components of networks with wireless interfaces.

Research has been carried out by dropping sensors (measuring current velocities, temperature, salinity, pressure, chemicals, etc.) into the ocean and physically retrieving them to download and process their gathered data. Real-time underwater monitoring requires underwater wireless sensor networks. Submerged wireless sensor network communication has drawn lots of attention, driven by numerous scientific, military, and commercial applications.

Routing Requirements of Low-Power Networks and IoT Applications

IoT/LLN networks may have different routing needs depending on the particulars of each application. The RoLL working group first submitted four informational RFCs outlining the requirements for various LLN groups. Urban LLN (U-LLN) routing specifications were stated in "Routing Requirements for Urban Low-Power and Lossy Networks," by Watteyne, T. et al.[4]. The network structure for applications that run in urban settings, like smart metering, pollution and weather monitoring, and general smart city applications, is provided by this type of LLN. The document identifies three types of devices that U-LLNs can display: sensors, actuators, and routers. The actuator and sensor nodes can measure physical data and, depending on their surroundings, take action. Conversely, routers are in charge of building the sensing infrastructure, connecting to the Internet, regulating energy consumption, and prolonging the network's lifespan. Of them, RFC 5548 deals with U-LLN (*urban low-power and lossy networks*) routing specifications.

Understanding Urban LLNs (U-LLNs)

Urban LLNs are made to supply network infrastructure for applications in smart cities that need scalable, low-power, effective communication. These networks are essential for many applications, including:

- **Smart metering:** Smart metering allows for automated measurements of gas, water, and electricity usage.
- **Pollution monitoring:** Monitoring pollution involves keeping an eye on carbon emissions, air quality, and other environmental factors.
- **Meteorological monitoring:** Meteorological monitoring is the process of gathering and disseminating meteorological data for climate research and forecasting.
- **General smart city operations:** Overarching smart city operations facilitates a range of IoT-powered applications that improve urban living.

Device Types in U-LLNs

Three main device categories, discussed in this section, make up the heterogeneous network architecture that U-LLNs depend on to operate effectively in an urban IoT environment.

Sensor Nodes and Low-Power Communication Protocols

In urban IoT contexts, sensor nodes are essential because they continuously collect environmental data like traffic patterns, temperature, humidity, and air quality. The usage of low-power communication protocols is crucial since energy efficiency is a key concern due to their implementation in large-scale networks. Sensor nodes can send data over great distances with low power consumption thanks to technologies like 6LoWPAN (IPv6 over low-power wireless personal area networks), Zigbee, and LoRaWAN (great range wide area network). Because LoRaWAN enables sensors to communicate over large regions with minimal power consumption, it is very helpful for smart city applications such as smart waste management and air quality monitoring.

Applications like smart lighting and industrial monitoring benefit greatly from Zigbee's low-power mesh networking characteristics, which make it ideal for energy-efficient, short-range communication. Likewise, 6LoWPAN enables IPv6-based communication across low-power wireless networks, guaranteeing sensor nodes' smooth integration into the larger IoT ecosystem. Sensor nodes that use these energy-efficient communication protocols can operate dependably for longer periods of time, lowering maintenance requirements and guaranteeing ongoing data collection in urban IoT contexts.

Actuator Nodes and Low-Power Communication Protocols

The execution layer of IoT systems is made up of actuator nodes, which respond to real-time input from sensor nodes by precisely acting to boost automation and efficiency. Actuator devices need to run with low power consumption to maintain long-term deployment, which requires utilizing low-power communication technologies like Z-Wave, Bluetooth Low Energy (BLE), and NB-IoT (Narrowband IoT). Z-Wave, being developed for low-power short-range application, is best suited for smart home and urban automation networks, (i.e., remotely actuated water valves in smart irrigation and automated security systems). BLE, with its low-energy profile, finds extensive applications in proximity-based use cases like smart locks and wearables for health monitoring that need sporadic but consistent data transfer. For scenarios involving long-distance connectivity with minimal power drain, NB-IoT is the preferred technology since it makes it possible for actuators like industrial automation systems and smart meters to operate optimally with low energy consumption. These low-power protocols make actuator nodes efficiently function in restricted power environments so that automated activities can be carried out reliably with the optimization of battery life.

Routers and Low-Power Communication Protocols

Routers are the foundation of city-wide IoT networks, providing uninterrupted communication among sensor nodes, actuator nodes, and cloud systems. For maximum energy efficiency and network performance, routers use protocols like RPL (routing protocol for low-power and lossy networks), 6LoWPAN, and Wi-SUN (wireless smart ubiquitous networks). RPL is particularly intended for lossy, low-power networks to allow routers to form energy-efficient routing paths with low data loss and increased network lifespan. 6LoWPAN enables routers to support IPv6-based communication across resource-limited wireless networks while ensuring low packet transmission with high efficiency. Wi-SUN, highly adopted for large-scale smart city use cases, enables energy-efficient, long-range connectivity and is hence suitable for public infrastructures like smart grid control and intelligent traffic management. By utilizing such low-power communication protocols, routers are also pivotal in ensuring network reliability, avoiding duplicate transmissions, and continuous data exchange among IoT devices. Such an energy-efficient practice assists in maintaining large-scale IoT deployments while keeping operational costs and power use to a minimum.

By combining low-power communication protocols between sensor nodes, actuator nodes, and routers, urban IoT networks can achieve a balance that is optimal for data efficiency, scalability, and energy saving. In terms of facilitating long-term automation and astute urban administration, this ensures the viability of smart city applications.

Key Considerations for U-LLN Routing

Owing to the particular difficulties associated with urban IoT deployments, U-LLN routing protocols need to:

- Reduce energy use to extend device life, as many nodes run on batteries.
- Support dynamic topologies, as nodes may frequently join or leave the network.
- Ensure reliable data transmission, even in environments with high interference and network congestion.
- Adapt to scalability requirements so that a single smart city deployment can effectively communicate with thousands of devices.

In order to ensure effective, dependable, and scalable communication in smart city applications, IoT-based *low-power and lossy networks* (LLNs) must meet certain routing requirements. Urban LLNs (U-LLNs) are the foundation of contemporary smart cities, utilizing a mix of sensors, actuators, and routers to facilitate automated data gathering, real-time decision-making, and smooth Internet integration. IoT-driven smart city solutions will be more successful as a result of ongoing improvements in energy-efficient networking technology and routing algorithms, which will further improve these networks' sustainability, resilience, and efficiency.

Building automation LLN (BA-LLN) routing standards were described in "Building Automation Routing Requirements in Low-Power and Lossy Networks," by Martocci, J. et al.[5]. Among the many applications for BA are the monitoring of fire alarms, elevator systems, intrusion detection systems, and control access.[6] Wireless devices have the potential to increase flexibility and reduce the costs associated with deploying applications. The network design should accommodate a minimum of 2,000 nodes, which should include sensors, actuators, controllers, and user interface devices for BA applications. Different, smaller applications running in many subnetworks connected by a backbone can make up a full *building management system* (BMS). Each subnetwork may have a different traffic pattern, device density, and a number of other network quirks.

For the installation and replacement of devices to be possible, the routing protocols must offer a self-organizing structure with zero configuration. In addition, they need to be scalable, support devices with limited resources, mobile, manageable, addressing, dynamic route selection, and secure.

By cleverly merging the data from the numerous inexpensive microsensor nodes, users can network hundreds or thousands of them together to precisely monitor a distant environment. Strong routing techniques with low latency and energy efficiency are necessary for these wireless networks.[8]

Devices in ad hoc networks must self-organize into a network in the absence of preexisting infrastructure. The creation of tiny, reasonably priced, low-power sensors, known as *microsensors,* that may be linked over a wireless network has been made possible by developments in sensor technology, low-power electronics, and low-power radio frequency (RF) design.[8]

LEACH (Low-Energy Adaptive Clustering Hierarchy) Protocol

The self-organizing, energy-efficient LEACH protocol was created for wireless sensor networks. Sensor nodes are grouped into clusters, and a cluster head (CH) oversees each cluster. The CH is in charge of gathering information from its member nodes, processing it, and sending the combined information to the base station (BS). LEACH uses less energy than traditional routing protocols, which permit all nodes to connect directly to the BS, by ensuring that only CHs control long-distance transmissions.

CHs are chosen at random in every round to balance energy consumption and keep some nodes from using up their energy too rapidly. To further improve network durability and efficiency, LEACH also uses data fusion and compression techniques to remove unnecessary transmissions.

Cluster-Based Communication vs. Traditional Routing

Every sensor node talks directly with the base station (BS) in conventional routing protocols, which uses a lot of energy, particularly for nodes that are far from the BS. By guaranteeing that only a small number of carefully chosen CHs manage long-distance transmissions, LEACH solves this problem and greatly lessens the communication load on individual nodes.

Random Selection of Cluster Heads (CHs)

The CHs are chosen at random in each round, which is one of LEACH's primary characteristics. The uniform distribution of energy consumption across all nodes over time is guaranteed by this randomization. In order to avoid early energy depletion of certain nodes, the selection procedure is based on a probability function that keeps the same nodes from being selected as CHs repeatedly.

Data Fusion and Compression Techniques

At the CH level, LEACH uses data fusion and compression techniques to further maximize energy efficiency. The CH aggregates, analyzes, and compresses the data prior to transmission, as opposed to sending the raw data from every node straight to the BS. By avoiding duplicate data transfers, this procedure lowers network traffic overall and saves energy.

Working Mechanism of LEACH

The working of LEACH is divided into two primary phases—the setup phase and the steady-state phase.

Setup Phase

Cluster formation and cluster head selection are handled during the setup phase. This phase occurs at the beginning of each round and involves the following steps:

- **Cluster head selection:** Each node independently decides whether to become a CH based on a probability function.

- **Cluster formation:** After the CHs are selected, they broadcast their status to the other nodes. After hearing these ads, non-CH nodes use the broadcast's signal strength to determine which CH to join. Clusters are then created by each node sending a join request to the selected CH.
- **TDMA scheduling:** To ensure effective data transfer free from collisions, the CH allots Time Division Multiple Access (TDMA) slots to each cluster member.

Steady-State Phase

The steady-state phase, during which actual data transmission occurs, starts once the clusters are created.

- **Data aggregation and collection:** During their designated TDMA slots, member nodes detect their surroundings and transmit the data they have gathered to the appropriate CHs. CHs reduce the overall number of transferred packets by performing data aggregation and compression in place of transmitting raw data.
- **Data transmission to base station:** CHs send the combined data to the BS following processing. Depending on the network design, this transmission can be either single-hop (direct communication) or multi-hop (via other CHs).
- **Cluster head rotation:** CH duties alternate on a regular basis to keep CHs from using up too much energy. This extends the network's total lifespan by guaranteeing that every node shares the energy load.

Advantages of LEACH

LEACH maximizes energy efficiency in WSNs. By using randomized CH selection and hierarchical clustering, it greatly extends a network's lifetime. The following sections outline some of its main benefits.

Energy Efficiency

- By creating clusters, where CHs compile and transmit data, LEACH lowers the number of direct transmissions to the base station.
- It lowers energy waste and extends battery life by minimizing redundant transfers.

Load Balancing

- Round after round, CHs are rotated at random to prevent any one sensor node from using up all of its energy in a short period of time.
- This results in a longer network life by providing regular energy utilization.

Scalability

- LEACH can grow effectively with large networks thanks to the clustering method.
- Communication overhead is decreased because nodes only speak to their individual CHs rather than to the BS directly.

Improved Data Transmission

- In order to minimize redundant data transfer, CHs compile and compress sensor data prior to delivering it to the BS.
- This increases network efficiency and bandwidth consumption.

Self-Organizing Capability

- LEACH arranges nodes into clusters dynamically and functions without centralized control.
- It is hence very flexible in response to modifications in network topology.

Reduced Latency

- Compared to multi-hop routing, LEACH lowers data transmission latency by creating localized clusters.
- Because of this, it may be used in real-time for tasks like environmental monitoring.

Fault Tolerance

- Network failures brought on by a single node's energy depletion are reduced because CHs fluctuate on a regular basis.
- Network resilience is ensured by having a backup node in case of a CH's death.

Enhanced Network Lifetime

- LEACH optimizes energy consumption across all nodes, thereby extending the operating life of WSNs.
- This is especially helpful in situations where changing the battery is not feasible.

Because of its improved communication efficiency, energy savings, and self-organizing capabilities, LEACH remains a fundamental protocol for energy-conscious WSNs. Its advantages make it a popular protocol in industrial IoT applications, healthcare monitoring, and environmental monitoring, despite certain disadvantages, such as uneven cluster dispersion.

Limitations of LEACH

LEACH has some drawbacks that reduce its effectiveness in large-scale or dynamic WSNs, despite its many advantages in reducing energy consumption and prolonging network lifetime. Random CH selection, one-hop communication, the equal energy assumption, and the lack of mobility assistance are some of these drawbacks.

Random Cluster Head (CH) Selection

LEACH's random CH selection technique is one of its fundamental drawbacks; while it aims to balance energy consumption, it occasionally results in an uneven distribution of CHs across the network. Because CHs are chosen probabilistically without regard to their spatial locations, some areas might have too many CHs, while others might have too few or none at all.

- Too many CHs in a localized area can result in overlapping coverage, which can be wasteful in terms of resources.
- If there are not enough CHs in some regions, some sensor nodes will be compelled to transmit data over long distances, leading to higher energy consumption and lower network efficiency.
- The absence of adaptive CH selection relying on node density or residual energy can result in ineffective clustering as well as inferior energy utilization.

Single-Hop Communication

LEACH presumes that all CHs can communicate directly with the base station via a single-hop transmission. This is okay for small networks but is very inefficient and unrealistic for large-scale WSNs.

- In the case of massive networks, remote CHs may spend too much energy on direct communication, exhausting their battery lives quickly.
- Nodes on the boundary of the network may have difficulty finding a CH within an optimal range, which will lead to increased transmission delays and packet loss.
- The absence of multi-hop routing means that LEACH is unsuitable for applications where sensor nodes are deployed over large geographical areas, such as smart cities or agricultural monitoring.

To address this issue, hierarchical or multi-hop routing versions of LEACH (such as LEACH-M and LEACH-C) have been proposed, but the original LEACH protocol lacks this capability.

Equal Energy Assumption

LEACH is based on the assumption that all sensor nodes have the same initial energy levels, which is not the case in real-world implementations. Sensor nodes in real deployments can have different battery capacities due to differences in hardware, environmental factors, and past workload.

- Nodes near the base station or often voted as CHs tend to exhaust their energy more rapidly, resulting in early network crashes.
- LEACH does not consider residual energy levels when selecting CHs, meaning a node with low battery might still be chosen as a CH, reducing overall network stability.
- Since energy consumption varies based on communication distance, processing, and data aggregation, assuming uniform energy availability leads to inefficient network performance over time.

To overcome this, energy-aware variations of LEACH have been developed, such as LEACH-E (Energy-aware LEACH), which selects CHs based on their remaining energy levels.

No Consideration of Node Mobility

LEACH is designed for static sensor networks, where nodes remain in fixed positions after deployment. It does not support mobile sensor nodes, making it unsuitable for applications that require mobility, such as:

- Vehicle tracking systems, where sensors move with cars or drones.

- Healthcare applications, where wearable sensor nodes monitor patient movement.
- Disaster management scenarios, where sensor nodes may shift due to environmental changes.

Since CHs are selected at the beginning of each round and remain fixed for the duration of that round, mobile nodes can cause frequent disconnections, leading to data loss, inefficient clustering, and increased network instability. LEACH does not have a mechanism to dynamically adapt to changing node positions, making it less effective for dynamic and mobile WSN environments.

Variants of LEACH

To overcome these limitations, several improved versions of LEACH have been developed:

- **LEACH-C (LEACH-Centralized):** Unlike LEACH, where CHs are selected randomly, LEACH-C uses a centralized approach where the BS selects CHs based on node location and energy levels.
- **LEACH-F (LEACH-Fixed):** In this version, clusters are formed once and remain fixed throughout the network lifetime, reducing setup overhead.
- **V-LEACH (Vice Cluster Head LEACH):** To increase reliability, V-LEACH adds a Vice CH to assume duties in the event that the primary CH fails.
- **E-LEACH (Energy-LEACH):** This algorithm ensures that nodes with higher energy have a higher probability of being CHs by modifying CH selection and taking residual energy into account.

These modifications strengthen the fundamental LEACH protocol and fix several flaws.

Applications of LEACH

LEACH is extensively utilized in many WSN applications, including:

- **Environmental monitoring:** Weather forecasting, pollution monitoring, and smart agriculture all use environmental monitoring.
- **Healthcare systems:** Wireless body sensor networks (WBSNs) use healthcare systems to keep an eye on patients' health.
- **Military surveillance:** Military surveillance is utilized in intrusion detection systems and battlefield monitoring.
- **Industrial automation:** Smart companies use industrial automation to keep an eye on machine conditions and avoid malfunctions.

LEACH's adaptability makes it the perfect option for a range of real-world situations.

The goal of the popular and essential LEACH hierarchical clustering technology is to increase the energy efficiency of wireless sensor networks. Longer network lifetimes are achieved by LEACH's considerable reduction in overall power consumption through the clustering of sensor nodes and the rotation of CHs. LEACH is still a mainstay in WSN research despite its shortcomings, and it has spawned many enhanced versions, such as LEACH-C and E-LEACH. Considering how well it balances energy use and eliminates redundant data, LEACH remains a useful protocol for energy-efficient wireless sensor applications.

Types of Low-Power Communication Protocols

Low-power communication protocols are made especially to reduce energy use while guaranteeing dependable and effective data transfer in embedded systems, IoT devices, and WSNs. In applications where devices depend on energy harvesting or battery power and must operate well for prolonged periods of time without frequent maintenance or recharging, these procedures are essential.

These protocols help increase network scalability, save operating costs, and prolong battery life by optimizing power utilization. Smart homes, industrial automation, healthcare monitoring, agriculture, and environmental sensing are just a few of the many IoT applications that depend on them. Enabling seamless connectivity while reducing power waste is the main objective of low-power communication protocols.

Categorization Based on Range and Functionality

Three primary types of low-power communication protocols can be distinguished by their application scenarios, power efficiency, and range:

- **Short-range low-power protocols:** These protocols are made for wearables, smart home appliances, and personal area networks (PANs), which need to communicate over a short distance (usually up to 100 meters). These protocols prioritize effective data transport and extremely low power consumption. Bluetooth Low Energy (BLE), Zigbee, Z-Wave, and Thread are a few examples.

- **Long-range low-power protocols:** Because these protocols are designed for wide-area coverage, devices can communicate across distances of kilometers while using very little power. They are employed in industrial IoT, asset tracking, smart cities, and agriculture. Sigfox, NB-IoT (Narrowband IoT), LoRa (Long Range), and LTE-M (LTE Cat-M1) are a few examples.
- **Medium-range low-power protocols:** Compared to conventional wireless technologies, these protocols offer a greater range while using less power because they strike a balance between coverage and power efficiency. They work well for logistics, smart agriculture, and industrial automation. Wi-Fi HaLow (IEEE 802.11ah) is one example.

Short-Range Low-Power Protocols

Short-range low-power communication protocols are primarily designed for indoor environments, smart homes, and personal-area networks (PANs). They focus on minimizing power consumption while maintaining efficient data transmission, making them ideal for wearable devices, home automation, healthcare monitoring, and industrial control systems. These protocols generally operate within the 2.4 GHz ISM band or sub-GHz frequencies, offering a good balance between power efficiency, data rate, and coverage. The following sections outline some widely used short-range low-power protocols.

Bluetooth Low Energy (BLE)

Bluetooth Low Energy, or BLE, is a power-efficient extension of the classic Bluetooth, designed for applications that require low power consumption, sporadic data exchange, and close-range wireless communication. BLE is widely adopted in wearables, fitness trackers, smart home appliances, medical sensors, and industrial IoT devices. BLE operates within the 2.4 GHz ISM band and is tailored for ultra-low power consumption, allowing devices to run for months or even years on small batteries.

Advantages of BLE:

- **Low power consumption:** BLE is designed to be extremely energy-efficient, with devices being able to operate on small batteries (e.g., coin-cell batteries) for long durations.
- **Fast connection setup:** BLE supports quick wake-up times and low-latency connections, which make it especially well-suited for use in applications where there is periodic but short data transmission needed.
- **Global standard and compatibility:** BLE is a broad industry standard, with interoperability across various devices and manufacturers.
- **Support for mesh networking:** BLE supports working in a mesh network, enabling many devices to talk to each other, which is great for smart home and industrial IoT use cases.
- **Secure communication:** BLE supports AES-128 encryption, enabling secure data transmission for secure use cases like healthcare and finance.
- **Cost-effective implementation:** BLE modules are inexpensive and easy to implement, making them perfectly suited for mass-market products.
- **Widely adopted ecosystem:** BLE is natively supported by all operating systems like iOS, Android, Windows, and macOS, and hence widely adopted.

Disadvantages of BLE:

- **Limited data transfer rate:** BLE is optimized for power and thus its peak data rate (2 Mbps) is lower compared to conventional Bluetooth (3 Mbps) and Wi-Fi.
- **Short range:** BLE offers a limited range (typically 10–50 meters indoors, up to 100 meters in the open air), and thus it is not feasible for extended distance communication.
- **Interference issues:** Since BLE operates on the 2.4 GHz ISM band, it is interfered with by Wi-Fi, microwave ovens, and other Bluetooth devices.
- **Not for ongoing streaming:** BLE is not designed for high-bandwidth applications like audio or video streaming; the classic Bluetooth is employed for them.
- **Maximum latency of certain other low-power protocols:** While BLE is low-latency, other protocols (like Zigbee or Z-Wave) may be better for certain specific industrial IoT use cases.

Zigbee

Zigbee is a low-data-rate, low-power wireless communication protocol using the IEEE 802.15.4 standard. It is mainly used for applications that demand low energy usage and secure communication over short ranges. Zigbee is extensively used in smart homes, industrial automation, and lighting control systems, where devices must communicate effectively with low power consumption.

One of Zigbee's prominent features is its mesh networking functionality, which permits devices to relay data across a network. Mesh networking provides broader coverage and strengthens network reliability.

Smart thermostats, light systems, and security sensors oftentimes utilize Zigbee due to its power conservativeness, scalability, and wireless communication stability.

Advantages of Zigbee:

- **Low power consumption:** Zigbee is optimized for use in applications in which energy efficiency is of utmost importance. Zigbee devices can run for months or even years on tiny batteries, thanks to its power-saving mechanisms, which makes it perfect for battery-powered smart home and industrial devices.
- **Mesh networking support:** Unlike other point-to-point communication, Zigbee is mesh network-enabled, meaning devices can relay data to other devices, increasing network range and reliability. If a node fails, the network can automatically reroute data, providing continuous connectivity.
- **Scalability:** Zigbee networks are capable of handling hundreds to thousands of devices, making it very scalable for massive IoT applications like smart homes, industrial automation, and smart cities.
- **Cost-effective:** Compared to cellular networks and Wi-Fi, Zigbee modules are cheap, and this makes them an economical option for IoT and home automation systems. The low-power consumption also helps in lowering maintenance costs by minimizing battery replacements.

- **Secure communication:** Zigbee features AES-128 encryption, making data transmission secure. This is a good option for applications that require data privacy and security, including home security systems and industrial monitoring.

Disadvantages of Zigbee:

- **Limited data rate:** Zigbee has a maximum data rate of 250 kbps, which is significantly lower than Wi-Fi or Bluetooth. This renders it inappropriate for use in applications involving high-speed data transfer (e.g., video streaming or large file exchange).
- **Shorter range compared to other protocols:** Whereas the range of Zigbee can be extended with mesh networking, the range of its individual devices is only 10-100 meters based on the environment. By comparison, LoRa or Wi-Fi HaLow protocols support longer-range communications.
- **Interference in the 2.4 GHz band:** Zigbee uses the 2.4 GHz ISM band, which is common with Wi-Fi and Bluetooth, and thus may cause interference in dense environments. This can impact network stability and necessitate meticulous frequency management.
- **Higher latency compared to some protocols:** Due to its multi-hop mesh networking, Zigbee may experience higher latency compared to direct point-to-point communication protocols like Bluetooth Low Energy (BLE), making it less suitable for real-time applications.

Z-Wave

Z-Wave is a wireless technology created especially for home automation, security, and smart home appliances. Whereas Zigbee uses the 2.4 GHz range, Z-Wave uses sub-GHz frequency ranges (such as 908 MHz in the US). This frequency selection reduces interference from common wireless technologies like Wi-Fi and Bluetooth, resulting in more reliable connections.

Because Z-Wave signals have a lower frequency than Zigbee signals, they can travel farther and pass through walls more effectively. Z-Wave can readily cover a large house or workplace without the need for numerous repeaters, thanks to its usual 100-meter range in the open.

Advantages of Z-Wave:

- **Reduced wireless interference:** Z-Wave avoids interference in the 2.4 GHz frequency, which is used by Bluetooth, Zigbee, and Wi-Fi, by operating in the sub-GHz spectrum, which is normally 868-928 MHz. In crowded Wi-Fi settings, this leads to more reliable communication and fewer connectivity problems.
- **Extended range:** Compared to Zigbee, Z-Wave signals may travel farther and pass through walls more effectively because of their lower frequency. Z-Wave can efficiently cover a large house or workplace without the need for as many repeaters because it typically has a range of 100 meters in open regions.
- **Optimized for smart home applications:** Z-Wave is ideal for smart security systems, lighting controls, thermostats, and other IoT devices because it was designed with home automation in mind. Because of its low power consumption, gadgets like sensors and smart locks can run on batteries for years.

- **Reliable and secure communication:** Z-Wave employs a source-routed mesh network, in which message delivery is facilitated by tightly regulated data transfer. Additionally, Z-Wave has AES-128 encryption, which provides a secure channel for critical applications like access control and home security.
- **High device compatibility:** Due to Z-Wave's high level of standardization, devices from different manufacturers can easily communicate with one another. This eliminates the possibility of incompatibilities and enables customers to effortlessly integrate many smart home devices.

Disadvantages of Z-Wave:

- **Lower data rate:** With a top data transfer rate of only 100 kbps, Z-Wave is significantly slower than Wi-Fi or Bluetooth and slower than Zigbee (250 kbps). Due to this, it is unsuitable for applications such as real-time data transfers or video streaming that require rapid or high-bandwidth transmission.
- **Limited number of connected devices:** Most home automation systems can utilize a single Z-Wave network with 232 devices, but it is not as scalable as Zigbee, which supports thousands of units. This limitation can be a hindrance for smart building projects that are large in scale.
- **Higher cost compared to Zigbee:** Gadgets that utilize Z-Wave tend to be pricier than their Zigbee equivalent, and Z-Wave chipsets are proprietary. Although Z-Wave

devices are restricted to certified manufacturers, Zigbee is an open standard allowing lower costs of production and broader implementation.

- **Regional frequency limitations:** Depending on the location, Z-Wave uses a different frequency (for example, 868 MHz in Europe and 908 MHz in the United States). This implies that devices bought in one nation might not function with networks in another, which could be a drawback for customers around the world.

Thread

Thread is a low-power, IPv6-enabled wireless communication protocol that was invented by Google's Nest Labs. Thread is specially created for smart home applications that are secure, trustworthy, and scalable. Unlike other smart home protocols, Thread is open standard-based and provides native IP support, thus ease of integration into the larger IoT environment. One of Thread's most interesting features is the mesh networking support, which enables devices to effectively communicate and stretch coverage while utilizing very little power. It is also optimized for use with other smart home protocols such as Matter, enhancing smart home device interoperability.

Advantages of Thread:

- **IPv6-based communication:** Thread supports IPv6, enabling devices to talk directly to each other over the Internet without the need for a gateway. This is easier to integrate with cloud services and other IP devices more straightforward.
- **Secure and reliable network:** Thread uses AES-128 encryption to secure device-to-device communication,

preventing unauthorized access and data corruption. It is also self-healing mesh networking, whereby if one device fails, traffic is rerouted through the other nodes to keep running without interruption.

- **Low power consumption:** Thread is power-frugal for devices, so that it's well-suited to battery-powered smart home devices such as sensors, door locks, and light switches. Devices may run for years on low-power batteries.
- **Supports mesh networking:** Thread's self-organization and self-healing mesh let devices communicate optimally, building network reliability and extending coverage without a central point. This destroys single points of failure and augments the smart home system overall performance.
- **Interoperability with Matter:** Thread is engineered to coexist flawlessly with Matter, the new smart home standard supported by Google, Apple, Amazon, and other industry leaders. This provides future-proof compatibility, enabling devices of various manufacturers to communicate seamlessly.

Disadvantages of Thread:

- **Limited device support (still growing):** As much as Thread is gaining adoption, it is not widely supported compared to Zigbee or Z-Wave. Many smart devices are still built around Wi-Fi, Zigbee, or Bluetooth, and therefore it is necessary to check for Thread compatibility before making purchases.

- **Requires a Thread Border Router:** Whereas Zigbee and Z-Wave employ dedicated hubs, Thread products need a Thread Border Router in order to attach to other non-Thread networks such as Wi-Fi or Ethernet. Though many Google Nest and Apple HomePod products can currently act as Thread Border Routers, the full connectivity will perhaps require some added hardware for certain users.
- **Higher initial cost:** Since Thread is relatively new compared to Zigbee or Z-Wave, compatible devices are more costly. As the adoption increases, prices will likely drop, but early adopters will have to pay a premium for Thread-enabled devices.
- **Complexity in Setup:** It requires the installation of a Border Router and proper configuration, which is likely more complex than connecting Wi-Fi or Bluetooth devices. People without experience with networking may not find it easy to install and use.

Long-Range Low-Power Protocols

Long-range low-power protocols are optimized for wide-area communication with minimal energy consumption. Such protocols are widely employed in applications like smart agriculture, industrial IoT, and environmental monitoring, where devices must send data over long distances while running on battery power for years. Some of the most widely used long-range low-power communication protocols are explained in this section.

LoRa (Long Range)

LoRa is a popular wireless communication protocol that applies spread spectrum modulation to provide long-range and low-power communication. LoRa uses unlicensed sub-GHz ISM bands (such as 868 MHz in Europe, 915 MHz in the United States) to support longer coverage in smart cities, agriculture, and industrial automation.

- **Battery life:** LoRa technology can run up to ten years on a tiny battery.
- **Network topology:** Compatible with star and mesh topologies with flexible deployment.
- **Use cases:** Used in remote sensor networks, smart irrigation, asset tracking, and environmental monitoring.

Advantages of LoRa:

- **Extensive communication range:** With a range of up to 15 km in rural areas and 2–5 km in urban areas, LoRa provides long-distance communication that is appropriate for wide-ranging applications like industrial IoT, smart agriculture, and environmental monitoring.
- **Low power consumption:** LoRa's extremely low power consumption is one of its main benefits; battery-powered devices can operate for up to ten years with very little energy use.
- **Operates in unlicensed frequency bands:** By using sub-GHz ISM bands (such as 868 MHz in Europe and 915 MHz in the United States), LoRa eliminates the need for expensive spectrum licensing fees, which reduces deployment costs.

- **Highly scalable for large networks:** LoRaWAN (LoRa's network protocol) is capable of handling thousands of connected devices, so it is very scalable for uses such as smart cities and industrial automation.
- **Flexible network topology:** It supports both star and mesh topologies, supporting flexible deployment according to the application needs. This facilitates effective communication and wide coverage.
- **Robust interference resistance:** LoRa employs spread spectrum modulation, which increases the signal strength against interference, allowing reliable communication in noisy conditions.
- **Ideal for IoT and remote applications:** LoRa is extensively employed in smart agriculture (irrigation monitoring), asset tracking, smart metering, and environmental monitoring, where low-power, long-range communication is needed.

Disadvantages of LoRa:

- **Low data transmission rate:** LoRa is at a low data rate (usually less than 50 kbps) and thus not applicable to applications where high-speed data transfer is needed, (e.g., video streaming or real-time monitoring).
- **Higher latency:** Due to its low data rate, LoRa networks may experience increased latency, which can impact real-time applications like live tracking and emergency response systems.

- **Limited downlink communication:** Most implementations of LoRaWAN make uplink messages (sensor to gateway) their priority, and downlink messages (gateway to sensor) are sparse, complicating bidirectional communication.
- **Interference and network congestion:** In tight deployments where there are numerous LoRa devices, congestion and packet collisions are possible, lowering communication efficiency.
- **Regulatory restrictions:** LoRa works in unlicensed spectrum that is governed locally and subject to duty cycle limitations, limiting how many transmissions one can have over a certain amount of time.
- **Requires a gateway infrastructure:** Although LoRa devices are themselves low power, deploying a LoRaWAN network involves gateways, which can add infrastructure costs based on the scale of deployment.

LoRa is a great low-power, long-range protocol for IoT applications that need wide-area coverage, low energy consumption, and low data rates. It is not ideal for high-speed or real-time applications because it has a low data transmission rate, higher latency, and network congestion risks in high-density deployments.

Sigfox

An ultra-narrowband communication system called Sigfox is designed for long-distance, low-power transmissions. It is perfect for sensors that send tiny amounts of data infrequently because it is made especially for low-data-rate applications.

- **Data rate:** It is not appropriate for high-bandwidth applications because it only supports very low data rates (up to 100 bps).
- **Battery efficiency:** The low power consumption of sensors allows them to function for several years on a single battery.
- **Use cases:** Environmental sensors, smart meters, and asset tracking are common uses.

Advantages of Sigfox:

- **Ultra-low power consumption:** Due to Sigfox's low energy consumption, devices can run on a small battery for five to ten years. This is advantageous for IoT applications when devices are placed in remote areas and battery replacement is expensive or challenging.
- **Long-range coverage:** Sub-GHz frequencies, such as 868 MHz in Europe and 902 MHz in the United States, are used by Sigfox, which offers a communication range of up to 50 km in rural areas and 10 km in urban areas. This makes it perfect for uses requiring wide coverage areas, such as environmental monitoring, logistics, and agriculture.
- **Low cost of deployment:** Sigfox does not require costly spectrum licenses because it uses unlicensed frequency ranges. Users can also take advantage of existing Sigfox networks, which eliminates the need for expensive infrastructure deployment.

- **Efficient for low-data applications:** Applications that need sporadic data transfer as opposed to constant communication are best suited for Sigfox. This makes it perfect for applications where little data packets are exchanged on a regular basis, such as environmental sensors, smart meters, and asset tracking.
- **Interference-resistant technology:** Sigfox reduces interference from other wireless signals by using ultra-narrowband (UNB) modulation. Even in locations with various radio frequency transmissions, this guarantees dependable connection.

Disadvantages of Sigfox:

- **Extremely low data rate:** The greatest data rate that Sigfox can provide is 100 bps, which is far less than that of other wireless communication methods. Because of this, it is not appropriate for applications that need real-time communication, streaming video, or huge data transfers.
- **Limited global coverage:** In contrast to cellular-based protocols (such as LTE-M or NB-IoT), Sigfox is only accessible in areas with established network infrastructure. Users cannot communicate if a region is not covered by Sigfox.
- **Restricted data transmission:** The daily message sending limit set by Sigfox is 140 uplink messages of 12 bytes and 4 downlink messages of 8 bytes. Because of this limitation, it is not appropriate for applications that need real-time monitoring or frequent updates.

- **Limited downlink communication:** Device-to-network (uplink) communication is Sigfox's primary focus, whereas downlink (network-to-device) communications are severely constrained. This indicates that it is not the best option for applications that need regular bidirectional connection or remote device control.
- **Dependence on Sigfox network operators:** For connectivity, Sigfox users must rely on outside Sigfox network providers. Sigfox necessitates subscription-based access to preexisting networks, which may restrict flexibility and raise operating costs in contrast to LoRa, which allows users to set up their own private networks.

NB-IoT (Narrowband IoT)

Operating on licensed LTE airwaves, NB-IoT is a cellular-based IoT protocol that provides dependable connectivity, low power consumption, and extensive indoor coverage. In contrast to Sigfox and LoRa, NB-IoT uses the current cellular infrastructure to offer a reliable and secure connection.

- **Coverage:** Effective in rural places, underground facilities, and urban areas.
- **Battery life:** Sensors can operate for years thanks to low-power optimization.
- **Use cases:** Use cases include connected wearables, industrial IoT, smart meters, and environmental monitoring.

Advantages of NB-IoT:

- **Excellent coverage:** NB-IoT can offer deep interior and underground coverage since it uses licensed LTE frequency. It is perfect for applications in smart cities, smart meters, and industrial monitoring where sensors must work in remote areas, tunnels, or basements.
- **Low power consumption:** Devices can operate for up to ten years on a single battery thanks to NB-IoT's long battery life optimization. Because of this, it can be used for low-power IoT applications like asset tracking and environmental monitoring.
- **Reliable and secure connectivity:** Compared to unlicensed protocols like LoRa and Sigfox, NB-IoT offers superior dependability, robust security (AES encryption), and low interference because it operates on cellular networks. For mission-critical applications like industrial automation and wearable healthcare technology, this is essential.
- **Leverages the existing cellular infrastructure:** By utilizing current LTE networks, NB-IoT eliminates the requirement for further infrastructure, in contrast to LoRa or Sigfox, which call for independent network deployment. This makes it possible for IoT solutions to be deployed more quickly and scalable.
- **Supports massive IoT deployment:** With the capacity to manage up to 50,000 connected devices per cell, NB-IoT is perfect for large-scale industrial IoT applications.

Disadvantages of NB-IoT:

- **Subscription costs:** In contrast to LoRa, which allows users to create private networks, NB-IoT necessitates a telecom provider subscription. For small-scale IoT deployments, this reduces cost-effectiveness by raising operating expenses.
- **Higher latency compared to LTE-M:** Due to its higher latency than LTE-M, NB-IoT is less appropriate for real-time applications that demand quick answers, like industrial automation, vehicle tracking, and voice communication.
- **Limited data transmission rate:** Applications like video surveillance and telemedicine that demand high-speed transmission cannot use NB-IoT because it only supports modest data rates (up to 250 kbps).
- **Restricted mobility support:** NB-IoT is intended for low-mobility or fixed devices, in contrast to LTE-M, which facilitates smooth handovers between cell towers. Because of this, it is less useful for tracking moving things, such as cars or drones.
- **Dependence on cellular network availability:** The performance of NB-IoT is dependent on the coverage of cellular networks. Connectivity may be erratic or nonexistent in places with poor LTE signals or where network providers have not implemented NB-IoT capability.

Smart meters, environmental monitoring, and industrial IoT are just a few of the stationary, low-power, long-range applications that benefit greatly from NB-IoT, a cellular IoT protocol that is extremely safe, dependable, and power-efficient. However, it is not appropriate for applications that need high-speed, mobile, or real-time communication because to its higher prices, constrained data rates, and lack of real-time capabilities.

LTE-M (LTE Cat-M1)

Advantages of LTE-M include the following:

- **Supports voice communication and mobility:** In contrast to NB-IoT, LTE-M offers in-cell handover and voice over LTE (VoLTE), making it appropriate for use in mobile apps, wearable technology, and vehicle tracking. It facilitates real-time communication for fleet management, emergency services, and healthcare.
- **Higher data rates:** Compared to NB-IoT, LTE-M has faster data transmission rates (up to 1 Mbps), enabling real-time applications like linked cars, smart healthcare, and industrial automation.
- **Low latency for real-time applications:** Compared to NB-IoT, LTE-M offers a shorter latency (<100 ms), which makes it appropriate for interactive and real-time monitoring applications like telemedicine, industrial IoT, and remote-controlled robotics where prompt reaction is essential.
- **Extended coverage and reliability:** Operating on licensed LTE airwaves, LTE-M offers strong indoor and subterranean coverage along with great reliability and security. This makes it beneficial for industrial monitoring, smart meters, and asset tracking.

- **Leverages existing LTE networks:** Since LTE-M can be implemented utilizing current 4G LTE networks, it eliminates the need for new infrastructure and lowers setup costs for extensive IoT applications.
- **Supports firmware updates over-the-air (FOTA):** By enabling over-the-air firmware updates, LTE-M facilitates remote maintenance and upgrades of IoT devices without the need for physical interaction.

Disadvantages of LTE-M include the following:

- **Higher power consumption compared to NB-IoT:** Since LTE-M uses more power than NB-IoT, its batteries don't last as long—usually around five years as opposed to NB-IoT's ten-year lifespan. It is therefore less appropriate for ultra-low-power uses, such as distant sensors.
- **Higher network costs:** Unlike LoRa or Sigfox, which can operate on private networks, LTE-M necessitates a cellular network subscription, which raises operating expenses.
- **Limited availability in some regions:** Despite being extensively supported, LTE-M's accessibility varies by cell operator and might not be available in all nations or in rural locations with inadequate LTE-M coverage.
- **More complex implementation:** LTE-M is less adaptable for small-scale IoT installations than LoRa or Sigfox since it requires integration with mobile networks and has a more complicated setup.

Wearables, car tracking, and industrial IoT are all made possible by LTE-M, a great low-power, long-range protocol that offers real-time connectivity, mobility, and high data rates. However, it might not be as appropriate for battery-sensitive and budget-conscious IoT applications because to its increased power consumption, network expenses, and restricted availability.

In general, long-range low-power protocols are perfect for sensor-based and IoT applications because they minimize power consumption while extending connectivity across large areas. Data transmission requirements, power consumption, cost, and network availability all influence the protocol selection:

- **LoRa:** Ideal for long-distance, private networks requiring less data.
- **Sigfox:** Perfect for applications requiring very little power and sporadic data transfer.
- **NB-IoT:** Ideal for dependable, long-term connectivity and extensive indoor coverage.
- **LTE-M:** Best for real-time applications that need mobility and faster data speeds.

Medium-Range Low-Power Protocols

Medium-range low-power protocols are perfect for supply chain management, smart agriculture, and industrial automation because they strike a compromise between communication range and energy efficiency. These protocols allow for dependable wireless communication over tens to hundreds of meters, guaranteeing smooth data transfer between IoT devices while using very little power. They are frequently utilized in applications like smart farming, warehouse monitoring, and industrial automation where equipment must run for lengthy periods of time between battery changes. Mesh networking, low-latency communication, and secure data transmission are just a few of the distinctive qualities that medium-range protocols like Bluetooth Low Energy (BLE), Zigbee, and Z-Wave offer. Applications requiring efficient communication, minimal power consumption, and moderate data speeds in confined or semi-open spaces frequently use these protocols.

Wi-Fi HaLow (IEEE 802.11ah)

An expansion of conventional Wi-Fi that uses less power, Wi-Fi HaLow (IEEE 802.11ah) is made to function in sub-GHz frequency ranges. In comparison to conventional Wi-Fi, this allows it to offer a longer range, improved penetration through obstructions and reduced power usage. It is especially helpful for applications like outdoor IoT, smart agriculture, and industrial automation, where traditional Wi-Fi is ineffective because of its shorter range and greater power requirements.

Wi-Fi HaLow supports faster data speeds than other low-power protocols like Zigbee or LoRa, which makes it ideal for applications that need safe, dependable, and quick data transfer while still maximizing energy efficiency. Wi-Fi HaLow is the perfect option for real-time monitoring, automation, and smart infrastructure deployments because of its long-range connectivity and minimal power consumption.

Advantages of Wi-Fi HaLow:

- **Extended range:** Utilizes sub-GHz frequencies for improved coverage and penetration via obstructions like walls.

- **Low power consumption:** More effective than conventional Wi-Fi, which makes it appropriate for IoT devices that run on batteries.

- **High data rates:** Allows for faster data transfer than other low-power protocols, such as LoRa or Zigbee.

- **Better security:** Uses Wi-Fi security technologies to provide secure and encrypted connection.
- **Supports large networks:** Can manage several linked devices, which is advantageous for applications in smart cities and industry.

Disadvantages of Wi-Fi HaLow:

- **Higher power consumption than LPWAN:** Battery life is limited because, despite its efficiency, it still uses more power than Sigfox, LoRa, or NB-IoT.
- **Limited deployment:** Wi-Fi HaLow adoption is still growing, and infrastructure support is not as widespread as traditional Wi-Fi or cellular IoT.
- **Interference in Sub-GHz band:** Can experience interference from other low-power networks, affecting reliability in dense environments.
- **Hardware costs:** Requires new chipsets and devices, leading to higher initial costs compared to traditional Wi-Fi solutions.

Wi-Fi HaLow is a promising, medium-range low-power protocol that offers a balance between range, power efficiency, and data rate, making it ideal for industrial IoT, smart agriculture, and smart cities where secure, high-speed, and energy-efficient communication is essential.

Applications of Low-Power Communication Protocols in the Real World

Low-power communication protocols such as LoRa, Sigfox, NB-IoT, LTE-M, Wi-Fi HaLow are widely used in various industries due to their energy efficiency, long-range coverage, and cost-effectiveness (see Figure 5-1). The following lists explain some key real-world applications.

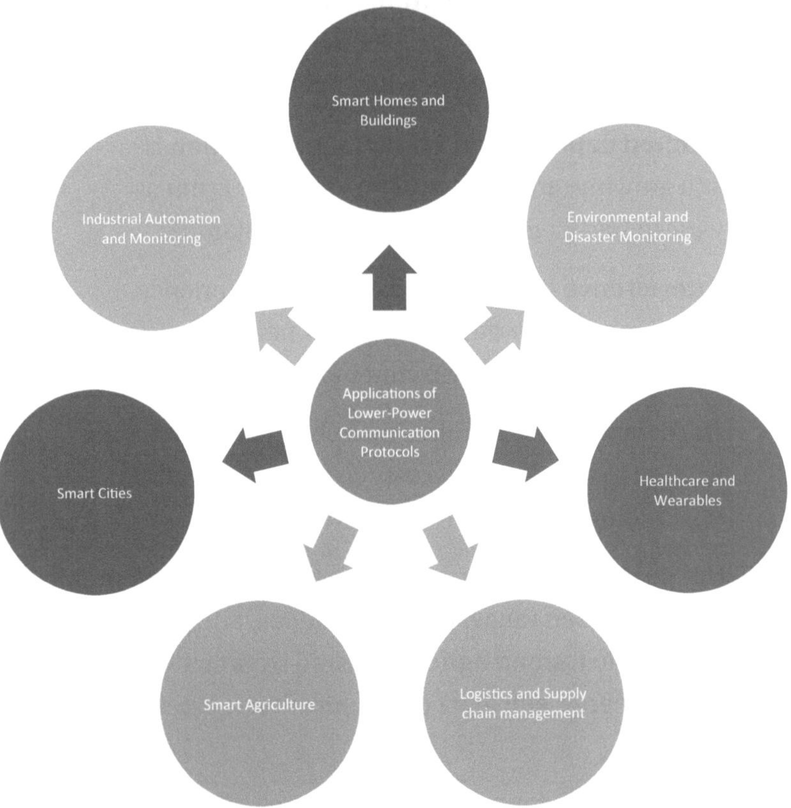

Figure 5-1. *The application of lower-power communication protocols in the real world*

Smart agriculture:

- **Soil and weather monitoring:** LoRa and NB-IoT sensors collect data on soil moisture, temperature, and humidity to optimize irrigation and crop yield.
- **Livestock tracking:** GPS-enabled Sigfox and LTE-M devices help monitor animal movements and health.
- **Automated irrigation:** LoRaWAN-based irrigation systems regulate water use efficiently based on real-time data.

Smart cities:

- **Smart street lighting:** LoRa and NB-IoT are used to remotely control and automate streetlights based on traffic and environmental conditions.
- **Waste management:** Waste collection crews can optimize pickup schedules by using smart garbage cans equipped with Sigfox/NB-IoT sensors to alert them when the bins are full.
- **Parking management:** Drivers can receive real-time availability data from IoT-enabled parking systems that use NB-IoT and LTE-M.

Industrial automation and monitoring:

- **Predictive maintenance:** LoRa and LTE-M sensors save downtime by identifying machine issues before they become serious.
- **Asset tracking:** Sigfox makes it possible to monitor tools, cars, and containers in warehouses in real time.
- **Air quality monitoring:** LoRa and NB-IoT are used by industrial facilities to monitor pollution and guarantee environmental compliance.

Healthcare and wearables:

- **Remote patient monitoring:** Elderly and chronically ill individuals can have their vital signs tracked in real time thanks to LTE-M and NB-IoT.
- **Smart wearables:** LTE-M is used by fitness bands and health monitors to transmit health data continuously.
- **Medical equipment tracking:** LoRa is used by hospitals to locate vital medical equipment, including as wheelchairs and ventilators.

Logistics and supply chain management:

- **Cold chain monitoring:** Perishable foods and vaccinations are examples of temperature-sensitive products that are monitored using Sigfox and NB-IoT sensors.
- **Fleet management:** Route optimization and real-time GPS tracking of delivery vehicles are made possible by LTE-M and LoRa.

Environmental and disaster monitoring:

- **Forest fire detection:** Alerts are sent via LoRa-based sensors that identify early indications of wildfires.
- **Flood Monitoring:** In regions vulnerable to flooding, Sigfox and NB-IoT sensors monitor increasing water levels.
- **Earthquake sensors:** Early warning systems get real-time seismic data from LTE-M networks.

Smart homes and buildings:

- **Energy management:** HVAC systems are automated and energy consumption is tracked via LoRa and NB-IoT sensors.
- **Home security:** Remote surveillance, motion detectors, and smart locks are supported via LTE-M and Wi-Fi HaLow.
- **Smart appliances:** Devices connected to the IoT communicate best with Wi-Fi HaLow and NB-IoT.

In summary, IoT and other smart applications depend on low-power communication methods. They are perfect for sectors including smart cities, healthcare, industrial automation, logistics, and environmental monitoring because they offer long-range, affordable, and energy-efficient connectivity. These protocols lower maintenance and operating expenses by enabling devices to run on little power for years. Low-power communication solutions promote automation, real-time monitoring, and effective resource management by guaranteeing dependable data transfer in both urban and rural locations, hence enhancing overall sustainability and productivity.

Advantages of Low-Power Communication Protocols

For many wireless applications, including smart cities, industrial automation, and IoT, low-power protocols are essential. They are appropriate for devices that require extended battery life, long coverage, and efficient data connection because of their many benefits, as illustrated in Figure 5-2.

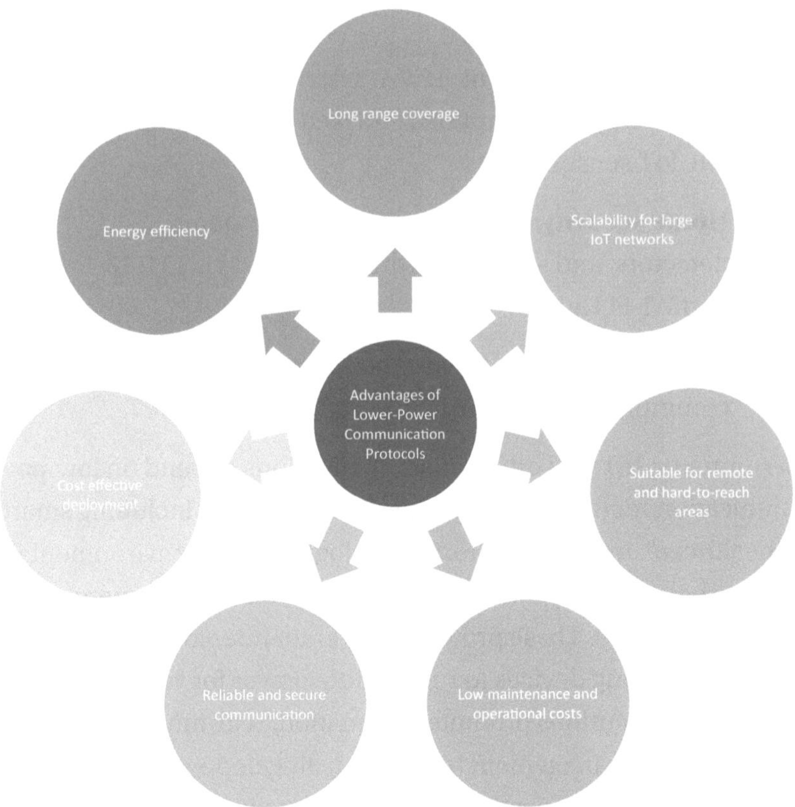

***Figure 5-2.** The advantages of low-power communication protocols*

The following section explains these main advantages:

- **Energy efficiency:** Low-power communication protocols are designed to consume low power, and devices can last for years on a single battery. Technologies such as LoRa, Sigfox, and NB-IoT employ sleep modes and low-duty cycles, lowering power consumption substantially. They are best suited for applications like smart meters, environmental sensors, and asset tracking, where battery replacement is not feasible at frequent intervals.

- **Long range coverage:** Most low-power protocols have sub-GHz frequency bands, allowing them to support long-range communication spanning several kilometers. LoRa is able to cover up to 10–15 km in rural settings. NB-IoT and LTE-M use cellular infrastructure, providing nationwide coverage. This makes them very well suited to applications such as agriculture monitoring, smart city infrastructure, and remote sensing.
- **Economical deployment:** LoRa and Sigfox protocols run on unlicensed frequency bands, minimizing the cost of expensive spectrum licenses.
    - LoRaWAN enables private network deployments, which means complete control over the infrastructure for business.
    - Sigfox is provided through a subscription model, and it decreases the upfront costs associated with IoT deployments. This is making low-power communication a low-cost solution for large-scale IoT networks as well as industrial deployments.
- **Large IoT network scalability:** Low-power protocols are capable of supporting thousands up to millions of devices in a single network. This makes them ideal for use in smart grid monitoring, industrial automation, and logistics tracking.
    - LoRaWAN provides support for large-scale IoT deployments by utilizing a star-of-stars topology.
    - NB-IoT coexists with current cellular networks, which makes it extremely scalable.

- **Trustworthy and secure communication:** Most low-power communication protocols employ adaptive data rate (ADR) and error correction techniques for improving reliability. These attributes render them appropriate for critical applications like healthcare monitoring, financial transactions, and industrial control systems.
    - NB-IoT and LTE-M provide robust encryption and authentication, guaranteeing secure data transport.
    - LoRaWAN and Sigfox have security features such as end-to-end encryption and network authentication.
- **Appropriate for remote and inaccessible places:** Given their low power consumption and long-range capabilities, the protocols are suitable for use in rural areas, underground sites, and remote places. NB-IoT and LoRa are appropriate for agriculture, mining, and environmental monitoring in areas with limited infrastructure.
- **Low maintenance and operating expenses:** Because low-power protocols maximize battery life, they minimize maintenance costs of frequent battery replacement and system downtime. This makes them an economical option for long-term IoT deployments in industries, healthcare, and smart homes.
    - Sigfox and LoRa devices have a battery life of ten years.
    - NB-IoT uses the existing mobile networks, so no extra infrastructure investments are required.

The Growing Importance of Low-Power Communication Protocols

Low-power communication protocols are transforming IoT, industrial automation, healthcare, and smart cities by making efficient, long-lasting, and scalable wireless connectivity a reality. Their advantages—energy efficiency, long-range communication, cost-effectiveness, scalability, security, and reliability—make them fundamental for today's connected ecosystems.

As the trend of IoT adoption gains momentum, the appropriate protocol is determined by parameters such as data rate, latency, security, and deployment cost to provide seamless and efficient communication for various applications.

Disadvantages of Low-Power Communication Protocols

Low-power communication protocols are essential for IoT, industrial automation, and smart city applications. However, they also come with several challenges that can impact their performance and usability, as illustrated in Figure 5-3.

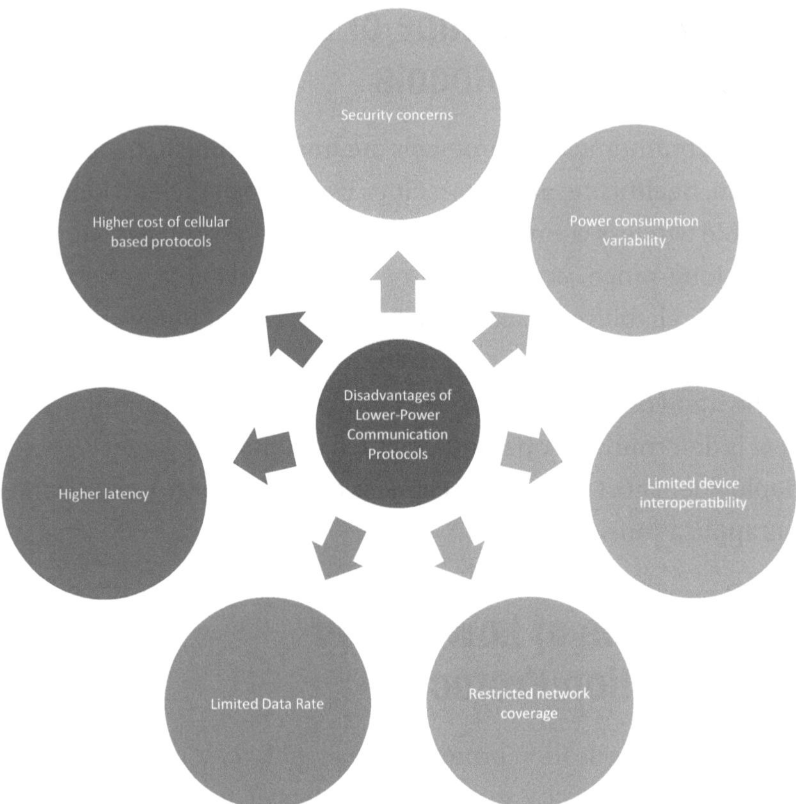

***Figure 5-3.** The disadvantages of lower-power communication protocols*

Here are some key disadvantages:

- **Limited data rate:** Low-power communication protocols such as LoRa, Sigfox, and NB-IoT are optimized for small, periodic data transmissions. They are not suitable for applications that require real-time communication or high-bandwidth data transfer, such as video streaming, voice calls, or large file sharing. The slow data rates make these protocols better suited for sensor-based applications rather than high-speed networking.

- **Higher latency:** Some low-power protocols, especially NB-IoT and Sigfox, experience delays in data transmission, leading to higher latency. This delay can be problematic for time-sensitive applications such as:
    - Emergency alert systems, where immediate notifications are crucial.
    - Live tracking in logistics, where real-time updates are needed.
    - Industrial automation, where quick response times improve efficiency.
- **Restricted network coverage:** Certain protocols, such as Sigfox and LoRa, rely on dedicated base stations or gateways for communication. These infrastructures are not available everywhere, particularly in remote or rural areas. Unlike cellular-based alternatives such as NB-IoT and LTE-M, which leverage existing mobile networks, these protocols require specific regional deployments, limiting their flexibility and scalability.
- **Limited device interoperability:** Different low-power communication protocols operate on different frequency bands and network architectures, leading to compatibility issues between devices from different manufacturers. This lack of standardization makes integration more complex and limits cross-platform compatibility. For example:
    - LoRa devices cannot communicate with Sigfox or NB-IoT devices.
    - NB-IoT devices require a cellular network, whereas LoRa operates on unlicensed frequencies.

- **Higher costs for cellular-based protocols:** Mobile network operators must provide subscription-based services for cellular-based choices like NB-IoT and LTE-M, while some low-power communication protocols (like LoRa and Sigfox) function on unlicensed frequency bands. These expenses raise operating costs, which reduces their cost-effectiveness for long-term IoT deployments.
- **Power consumption variability:** Certain protocols, like LTE-M, use more power than alternatives like Sigfox or LoRa, despite the fact that low-power protocols are meant to be energy efficient. Frequent data transmission devices may deplete their batteries more quickly, shortening their operating life and requiring more maintenance.
- **Security concerns:** Compared to cellular-based protocols (NB-IoT, LTE-M), low-power networks that operate in unlicensed frequency bands (such as LoRaWAN and Sigfox) frequently use inferior encryption techniques. As a result, they are more susceptible to online dangers such as:
    - *Eavesdropping:* When hackers can intercept data that isn't secured.
    - *Data tampering:* Unauthorized changes to data that has been transferred.
    - *Denial-of-Service (DoS) attacks:* Attacks that overload the network to prevent communication.

Evaluating Low-Power Communication Protocols

Low-power communication protocols are nevertheless necessary for IoT, smart cities, industrial automation, healthcare, and logistics, notwithstanding their shortcomings. A number of considerations must be balanced while selecting the best protocol, including:

- **Power efficiency:** Ideal for battery-powered sensors (e.g., Sigfox, LoRa).
- **Data rate and latency:** Critical for real-time applications (e.g., LTE-M).
- **Network coverage:** Cellular-based protocols (NB-IoT, LTE-M) provide better global coverage.
- **Security:** Compared to LoRaWAN, NB-IoT provides more robust encryption.

Every protocol has distinct advantages and disadvantages, and the best one to use will depend on the needs of the application, including price, power use, security, and network accessibility.

Discussion

For dependable and long-lasting wireless connectivity in IoT, industrial automation, healthcare, and smart cities, low-power efficient communication protocols are essential. Certain protocols, like LoRa, NB-IoT, Zigbee, and Wi-Fi HaLow, are designed to conserve energy without sacrificing affordable, long-range communication. Because of their effectiveness, battery-powered and remote sensing devices can be widely deployed, making them appropriate for uses such as asset tracking, smart agriculture, and environmental monitoring. However, there are disadvantages, including low data speeds, higher latency, security, and incompatibility. By doing away with duplicate data transmission and network load balancing, the LEACH protocol—a clustering protocol in wireless sensor networks (WSNs)—significantly increases energy efficiency.

Routing efficiency is a crucial component of low-power networks and IoT applications, as it directly affects device life and network performance. Energy conservation, scalability, and adaptive data transfer are the main routing requirements in these networks so that nodes may communicate without wasting power. Due to their high overhead and complexity, current routing protocols may not be suitable for IoT ecosystems with limited power. To increase network durability and dependability, routing techniques that are lighter, more flexible, and energy-efficient must be created. Future developments in AI-based routing algorithms, edge computing, and machine learning will continue to optimize data processing and energy efficiency in low-power networks, making them more scalable, secure, and resilient.

Conclusion

The selection of a low-power communication protocol depends on a number of factors, including data rate, power consumption, and application-specific needs. Short-range protocols, such as BLE and Zigbee, offer efficient data transfer in indoor settings and minimal battery consumption, making them ideal for smart home and personal products. With their broad coverage and low power consumption, long-range protocols like LoRa and Sigfox are appropriate for smart cities, rural surveillance, and IoT in agriculture. Wi-Fi HaLow and other medium-range protocols balance communication range and power efficiency, making them suitable for supply chain management and industrial automation. Engineers and developers may design reliable, scalable, and energy-efficient IoT systems tailored to real-world applications by understanding the advantages and disadvantages of each protocol.

CHAPTER 6

Data Management Techniques in IoT Using API

The Internet of Things (IoT) is transforming daily-use hardware—such as air conditioners, refrigerators, water heaters, water kettles, projectors, and fitness bands—into intelligent, inter-associated systems that generate massive volumes of real-time data. To efficiently manage this data, APIs are used to facilitate structured collection, filtering, storage, security, and analytics. The Cisco seven-layer IoT model provides a clear framework for this architecture, from physical hardware sensing to business intelligence integration. IoT data management involves several techniques, including temporal and spatial aggregation, secure access control, and scalable storage solutions. Communication protocols like MQTT and RESTful APIs play a key role in data transfer across layers. Technologies such as edge and fog computing support early-stage data processing, while cloud platforms handle long-term analytics and decision-making. Security remains a critical concern, with emphasis on confidentiality, access control, and license management. This chapter explores these dimensions, demonstrating the importance of efficient data handling to support real-time applications, smart grids, and industrial automation. IoT associates everyday hardware like air conditioners (AC), fridges, water heaters, ovens,

Dr. D. Sharma and Dr. B. Pandey, *Eco-Networking for IoT*,
https://doi.org/10.1007/979-8-8688-2317-6_6

projectors, vehicles, washing machines, fitness bands, wristwatches, and even shoes to the Internet. IoT systems generate a high volume of data, and cloud computing facilitates that data to reach its destination with the help of the IoT communication protocol. A large amount of data is always transmitted from IoT hardware to another IoT hardware (such as edge, fog, cloud, or database server) using the IoT communication protocol.

For instance, a fitness or activity tracker represents a simple use of IoT technology but collects data such as the distance you walked, ran, cycled, or swam, your pace, your pulse rate, your stroke count during the swim, calories burnt, your sleep quality, and so on. IoT information management techniques using APIs involve structured methods for collecting, processing, storing, and securing IoT data. Key techniques in information management inside IoT include data collection APIs, data filtering and aggregation, storage management, access control and security, data querying and analytics, and interoperability and integration.

In the IoT architecture, the layer used for collecting data from sensors is the *perception layer* (also known as the *sensing layer*). This layer on IoT systems consists of sensors, actuators, RFID tags, cameras, and other data acquisition hardware. This layer collects real-world data such as temperature, humidity, motion, pressure, and so on. This perception layer converts physical signals into digital data for further processing. It acts as the interface between the real world and the virtual world in an IoT system.

After data is collected, it is transmitted to the network layer, which is responsible for communication and data transmission to other layers for processing and storage. The BI systems are transforming unprocessed data into meaningful insight. These days, we commonly use APIs to access third-party and proprietary data. The API usually handles data applicability and efficiency of Python in handling API data for BI by demonstrating a case study using data from e-commerce sales.[1] The integration of security in information management on the Internet is an imperative task. Secure information management consists of Confidentiality, access control, and license management.[2]

Confidentiality of IoT information management ensures that data goes through the process of encryption and hashing to enhance its security. Access control in IoT information management applies different access rights to different users. The data owner usually delegates these accesses. The license management in IoT information management verifies granted license (keys, authentication code, etc.) to authorized users. Above all, licenses are used to determine access conditions (including access times, frequencies, and lifetime).[2]

Researchers highlight the necessity of efficiency in large-scale data management in smart grids.[3] A smart grid is a cyber-physical system of various domains that consists of power generation devices, smart meters, transmission equipment, distribution services, information management substations, and communication systems.[3] In Bramantyo, H. A., et al. (2022)[4], a system was designed to remotely access and transmit data from oil and gas refineries, displaying conditions in real time. In Ferreira, C. M. et al. (2021)[5], researchers developed the blockchain API gateway project. This gateway is essentially a daemon running in Bastion, primarily designed to protect the application network. The daemon receives the IoT edge API gateway payloads. The message follows the protected application network's information management server address if and only if the sender is verified. Their project also has a testbed with real hardware and IoT information management project as evidence.

In Naghib, A., et al. (2023)[6], large-scale Information management in IoT is used for intelligent decision-making and knowledge discovery. ML4IoT is a container-based machine learning methodology for IoT data analytics and machine learning management. The ML4IoT framework is divided into ML4IoT information management and ML4IoT core layer. This layer trains machine learning models and consists of container-based components, a designer-orchestrator-scheduler of workflow, and above all, a distributed data processing engine. ML4IoT information is equipped for data ingestion and storage. A messaging system, a distributed file system, and a NoSQL database are three subsystems of the ML4IoT system.[6]

Data Collection APIs

Data collection APIs usually facilitate real-time data ingestion from IoT sensors and hardware (e.g., RESTful or MQTT-based APIs). Researchers in "Application of RESTful APIs in IoT: A Review," (2021)[7] briefly examined the interpretation of RESTful APIs, their methods, and their responses. They explained the reasons that make REST (Representational State Transfer) better than SOAP (Simple Object Access Protocol). Most of the IoT hardware is not directly related. IoT equipment is usually associated with services that provide interfaces to users. In Maurya, R., et al. (2021) [7], the researchers addressed how IoT gets benefits from APIs. Extensible Markup Language (XML) was developed for the exchange of data. XML was a popular method for API integration, but JSON is now replacing XML. JSON is lightweight compared to XML, as it has a compact structure consisting of key-value pairs, and it is considered more legible. While working with complex systems, JSON is a good choice for RESTful APIs. JSON objects are easily accessed, whereas XML data needs to be parsed. [7] There are different communication protocols for the transmission of data on IoT and M2M systems. The MQTT (Message Queuing Telemetry Transport) protocol was developed by OASIS in 2013.[8] Version 3.1.1 in 2014 became standard. MQTT is the most well-known M2M/IoT protocol in comparison to other M2M protocols (AMQP and CoAP).[8]

Cisco's seven-layer IoT model provides a framework for understanding and designing IoT systems. Figure 6-1 represents the Cisco seven-layer IoT reference model intended to guide the design and implementation of IoT architectures. Level 1 is the physical hardware and controllers layer, also known as the foundation layer, and it includes sensors, actuators, and hardware that collect or act on data from the physical environment. Level 2 is the associativity layer that provides network associations (wired/wireless) to transmit data between hardware and other layers. Level 3 is the edge (fog) computing layer that performs local processing of data near the source to reduce latency and bandwidth usage. Level 4 is a data accumulation layer that aggregates and stores data for further analysis, transforming real-time data into "data at rest." Level 5 is a data abstraction layer developed to organize and process stored data into usable formats for applications; it handles querying and indexing. Level 6 is an application layer that delivers IoT services to end users, such as smart cities, industrial automation systems, and healthcare solutions. Level 7 is a collaboration and process layer that integrates IoT insights into business processes and decision-making workflows. The arrow on the right signifies the transition between data in motion (lower levels) and data at rest (higher levels), highlighting how raw data is collected, transmitted, stored, and utilized.

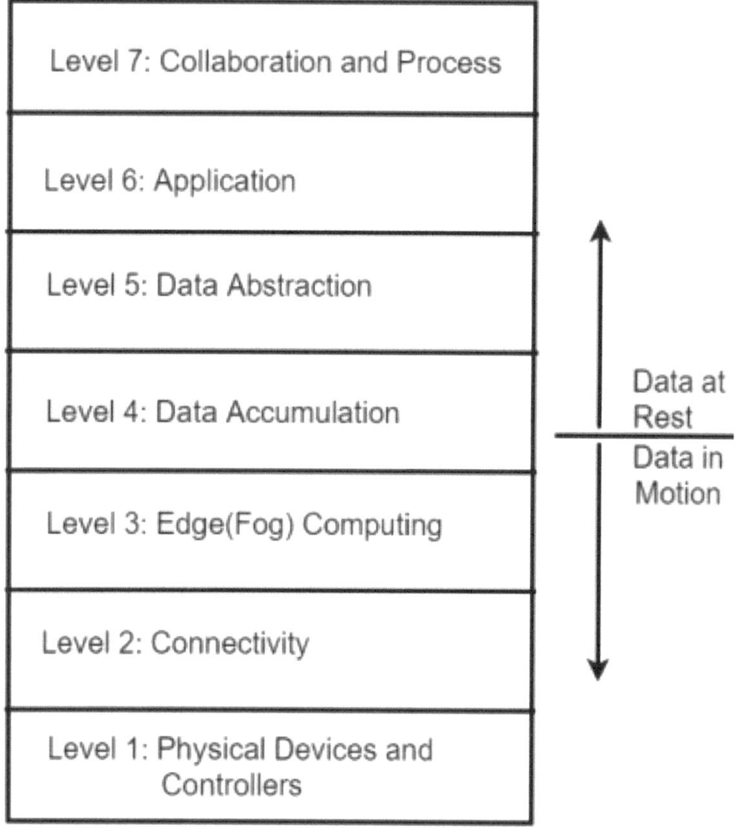

Figure 6-1. *The seven layers of the IoT reference model[8]*

Data Filtering and Aggregation

Data filtering and aggregation APIs help preprocess data at the edge or cloud to reduce redundancy and enable efficient storage and analysis. With IoT, data has a pivotal role in the decision-making process. Filtering on the collected raw data value makes it feasible.[9] The ECG signals are processed via frontend hardware that filters noise due to power supply, low pass filter, DC offset compensation, amplification, and digital conversion. There are many other ways of filtering, such as Kalman Filtering, Particle filtering, Extended Kalman Filtering, and so on.[9] After filtering, we start the aggregation process to reduce data volume. Temporal aggregation and spatial aggregation are two types of data aggregation used to aggregate data received from IoT hardware. *Temporal aggregation* refers to summarizing data over time intervals (e.g., hourly or daily averages). In contrast, *spatial aggregation* involves summarizing data across multiple origins or locations (e.g., averaging sensor readings from different rooms or regions). They different in terms of focus, as shown in Table 6-1, but both are useful in IoT to reduce data volume and extract meaningful patterns from raw data.

Table 6-1. *Difference Between Temporal and Spatial Aggregation*

	Temporal Aggregation of IoT Data	**Spatial Aggregation of IoT Data**
Aggregate data	Over time	Across space or origins
Example	Averaging temperature readings from a single sensor every hour.	Averaging temperature readings from multiple sensors in different rooms at the same time.
Focus	When the data was collected	Where the data was collected

In MQTT+, the broker performs temporal aggregation by storing K statistical tuples per topic for specified intervals (e.g., 15, 60, 1440 minutes).[10] Each tuple includes the count, sum, average, max, and min of published values over its time window. This enables low-frequency data access and has linear memory complexity relative to the number of topics.

Storage Management

Storage management APIs interface with cloud or local databases (e.g., InfluxDB, AWS IoT) for structured, scalable storage. There is no direct communication link from data collection systems to data storage. Also, the endpoint for data storage is not always compatible with data received from sensors, as shown in Figure 6-2.[11]

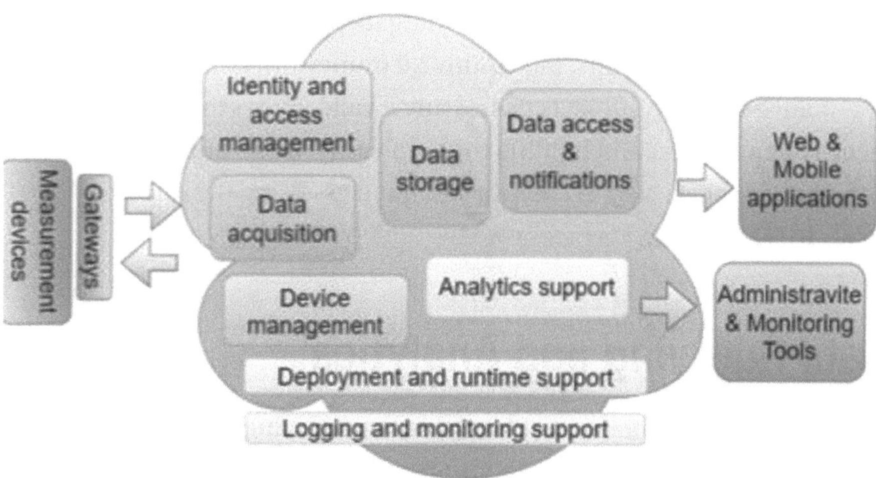

Figure 6-2. *Data storage in IoT architecture[11]*

Access Control and Security

Access control and security APIs enforce authentication, encryption, and role-based access to guarantee data integrity and privacy during data management in IoT. The Policy Decision Point (PDP) API offers an interface to obtain authorization decisions made by an access control engine that is compliant with eXtensible Access Control Markup Language (XACML). The Policy Administration Point (PAP) API provides an interface to apply XACML rules used by the PDP to make access control decisions. The implementation provides an API to get authorization decisions based on authorization policies and authorization requests from PEPs (Policy Enforcement Points). The API follows the REST architecture style and is compatible with XACML v3.0.[12] Most IoT solutions, such as oneM2M and Future Internet Ware (FIWARE), utilize REST APIs to access resources. To prevent unauthorized access and mitigate potential security risks associated with REST APIs, the OAuth 2.0 framework is implemented. To enhance security, subjects possessing a valid access token for the security department and holding the "professor" role—authorized to take lectures—are permitted to create a student class using the university's IoT server REST API.[13]

Data Querying and Analytics

Data querying and analytics APIs enable the querying of historical or real-time data for insights and decision-making (e.g., via GraphQL or SQL-like APIs). Facebook released GraphQL as an alternative to traditional web services based on REST architecture. GraphQL was developed in 2012 and was used only by Facebook from 2012 to 2015 before becoming open-sourced.

In Khan, R., & Noor Mian, A. (2020)[14], researchers used Google Cloud services and created a testbed using Contiki OS, Z1 IoT motes, and GraphQL web framework. They also proposed a scheme based on interfacing cloud services with a constrained application protocol and an efficient web framework. GraphQL is used for duty cycling-based sensor networks to utilize round-trip savings for optimization of active time slots.[14] Spark Core hosts the API and defines a distributed collection of objects with immutability as a *resilient distributed dataset* (RDD). The Spark code, regardless of the API used (Java, Python, Scala, SQL), breaks down into a highly compacted bytecode. The same Spark code is executed across the cluster. Spark SQL is an Apache Spark module that integrates relational processing based on Spark's functional programming API. These SQL variants provide the opportunity to manipulate dataframes. Also, these APIs were able to query data using SQL-like queries integrated with Spark's Structured Streaming application programming interfaces. Spark SQL is an ANSI SQL 2003-based SQL variant.

Interoperability and Integration

Interoperability and integration APIs standardize data formats (e.g., JSON, XML) and protocols, enabling communication between heterogeneous IoT systems. In Escarda-Fernández, M., et al. (2024)[16], researchers integrated fine-tuned LLMs into the Flythings Technologies platform. Their chat-based application enabled users to submit queries in natural language, which the model then processed. The model's task was to extract relevant information from each query by identifying and mapping it to the appropriate Flythings API input fields. It then generated a well-structured JSON output that adhered to a predefined schema. This allowed seamless interaction with the Flythings API, enabling real-time monitoring and visualization of IoT hardware details.

The JSON schema used for output validation is structured into two main components. First, the series field contained information about the specific IoT hardware being queried. Second, the visualization properties defined the necessary parameters for representing the series data visually within the virtual assistant interface, as shown in Figure 6-3.

```
{                                              Json Schema
    "series":[
        {
            "property": String,
            "foi": String,
            "module": String,
            "asIncremental": Boolean
        }
    ],
    "visualization":{
        "config":{
            "type": Enum,
            "subtype": Enum
        },
        "body":{
            "period": Enum,
            (...)
            (...)
            "temporalScaleType": Enum
        }
    }
}
```

Figure 6-3. *JSON schema of Flythings*

XML is a text-based format for sharing structured information among IoT devices. XML is stored in a hierarchical format. XML documents will not be processed if there are errors. In XML, each data element is denoted in a name-value pair (also called *key-value pair*) with the value situated between start-tags: and end-tags: . Figure 6-4 shows an example: `<value>5006</value>`. The value is the defined attribute or property name specified in the document, while the 5006 represents its current content or state.[17]


```
<Data SessionID="2022-01-16T11:47:16Z">
    <Time>2022-01-16T16:03:13.2177045Z</Time>
    <RecordNumber>3064</RecordNumber>
    <SensorData ID="SN100-0" Descr="System Parameters" SerialNo
        ="0" ProdNo="SN100" ProdName="System Node" ProtocolVer=
        "4">
        <Parameters>
            <Point ID="0" Descr="Battery Voltage" Type="VT_R4"
                Format="" Unit="V" RangeMin="0" RangeMax="15">
                <Value>2.124000</Value>
            </Point>
            <Point ID="1" Descr="Memory Used" Type="VT_I4"
                Format="" Unit="Bytes" RangeMin="0" RangeMax="
                12455936">
                <Value>8806400</Value>
            </Point>
            <Point ID="2" Descr="Interval" Type="VT_I4" Format=
                "" Unit="ms" RangeMin="" RangeMax="">
                <Value>5006</Value>
            </Point>
        </Parameters>
    </SensorData>
```


Figure 6-4. *XML data of sensor readings[17]*

Conclusion

IoT has evolved into a highly dynamic and data-intensive ecosystem that associates millions of pieces of hardware, each producing diverse types of information. Effective information management through APIs is central to maintaining performance, reliability, and security across such systems. From the initial perception of data using sensors to its aggregation, filtering, transmission, storage, querying, and final integration into business processes, every step requires intelligent handling and coordination. The Cisco seven-layer IoT reference model helps logically organize these operations. Data collection APIs allow real-time sensor data ingestion, while filtering and aggregation techniques, including temporal and spatial aggregation, reduce data overload and enhance efficiency. Storage management ensures that this data is securely and scalably preserved, while access control enforces data privacy through encryption and authentication. Interoperability APIs enable seamless communication across heterogeneous systems using formats like JSON and XML. With the inclusion of technologies like edge and fog computing and emerging paradigms like ML4IoT, the landscape of information management on IoT is rapidly advancing. Security measures such as license management and role-based access are essential in safeguarding sensitive data.

As demonstrated through case studies and research, effective IoT information management is not just a technical necessity but a strategic enabler of real-time, intelligent decision-making across domains such as smart grids, industrial automation, and healthcare. In the future, AI and machine learning will play a pivotal role in advancing big data analytics by automating complex tasks such as index querying and optimizing MapReduce frameworks. Deep learning will enable more efficient data partitioning, reduce redundancy, and enhance storage and retrieval processes. For OLAP systems, machine learning techniques will offer predictive caching and intelligent summarization, leading to faster queries and more accurate insights.

The future of IoT information management lies in further advancing intelligence, scalability, and security. As IoT hardware continues to grow in number and complexity, the demand for real-time, low-latency processing will intensify, prompting more widespread use of edge AI and fog-based analytics. APIs will evolve to support dynamic, self-adaptive integration across heterogeneous hardware and platforms. Enhanced semantic interoperability, powered by AI-driven metadata mapping, will enable more meaningful data exchange between different vendors and systems. Blockchain integration will strengthen trust and transparency in access control and license management. Future architectures will likely incorporate self-healing systems that autonomously detect and mitigate faults. In addition, the growing adoption of 5G and beyond will provide robust, high-speed communication infrastructure for massive IoT deployments. Research will continue to explore energy-efficient data handling, especially for battery-constrained edge hardware. Altogether, the future holds promise for smarter, more resilient IoT ecosystems through continuous evolution in API-driven information management.

CHAPTER 7

AI-Based Power Management in IoT

The rapid advancement and progress of IoT devices is creating an urgent need for efficient power management strategies, particularly in battery-powered and remote applications. Traditional power-saving methods often fall short in dynamic, data-intensive environments. This chapter explores the integration of AI techniques to enable intelligent, adaptive power management in IoT systems. The AI is itself an integration of ML (machine learning), DL (deep learning), FL (federated learning), and RL (reinforcement learning); therefore, this chapter uses artificial intelligence as a combination of ML&DL&FL or ML&DL&RL.

By leveraging predictive analytics, ML, and real-time decision making, AI (ML&DL&FL) can optimize energy demand and supply based on device behavior, environmental conditions, and user patterns. Applications in smart homes, industrial IoT, and agriculture demonstrate the practical benefits of AI (ML&DL&FL)-based energy control, including prolonged device lifespan and reduced operational costs. Furthermore, the adoption of edge computing and federated learning offers promising avenues for decentralized, privacy-preserving energy optimization. The study concludes that AI (ML&DL&FL)-driven power management is essential for building scalable, sustainable, and autonomous IoT ecosystems and highlights future directions for enhancing energy-aware intelligence in connected environments. With the explosive growth of IoT devices

Dr. D. Sharma and Dr. B. Pandey, *Eco-Networking for IoT*,
https://doi.org/10.1007/979-8-8688-2317-6_7

across various sectors, efficient power management has become a significant challenge. AI (ML&DL&FL)-based power management offers intelligent, adaptive solutions to optimize energy consumption without compromising the performance and responsiveness of connected devices.

Figure 7-1 shows a dual-layer adaptive control mechanism that optimizes power consumption and transmission efficiency in IoT networks. If parameters are not sufficient, the system either increases them or adjusts and monitors them, eventually converging on optimized energy usage. To apply AI in the dual-layer adaptive control mechanism for energy optimization in IoT networks (as shown in Figure 7-1), we can integrate ML and RL techniques to make intelligent, data-driven decisions rather than rule-based ones. We can use supervised or unsupervised ML models to predict the optimal transmission power and data rate based on network traffic conditions, device mobility, battery level and historical communication patterns. A regression or classification model can predict whether current settings are sufficient. If they are not enough, then an AI model (e.g., RL) can suggest how much power transmission or data rate is needed. We can also use RL agents to learn from transmission success/failure and adapt dynamically. AI can monitor channel conditions (e.g., congestion and collisions), allocate transmission slots efficiently, and adapt retry limits and backoff strategies. For example, an intelligent irrigation sensor network can use an RL agent to optimize transmission intervals and power based on soil moisture levels, battery health, and gateway distance, thus extending battery life without compromising data accuracy.

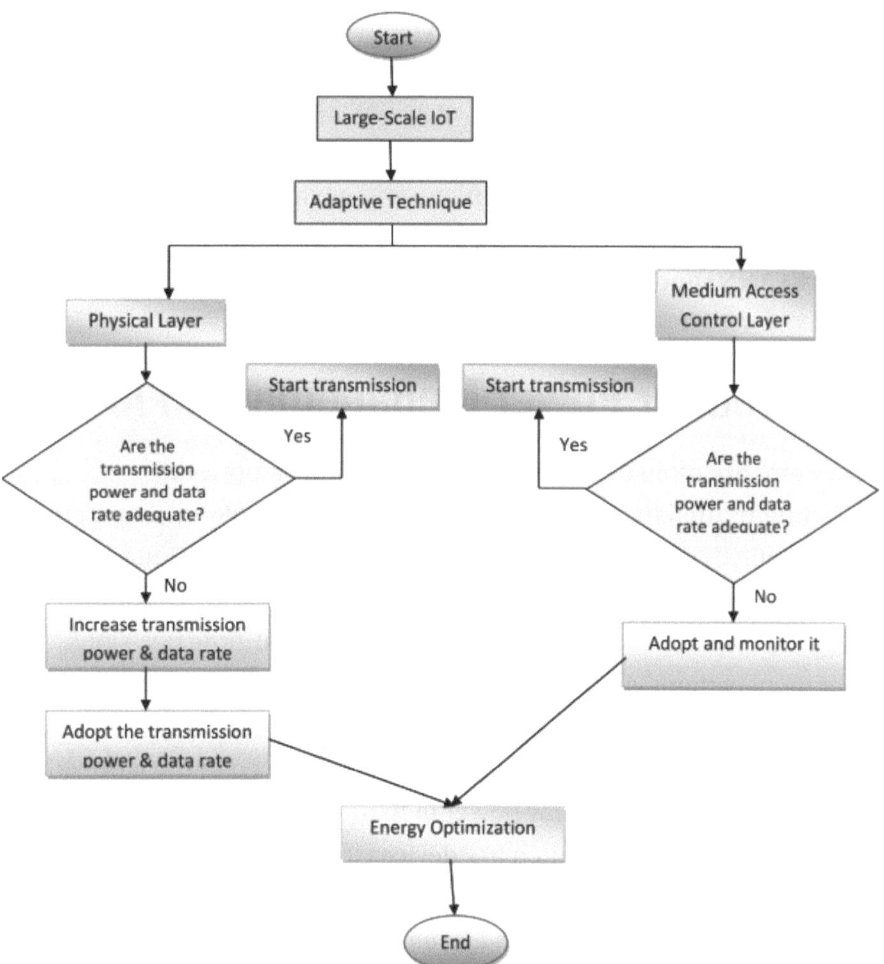

Figure 7-1. *Power optimization techniques in IoT[1]*

In Rochd, A., et al. (2021)[2], researchers proposed a methodology for designing an AI-based IoT Home Energy Management System (HEMS), as showcased in the Living Lab Green & Smart Building Park. The prediction of power generation (PG) from renewable sources plays an important role in the energy management of intelligent smart cities. There are many challenges in using edge intelligence in regulated IoT systems. To tackle this, they proposed a mixed deep autoencoder (AE) model based on multi-head attention (MHA) with a gradient boosting (XGB) machine learning algorithm.[3] In Raju, M. P. et al. (2022)[4], researchers attempt to present an IoT-based HEMS to accommodate AI-based integration of distributed generation in a smart micro-grid environment. They estimate total power (PT) and peak clipping power (PTh) using an Artificial Neural Network (ANN) and ML algorithms to perform AI-based DG integration.

The Need for Power Management in IoT

IoT systems are often deployed in remote or battery-powered environments, making energy efficiency crucial for prolonged operation and reliability. Traditional static power-management techniques are inadequate in dynamic and data-driven IoT scenarios, necessitating intelligent, context-aware systems that can make real-time decisions. Power management is becoming very important for IoT systems that use application-based sensors. Sensors in IoT systems get energy from small batteries for a long duration. The semiconductors used in the fabrication of this equipment must be low power in nature.[5] Critical factors affecting the power management of such IoT devices include voltage accuracy, sleep and shutdown capabilities, efficiency, built-in energy-efficient modes, high light load efficiency, ageing, scalability, and power timing and sequencing. See Figure 7-2.

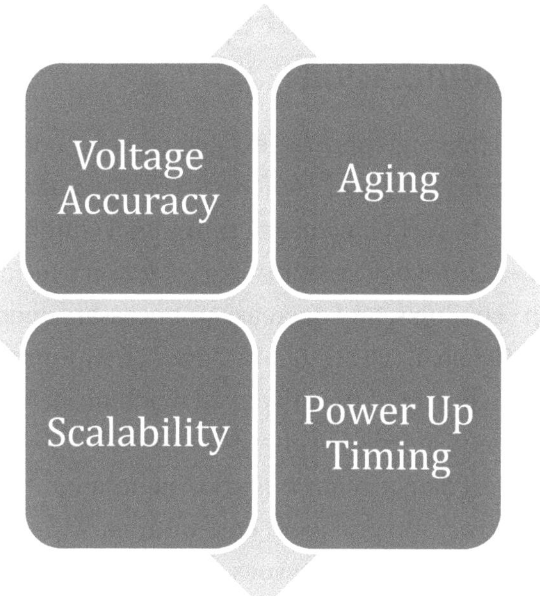

Figure 7-2. Factors affecting power management of IoT devices

Methodologies for power management include power grating, power matching, simultaneous power control and power management (SPCPM), new measurement solutions, predictive energy allocation techniques, and power mapping; see Figure 7-3.

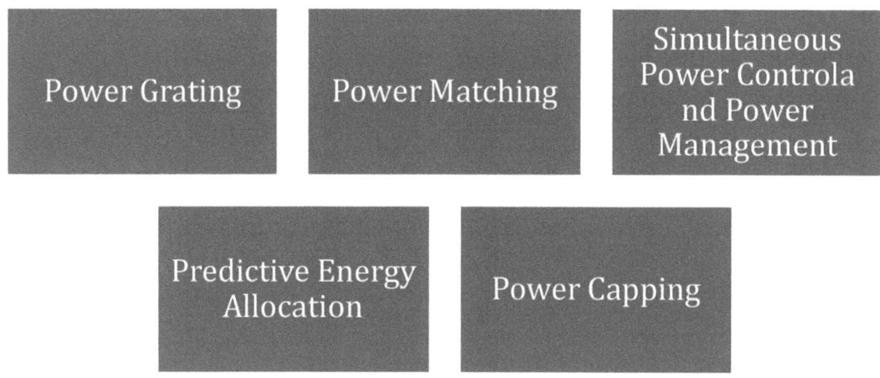

Figure 7-3. Methodologies for power management

The Role of AI (ML&DL&FL) in Energy Optimization

AI enhances power management by leveraging techniques such as ML, DL, federated learning (FL), and reinforcement learning (RL). These models predict hardware behavior, environmental conditions, and usage patterns to control device status (e.g., sleep, active, idle), change communication schedules, and decrease unnecessary energy use. In Stecyk, A., & Miciuła, I. (2023),[6] ML-based energy optimization techniques, especially CEOP, use advanced machine learning to optimize the distribution and dispersion of energy across the system. AI algorithms get training from real data, which consists of generation capacity, power consumption patterns, and grid load. Post-training, ML models predict power demand, identify potential issues, and optimize flows of energy. The AI methodology takes care of consumer requirements, weather changing, and policy goals to develop power management planning.

The energy Internet, unlike traditional power systems, enables integrated coordination across power sources, loads, transmission, and storage, promoting efficient use of diverse energy resources through multi-energy complementarity. Energy units have evolved from simple consumers to prosumers, energy cells, and now to We-energy. Prosumers both consume and produce energy, operating in a half-duplex mode, while energy cells include local generation, storage, and controllable loads. We-energy is a full-duplex model. It allows interaction among multiple energy forms and other entities using advanced control, conversion, and communication technologies, with adaptive capabilities and auto learning to optimize power use dynamically, as shown in Figure 7-4.

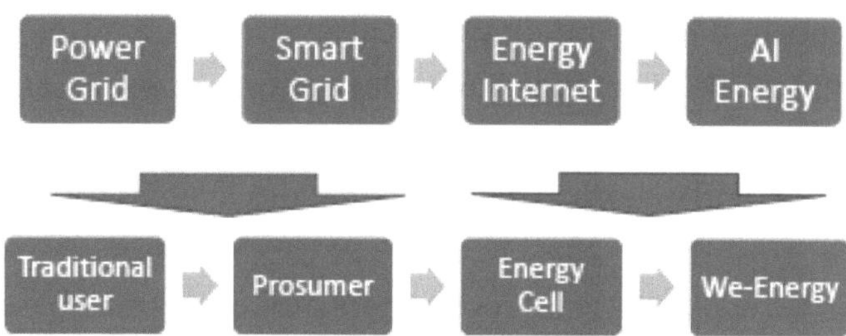

Figure 7-4. *Latest energy units and terminology[6]*

In Raval, M., et al. (2021),[7] researchers claimed that using AI in the protocol's negotiation mechanism results in significantly lower energy consumption. The AI-based techniques get experience from events and deliver output, productivity, and energy efficiency without human involvement. These were RL-based adaptive systems integrated with genetic algorithms in real time to optimize the power dissipation of groups of IoT devices.[7]

Implementation in Real-World Applications

AI (ML&DL&FL)-based energy management can be applied in different IoT areas, including smart homes, industrial IoT, smart agriculture, and wearables. The following sections explain some of those implementations.

Smart Homes

In smart homes, AI (ML&DL&FL) adjusts lighting, appliances, and HVAC based on occupancy and user preferences, which are visible in a IoT power management grid. HEMS connects the users and the grid. The intelligent terminal of HEMS enables users to read, process, and display information such as household electricity and water consumption, guiding them in using both water and electricity reasonably and saving both water and energy. Users can also remotely monitor home appliances via the Internet, cellular phones, and other devices. An advanced sensor senses changes in the surroundings in real time and communicates with humans in time. The AI enables power devices to process the sensed information, presenting it to the user as notifications or alerts. AI analyzes real information and historical data and provides insights for long-term decisions.[8]

In Kwon, K., et al. (2021),[9] researchers proposed an AI-based HEMS (AI-HEMS) that delivers power savings and resident satisfaction. To increase the validity of this research, a treatment group (100 households) and a control group (2,281 households) were created to compare the power savings of the treatment group and the control group. In a 48-day evaluation, AI-HEMS provided a 14% power savings and 91% better resident satisfaction.[9]

Industrial IoT (IIoT)

IIoT includes predictive maintenance and optimizes machine uptime. In Dini, P., et al. (2024),[10] processing data on embedded platforms decreased overall system energy requirements by not transmitting data over long distances and running complex AI methodologies on remote servers. Also, optimizing the resources of IoT devices allows for the efficient implementation of AI models. The AI-based control systems actively manage physical parameters such as temperature, speed, and pressure to optimize production processes and maintain quality. Therefore, such a predictive maintenance methodology can predict machinery failures. This allows for proactive maintenance interventions to reduce costly breakdowns. AI-based machine control and optimization delivers operational excellence in industrial environments.

Smart Agriculture

Regarding smart agriculture, AI (ML&DL&FL) can manage irrigation and sensor activity based on weather forecasts and soil data. In Doshi, M., & Varghese, A. (2022),[11] researchers discussed how the hybridization of energy generation from renewable resources and the field of AI improved recent practices followed by farmers. They proposed the concept of harnessing natural and artificial wind energy from the turbulence produced by the displacement of air due to the motion of objects such as trains, buses, cars and so on. This energy is used to power IoT devices that enable AI-based agritech IoT systems.

Wearables

Wearables include efficient data sampling and transmission to extend battery life. Wearable devices are facing challenges in maintaining battery life, along with performance that demands regular recharging and lower user satisfaction. In Kumar, A., et al. (2024),[12] researchers proposed the SmartAPM (Smart Adaptive Power Management) framework. The SmartAPM is an innovative approach that uses deep reinforcement learning (DRL) to achieve efficient power management in wearable devices. The primary purpose of SmartAPM is to provide longer battery life and a better user experience. They developed a detailed dataset based on user activity, sensor readings, and energy consumption metrics from different sources. Synthetic power profiles were also integrated into the dataset to increase epochs of training. The SmartAPM uses a multi-agent DRL framework that integrates on-device and cloud-based ML, in addition to transfer learning, to improve the user experience. Simulations on wearable devices have proved that SmartAPM is extending battery life by 36% compared to traditional methods, in addition to increasing user satisfaction by 25%.[12]

Conclusion

AI (ML&DL&FL)-based power management represents a transformative approach to addressing the energy challenges in IoT ecosystems. Unlike conventional methods, which often rely on fixed rules or manual configurations, AI (ML&DL&FL) leverages data-driven insights to adapt dynamically to changing conditions. By predicting usage patterns, monitoring environmental variables, and making intelligent decisions about device operation, AI (ML&DL&FL) significantly reduces unnecessary power consumption. This leads to enhanced battery life, reduced maintenance, and increased operational efficiency. As IoT devices become more ubiquitous and diverse, AI (ML&DL&FL)-driven strategies will be essential for mAI (creating energy-efficient, sustainable, and cost-effective deployments across various sectors such as healthcare, industry, agriculture, and smart cities).

Looking ahead, the integration of AI (ML&DL&FL) in IoT power management is expected to evolve rapidly, driven by advancements in machine learning models, edge computing, and energy-efficient hardware. One promising area is federated learning, which allows AI (ML&DL&FL) models to be trained across distributed devices without centralizing data, improving both efficiency and privacy. Edge AI (ML&DL&FL) will further enable real-time decision-making directly on devices, reducing latency and cloud dependency while conserving energy. Additionally, the development of ultra-low-power microcontrollers and AI (ML&DL&FL) accelerators will support the deployment of more sophisticated models, even on constrained IoT nodes. As these technologies mature, we can envision self-regulating IoT systems that autonomously optimize energy consumption, adapt to new contexts, and collaborate with other devices to balance network-wide power usage—paving the way for truly intelligent and autonomous IoT infrastructures.

CHAPTER 8

Advanced IoT Network Design Using AMQP, MQTT, Ktor and Retrofit

This chapter presents an advanced IoT network architecture integrating Message Queuing Telemetry Transport (MQTT) and Advanced Message Queuing Protocol (AMQP) protocols with Ktor and Retrofit. The main motive behind integrating these techniques is to get efficient communication, scalability, and real-time data handling in an IoT network. MQTT enables lightweight device communication in an IoT network. AMQP ensures reliable message routing and delivery. Ktor facilitates non-blocking backend services. Finally, Retrofit provides seamless client-side integration. A system based on MQTT, AMQP, Ktor, and Retrofit is designed to bridge limited IoT devices with scalable cloud microservices, enabling secure and efficient data processing across various applications, including smart cities, industrial automation, and remote monitoring.

Dr. D. Sharma and Dr. B. Pandey, *Eco-Networking for IoT*,
https://doi.org/10.1007/979-8-8688-2317-6_8

Ktor is a Kotlin-based framework for building lightweight, high-performance, non-blocking services suitable for IoT networks. Retrofit is a type-safe HTTP client for Android and Java, enabling efficient communication between IoT edge devices and cloud services via REST APIs. An advanced IoT network consists of AMQP, MQTT, Ktor, and Retrofit. Such an IoT network integrates message queuing, lightweight publisher or subscriber communication, and robust client-server interaction for modern, scalable applications, as shown in Figure 8-1.

MQTT is an application layer protocol in the IoT. The MQTT protocol is used to ensure reliable security.[1] Field gateways use protocols such as TLS RSA/PSK, IPSec, and RFC 4279 to transform into a cloud gateway. On the communication path, the field gateway and the cloud work interdependently. The gateway implements security on a protocol level (MQTT/AMQP/HTTP/CoAP).

Retrofitting in a IoT refers to the process of upgrading conventional systems with IoT devices, without replacing the whole system. This permits older machines to be connected, monitored, and optimized using modern digital tools and the Internet. In the context of IoT, retrofitting involves integrating sensors, controllers, and communication devices to existing conventional machines to enable data collection (e.g., temperature, vibrations, and energy usage), predictive maintenance, and remote monitoring.[1] In distributed networks, particularly within IoT applications, AMQP is widely used as a standard for messaging. It offers a flexible and reliable messaging framework that provides asynchronous communication between applications or components across the network. [2] AMQP is an open standard messaging protocol designed to enable asynchronous communication between components or applications in distributed networks. AMQP was initially developed in 2003 by John O'Hara at JPMorgan Chase, and it has since been expanded and supported by the OASIS Working Group, which also created the MQTT protocol.[2]

In Figure 8-1, microservices are part of the cloud backend, built using Ktor or similar frameworks. They consume messages from the message broker (via AMQP), process them (e.g., for storage, analytics, alerts), and expose APIs for the client applications (accessed via Retrofit). AMQP is designed to ensure reliable message delivery using features like acknowledgements (ACKs), message persistence, transactions, and flow control. MQTT is a lightweight protocol ideal for IoT; it uses a publish/subscribe model.

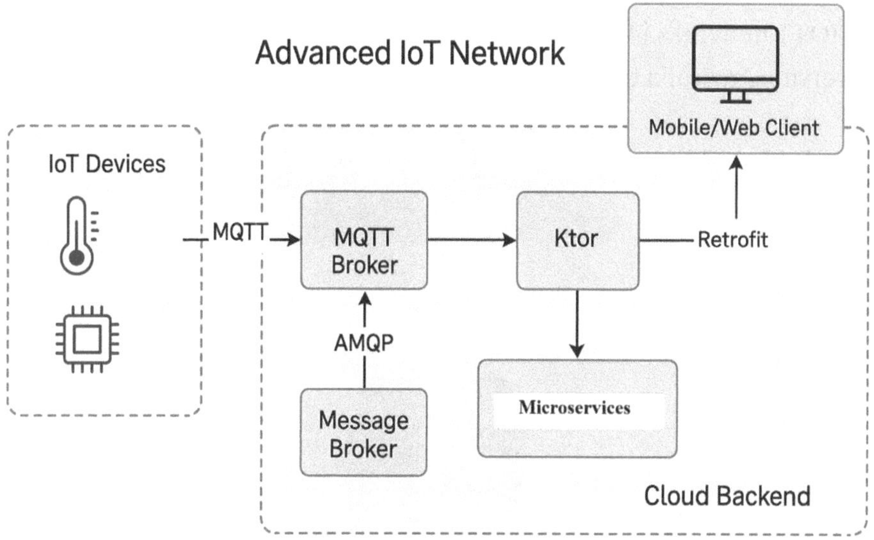

***Figure 8-1.** Advanced IoT network design using Ktor and Retrofit*

As shown in Figure 8-2, MQTT offers three quality of service (QoS) levels for message delivery. Quality of service 0 provides no guarantee and messages may be lost, quality of service 1 ensures at least one delivery but may result in duplicates, and quality of service two guarantees exactly one delivery without duplication. The first level of service is quality of service 0 (fire and forget), in which the receiver does not acknowledge receipt of a message, and the sender does not attempt to store or retransmit the message.[4] This level can be applied in IoT environments with severely resource-constrained MQTT components. In the second level, quality of service 1, the recipient acknowledges the sender after receiving the message. This level ensures that messages are delivered at least once to the receivers, while the recipients can receive the same message multiple times. The third level, known as quality of service 2 (QoS 2), employs a four-way handshake technique to ensure that a message is transmitted accurately to the sender and the receiver. This is the highest level of service in MQTT—no messages are lost and duplicate delivery of messages is prevented. However, this mode of operation may result in increased traffic on MQTT networks.[4] IoT-MQTT was used by researchers at Edith Cowan University, Australia to model and detect denial-of-service attacks.[5]

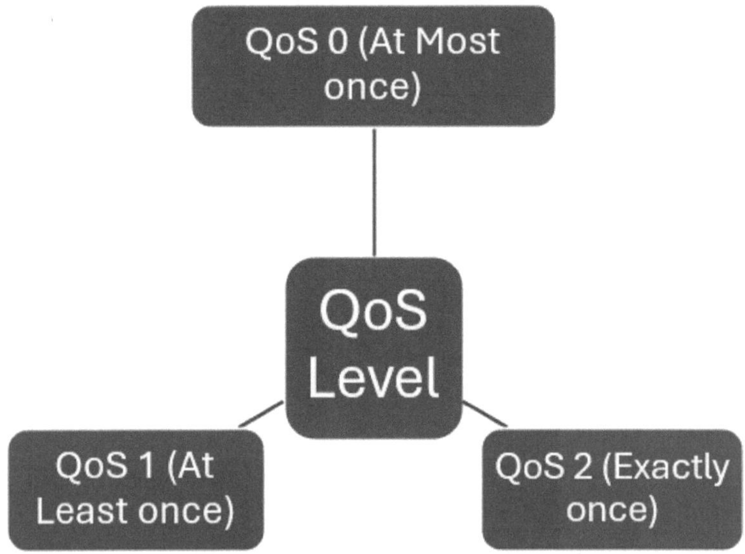

Figure 8-2. *MQTT quality of service level*

Ktor is a Kotlin-based asynchronous framework, ideal for writing microservices or APIs. It builds asynchronous server-side and microservices and serverless functions.[6] The Ktor framework is developed by JetBrains. It is used to create Kotlin web applications that use coroutines for both scalability and idiomatic API.[7] Retrofit is a type-safe HTTP client for Android/Kotlin, suitable for REST communication between devices and backends. Commercial IoTs are proprietary systems. These system does not offer flexibility for modifying the hardware and software of integrated devices. After deployment, retrofitting such systems to a newer functionality requires changing all the devices. This process is highly time consuming and not economically feasible.[8] Open analogue and digital ports, along with cloud API support, empower users to change IoT platforms to suit their own needs at a lower cost and with fewer design tasks. Smart building Retrofit can merge and scale various systems and equipment. This process of retrofitting also provides the ease of accessing data in addition to saving development and maintenance costs.[9]

Table 8-1 highlights how Kotlin-based tools and libraries can be effectively used to develop scalable, performant, and maintainable applications in the IoT and backend domains. The major benefits of building Retrofit, as a part of the IoT, are achieved with the help of reliable communication methodologies, such as Narrowband, Wi-Fi, Zigbee, LoRa or Sigfox.[9] These communication methodologies are essential for data gathering and control of remote systems. Three communication have been used in their research. Wi-Fi is the most popular indoor wireless connection methodology. Wi-Fi is widely tested, and a variety of affordable devices that implement Wi-Fi are easily available. Narrowband-IoT (NB-IoT) is an energy-efficient Wide Area Network (WAN). The NB-IoT enables a wide range of devices and services, specifically focused on indoor coverage, using third-party networks. Zigbee is a specification-based protocol mainly used to create Personal Area Networks (PANs) with energy-efficient devices.

***Table 8-1.** Benefits of Advanced IoT Network Design*

Feature	Technology	Benefit
Lightweight IoT comm	MQTT	Minimal overhead, ideal for constrained devices
Reliable backend messaging	AMQP (RabbitMQ)	Durable queues, routing, and delivery confirmation
Reactive services	Ktor	High-performance, non-blocking backend
Easy frontend integration	Retrofit	Type-safe, clean REST consumption on clients

Table 8-2 outlines the technology stack used across various layers of an IoT architecture, highlighting the tools and frameworks utilized at each level. IoT devices are the first level, where the system utilizes hardware platforms such as ESP32 and Raspberry Pi, which are popular for their low cost, wireless capabilities, and suitability for edge computing in IoT projects. Protocols manage communication between devices and systems using lightweight and reliable messaging protocols, such as MQTT (for low-power, publish-subscribe messaging) and AMQP (for more robust message delivery). Gateway is a Ktor server that acts as the gateway, handling both MQTT and REST communication. This allows it to bridge communication between IoT devices and backend systems, offering flexibility in protocol support. The architecture works as a broker, including Mosquitto as the MQTT broker and RabbitMQ for AMQP, enabling reliable and scalable message brokering between devices and backend services. The backend is the core logic. The processing is handled by Ktor microservices, which provide high performance. Some non-blocking backend services are created using Kotlin. Client applications include Android apps that use Retrofit for API communication. There are some web apps that utilize Axios or Retrofit to consume RESTful services. Database and storage are managed using a combination of PostgreSQL (for relational data), InfluxDB (for time-series data), and MongoDB (for document-based storage). This combination of database technologies ensures flexibility and efficiency in handling various types of data generated by IoT systems.

Table 8-2. *Tech Stack Suggestion*

Layer	Technology
IoT devices	ESP32, Raspberry Pi
Protocols	MQTT, AMQP
Gateway	Ktor server (MQTT/REST)
Broker	Mosquitto (MQTT), RabbitMQ (AMQP)
Backend	Ktor microservices
Clients	Android (Retrofit), web (Axios/Retrofit)
DB/Storage	PostgreSQL, InfluxDB, MongoDB

In Table 8-2, there is an illustration of a modern, scalable, and Kotlin-centric architecture for building IoT solutions. In IoT architecture, the layer used to collect data from sensors is said to be the *perception layer* (also known as the *sensing layer*). The perception layer (sensing layer) consists of sensors, actuators, RFID tags, cameras, and other data acquisition devices. It collects real-world data, such as temperature, humidity, motion, and pressure, among others. It converts physical signals into digital data for further processing. This layer acts as the interface between the physical world and the digital world in an IoT system.

After the data is collected, it is transmitted to the *network layer,* which is responsible for communicating and transferring data to other layers for processing and storage. IoT devices (edge layer)—sensors and microcontrollers—use MQTT to publish sensor data to an MQTT broker. Devices are lightweight and maintain persistent TCP connections with the broker. Gateway/middleware layer acts as a bridge between the lightweight MQTT devices and more robust backend systems. This layer translates MQTT to AMQP (if needed), aggregates data, handles device registration and security, and uses a Ktor server on edge hardware or a gateway for REST APIs, processing MQTT/AMQP messages and WebSocket communication with the dashboard/frontend. The cloud backend (core layer) message broker (RabbitMQ/Apache Qpid) utilizes AMQP to route messages to the appropriate services (e.g., storage, analytics)—enabling durable queues and delivery guarantees for Ktor microservices, thereby facilitating API exposure. Real-time alerts and device control commands are supported. Retrofit is used on Android client apps and web dashboards to consume Ktor-based REST APIs, allowing secure HTTPS access, JSON parsing, and easy integration.

AMQP in Advanced IoT Network Design

Advanced Message Queuing Protocol (AMQP) is an open standard for message-oriented middleware that supports reliable, secure, and flexible communication patterns. In the context of advanced IoT network design, AMQP plays a vital role in control-plane communications, particularly in cloud and edge server coordination, due to its support for guaranteed delivery, transactional messaging, and typed routing.[10],[11]

However, due to its binary framing overhead and protocol complexity, AMQP is less suited for constrained devices typical in IoT environments, where lightweight protocols such as MQTT or CoAP are often preferred. [10],[11],[12]

Recent research shows that integrating AMQP 1.0 over QUIC transport significantly reduces latency, communication time, and energy consumption, compared to traditional TCP transport, making it more viable for mobile and lossy wireless environments.[13],[14] Additionally, AMQP outperforms MQTT and ZeroMQ in specific federated learning scenarios, reducing communication overhead by a factor of 2.5 while maintaining model accuracy.[15]

Table 8-3 provides a concise overview of six key research studies evaluating AMQP's role in IoT networks. It highlights each study's main contribution, such as performance analysis, protocol comparisons, and enhancements, including C transport or federated learning.

Table 8-3. *Summary Table of Referenced Research on AMQP in IoT Networks*

Ref	Key Contribution
[10]	Evaluated AMQP for constrained IoT devices and found it reliable but resource-intensive.
[11]	Compared messaging protocols for IoT, highlighting AMQP's routing and quality of service benefits.
[12]	Found AMQP well-suited for backend services in IoT, but not optimal for constrained sensor nodes.
[13]	Demonstrated performance gains using AMQP 1.0 over QUIC vs TCP.
[14]	Validated improved throughput, latency, and energy efficiency of AMQP over QUIC.
[15]	Benchmarking of AMQP in federated learning; improved communication efficiency vs. TCP.

Role of MQTT in Advanced IoT Network Design

MQTT (Message Queuing Telemetry Transport) is a lightweight, publish-subscribe messaging protocol designed for resource-constrained IoT devices. It offers minimal protocol overhead, support for retained messages and "will" notifications, and reliability through quality of service levels 0, 1, and 2. It excels at telemetry in constrained, lossy environments and large-scale device deployments, thanks to its simplicity, scalability, and ecosystem support.

Table 8-4. *Summary Table of Referenced Research on AMQP in IoT Networks*

Ref	Key Contribution
[16]	Evaluated MQTT performance in terms of latency, throughput, and packet loss for lightweight IoT applications.
[17]	Conducted security assessment of open-source MQTT implementations, identifying potential standard non-conformance and exploit risks.
[18]	Proposed MQTT-ST, a spanning-tree-based distributed broker architecture to reduce latency and support edge clustering.
[19]	Introduced MQTT+, extending MQTT brokers with filtering, aggregation, and processing features to reduce client-side resource usage.
[20]	Designed SDFLMQ, a semi-decentralized federated learning framework using MQTT for load-balanced edge clustering in IoT.

Table 8-4 presents five pivotal studies that explore MQTT's applicability in IoT, focusing on performance evaluation, security assessment, broker scalability enhancements (such as spanning-tree clustering), protocol extensions (MQTT+), and its role in edge-based federated learning frameworks, including SDFLMQ. These works collectively emphasize MQTT's strengths—lightweight telemetry, scalability, and adaptability for advanced IoT network design—while also highlighting areas of concern, such as security and broker architecture optimization.

IoT Network Design for Water Supply System and NLP-Based Device Control

In Pandey, B., et al. (2019)[21], the researchers are most directly focused on IoT network design. The paper presents an IoT-based water management system leveraging multiple network protocols (Ethernet, Wi-Fi 802.11n, Modbus). Key contributions include a comparative analysis of network protocols for industrial IoT (IIoT) applications; design of a hybrid communication network to enable fault-tolerant, real-time water management; and evaluation of protocol efficiency, latency, and interoperability. It covers protocol-level design, system architecture, and real-world implementation challenges—key components of IoT network design.

Pandey, B. K. (2019).[22] describes a simulation-based IoT training environment that mimics water supply systems using cyber-range infrastructure. It involves designing and simulating network topologies for cyber-physical systems. Their system utilizes emulated sensor-actuator networks over communication protocols, delivering simulation-based network design and training architectures in IoT environments. Khanna, A., et al. (2016)[23] focuses on interface and scripting tools for IoT platforms. While not directly about hardware network protocols, this paper contributes to IoT network usability by proposing an NLP-based script system for device control. Their research is more software- or platform-focused, but it also touches on network control layers.

Conclusion

This chapter discussed IoT architecture and its integration with lightweight and enterprise-grade protocols with modern Kotlin-based frameworks to deliver a reliable, scalable, and responsive network. Real-time communication, low overhead, and modular microservices enable effective device-to-cloud integration. The use of Ktor and Retrofit further simplifies API communication and client interactions, making the system suitable for mobile and web platforms. This chapter emphasized the use of an advanced IoT network architecture that integrates the MQTT and AMQP protocols.

Future Scope

Future enhancements include AI-based edge analytics, dynamic device provisioning, blockchain-based data security, and support for additional protocols like CoAP and LoRaWAN. Integrating a visual dashboard, auto-scaling cloud functions, and predictive maintenance capabilities will further broaden this network's utility across smart agriculture, healthcare, and logistics sectors. Cross-platform compatibility and OTA (over-the-air) updates are also key areas for future development.

CHAPTER 9

Case Studies in Green IoT

IoT has a significant economic and environmental impact owing to the billions or trillions of interconnected devices that use various types of sensors to communicate through the Internet. It is widely known that every sensor needs a little energy to operate, but with billions of sensors, energy use can be considerable. Thus, it is important to create energy-efficient IoT technology and green solutions. Four framework principles for this are presented:

- Energy-efficient machine-to-machine (M2M) communications
- Energy-efficient and eco-sustainable wireless sensor networks (WSN)
- Energy-efficient radio-frequency identification (RFID)
- Energy-efficient microcontroller units and integrated circuits (IC)[2]

Consumption of energy by cellular networks has been a concern for both the industry and academia because of its potential large-scale economic and environmental impact. Environmental compatibility and sustainability are based mainly on energy efficiency and renewable power.[5]

Dr. D. Sharma and Dr. B. Pandey, *Eco-Networking for IoT*,
https://doi.org/10.1007/979-8-8688-2317-6_9

Information-centric networking (ICN) is an emerging Internet architecture design, regarded as the world-scale future internet (FI) paradigm. Despite ICN possessing significant advantages compared to the current IP-based Internet architecture, its real-world practical deployment remains subject to numerous issues, particularly with high congestion and low power in a sensor enabled-network for the IoT era. This chapter introduces an intelligent congestion control mechanism to reduce the network congestion rate, lower sensor power consumptions, and improve the network performance of ICN simultaneously to achieve a full green and efficient ICN-based sensor networking model.[3]

The goal of the *Green IOT* (GIoT) initiative is to improve energy efficiency across IoT systems. It works toward making everything in the IoT more energy efficient, from initial design to implementation.[1]

Mobile networks are the largest drivers of the large rise in energy consumption in the telecom sector.[4] According to Suarez, Luis, et al. (2012)[4], the amount of carbon dioxide (CO_2) emitted by the mobile sector will rise to 179 MtCO2 by 2020, which accounts for 51% of the total carbon footprint of the information and communication technology sector. Thus, the energy-efficiency issue in cellular networks is increasingly important because of its significant potential economic and ecological influence.

IoT is a revolutionary technology that interlinks billions of devices to gather, share, and analyze data to make intelligent decisions. IoT has had a deep impact on various industries, including healthcare, transportation, agriculture, and smart cities. Yet, with IoT devices expanding in quantity and complexity, issues concerning energy consumption, carbon emissions, and electronic waste (e-waste) have arisen.

To overcome these issues, the idea of Green IoT has been proposed, which aims to make IoT energy-efficient, eco-friendly, and sustainable. Green IoT intends to minimize the environmental footprint of IoT by streamlining power usage, leveraging renewable energy sources, and developing eco-friendly hardware and networks.

Literature Review

Albreem, Mohammed A., et al. (2021)[1] put forward an exhaustive review of GIoT, including its applications, prevailing practices, awareness levels, and the related challenges. The research focused on integrating energy-efficient protocols and the role of sustainable practices in IoT ecosystems. Alsharif, Mohammed H., et al. (2023)[2] explored the challenges posed by the high energy consumption of IoT devices and proposed strategies to improve sustainability. Their study focused on key areas such as energy-efficient machine-to-machine (M2M) communication, eco-friendly wireless sensor networks (WSNs), low-power radio-frequency identification (RFID) systems, and sustainable microcontroller units and integrated circuits (ICs). Their research highlights the role of renewable energy sources, AI-driven optimizations, and biodegradable hardware in reducing IoT's environmental footprint. Additionally, the paper outlines future research directions aimed at making IoT networks more sustainable while maintaining their efficiency and scalability. Sukjaimuk, Rungrot, et al. (2018)[3] proposed a smart congestion-control mechanism tailored for Green IoT sensor-enabled information-centric networking. Their research aimed at enhancing data transmission efficiency while minimizing energy consumption in IoT networks. Suarez, Luis, et al. (2012)[4] presented an overview and taxonomy of research methodologies in green wireless networks. Their paper classified different methodologies that focus on decreasing energy consumption in wireless communication systems toward the larger objective of sustainable IoT deployments. Alsharif, Mohammed H. (2017)[5] performed techno-economic analysis of a solar power-based standalone power system and battery storage for a global system mobile communication base station. His work highlighted the viability and cost-effectiveness of harnessing renewable energy sources in powering communication networks, in conformity with the values of Green IoT. These researchers cumulatively highlight the importance of integrating energy-efficient principles, renewable energy resources, and innovative technologies such as AI and machine learning in advancing sustainability in IoT environments.

Yang, Zhai, et al. (2021)[6] explored the role of GIoT and big data in the development of smart cities. Their study highlights how sustainable technologies, combined with big data analytics, contribute to enhancing urban infrastructure efficiency, reducing carbon footprint, and promoting environmental sustainability. The authors emphasize the integration of smart energy management and environmental monitoring systems to drive green innovation in urban settings. Memić, Belma, et al. (2022)[7] presented an overview of Green IoT, focusing on sustainable environments and emerging technologies. Their work discusses how IoT technologies can be optimized for energy efficiency while supporting environmentally conscious practices. They delve into the technological advancements necessary for building sustainable ecosystems powered by Green IoT solutions. Dalal, Sandeep (2021)[8] conducted an investigative study on IoT and Green IoT as key drivers for sustainable development. The research outlines futuristic approaches where IoT technologies support environmental sustainability by reducing energy consumption, enhancing resource management, and promoting eco-friendly practices. Dalal further examines the role of renewable energy sources in IoT deployments. Fraga-Lamas, Paula, et al. (2021)[9] discussed how Green IoT and edge AI serve as pivotal enablers in the transition toward a smart circular economy. Their study explores industry 5.0 use cases, highlighting the potential of edge computing in reducing data processing loads, minimizing energy consumption, and supporting sustainable industrial operations. Almalki, Faris A., et al. (2023)[10] examined Green IoT applications for eco-friendly and sustainable smart cities. The authors identified future directions and opportunities in leveraging Green IoT for urban development, focusing on smart grids, intelligent transportation, and green building technologies to achieve sustainable urban environments.

Ref.	Author(s) and Year	Focus Area/ Framework	Key Contributions/Findings
[1]	Mohammed A. Albreem, Ahmed M. Sheikh, Mohammed H. Alsharif, Mohd Jusoh, and Mohd N. Yasin (2021)	Green Internet of Things (GIoT) review	Provided a comprehensive review of GIoT applications, practices, and challenges; emphasized integrating energy-efficient protocols and sustainable IoT practices.
[2]	Mohammed H. Alsharif, Abu Jahid, Anabi Hilary Kelechi, and Raju Kannadasan (2023)	Sustainable IoT systems	Proposed strategies to address IoT energy consumption challenges; focused on M2M communication, WSNs, RFID, renewable energy use, and AI-driven sustainability.
[3]	Rungrot Sukjaimuk, Quang Ngoc Nguyen, and Takuro Sato (2018)	Smart congestion control for Green IoT	Introduced a smart congestion control mechanism for energy-efficient data transmission in sensor-enabled networks.
[4]	Luis Suarez, Laurent Nuaymi, and Jean-Marie Bonnin (2012)	Green wireless networks	Classified methodologies for reducing energy consumption in wireless systems to support sustainable IoT deployments.
[5]	Mohammed H. Alsharif (2017)	Solar-based GSM base station	Conducted a techno-economic analysis of solar-powered base stations, validating renewable energy as a feasible solution for communication networks.

(*continued*)

Ref.	Author(s) and Year	Focus Area/ Framework	Key Contributions/Findings
[6]	Zhai Yang, Liu Jianjun, Humaira Faqiri, Wasswa Shafik, Alanazi Talal Abdulrahman (2021)	Green IoT and big data for smart cities	Explored big data integration in Green IoT to enhance urban sustainability, focusing on smart energy management and environmental monitoring.
[7]	Belma Memić, Adisa Hasković Džubur, and Elma Avdagić-Golub (2022)	Sustainable Green IoT ecosystems	Discussed IoT energy optimization and technological innovations fostering eco-friendly IoT systems.
[8]	Sandeep Dalal (2021)	IoT and Green IoT for sustainable development	Analyzed IoT's role in reducing energy consumption, improving resource management, and using renewables for sustainability.
[9]	Paula Fraga-Lamas, Sérgio Ivan Lopes, and Tiago M. Fernández-Caramés (2021)	Edge AI and Green IoT in industry 5.0	Examined Edge AI's role in reducing energy use, enabling smart circular economy transitions and sustainable industrial processes.
[10]	Faris A. Almalki et al. (2023)	Green IoT for smart cities	Studied smart grid, transportation, and green building technologies using Green IoT for sustainable urban environments.

(*continued*)

Ref.	Author(s) and Year	Focus Area/ Framework	Key Contributions/Findings
[11]	Lalit Mohan Saini, Prerna Ajmani, V. Asha, Khobragade Pithamber, and N. Sreevani (2024)	KubeEdge for scalable IoT	Proposed a scalable edge computing framework that enhances IoT performance and energy efficiency in large-scale deployments.
[12]	Vaishali Aggarwal, Kashvi Goel, Ishika Gupta, and Prerna Ajmani (2024)	CleanComm (ACO-WOA-MOA Model)	Introduced a hybrid optimization model improving communication efficiency and sustainability in IoT networks.
[13]	Prerna Ajmani, Vandana Sharma, Prithi Samuel, K. Somasundaram, and V. Vidhya (2022)	Internet of Medical Things (IoMT)	Investigated energy-efficient health monitoring using Green IoT with predictive analytics for healthcare optimization.
[14]	Dayu Wang, Daojun Zhong, and Alireza Souri (2021)	IoT energy management	Reviewed energy optimization techniques to enhance IoT device longevity and operational efficiency.
[15]	Arash Heidari, Nima Jafari Navimipour, Mohammad Ali Jabraeil Jamali, and Shahin Akbarpour (2023)	IoT-edge-cloud offloading	Proposed energy-efficient, secure, and intelligent task offloading for sustainable resource management.
[16]	Sakshi Popli, Rakesh Kumar Jha, and Sanjeev Jain (2022)	Green IoT Survey	Reviewed advancements in energy-efficient protocols, low-power sensors, and sustainable architectures.

(*continued*)

Ref.	Author(s) and Year	Focus Area/ Framework	Key Contributions/Findings
[17]	Ramanjeet Singh and Amit Jain (2021)	Energy efficiency in Green IoT	Presented techniques for energy-aware routing, hardware design, and power-saving mechanisms.
[18]	Sha Zhu, Kaoru Ota, and Mianxiong Dong (2021)	Green AI in Industrial IoT (IIoT)	Discussed AI integration for improving industrial energy efficiency and operational sustainability.
[19]	Pallati Narsimhulu et al. (2024)	FL-based route optimization for ITS	Developed a federated learning-based model for sustainable, congestion-free vehicular communication using Green IoT.
[20]	Mudita Sinha, Elizabeth Chacko, Priya Makhija, and Sabyasachi Pramanik (2021)	Green IoT for smart cities	Proposed strategies for smart infrastructures, renewable energy integration, and sustainable urban planning.
[21]	Ajmani et al.	Internet of Vehicles (IoV)	Explained IoV protocols analogous to IoT, supporting connectivity and automation in vehicular networks.
[22]	Authors in [22]	Blockchain and smart contracts in IoT	Presented blockchain-based IoT systems that ensure security, transparency, and energy-efficient operations.

Why Is Green IoT Important?

IoT is transforming industries by allowing smart connectivity and automation in various industries (see Figure 9-1). With this accelerated growth, there are environmental issues associated with it in the form of high energy use, higher electronic waste (e-waste), a large carbon footprint, and depletion of resources. Green IoT is introduced to counteract these issues with energy-efficient techniques, sustainable hardware, and green computing practices.

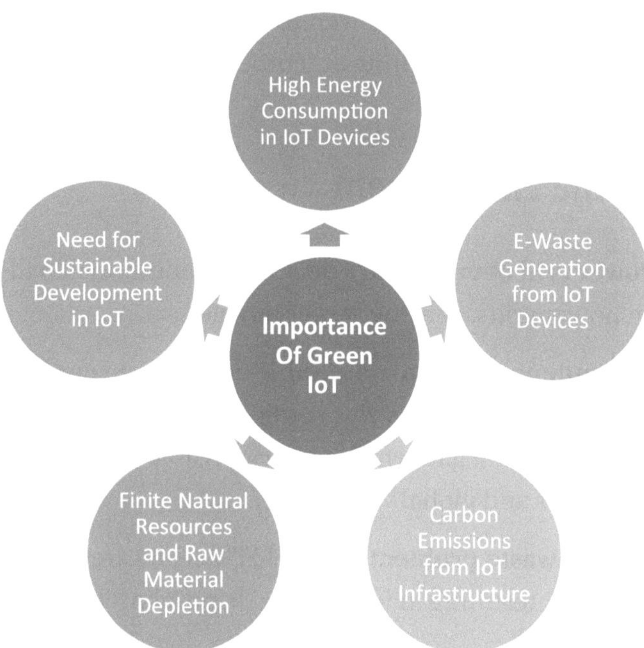

Figure 9-1. *The importance of Green IoT*

High-Energy Consumption in IoT Devices

The rapid expansion of IoT devices has created an enormous power demand. Billions of smart devices such as sensors, actuators, and Internet-enabled appliances must consume power continuously to function. The rising demand profoundly affects electricity usage worldwide.

Energy Consumption in IoT Networks

IoT devices interact with gateways, cloud platforms, and edge computing systems, all of which need to be powered. Networks like 5G, LPWAN, and Wi-Fi use power while transmitting and processing data, adding to the energy footprint.

Impact on the Environment

- **Power grid overload:** IoT devices put additional load on power grids, causing power outages.
- **Dependence on non-renewable energy sources:** Most IoT-driven industries continue to rely on coal, oil, and natural gas, which are responsible for carbon emissions and global warming.
- **Battery waste problems:** Most IoT sensors are battery-powered, resulting in toxic waste disposal problems.

Green IoT Solutions to Reduce Energy Consumption

- **Energy-efficient protocols:** Utilization of low-power networks such as Zigbee, LoRaWAN, and Bluetooth Low Energy (BLE) can reduce power consumption.

- **Intelligent sleep mechanisms:** Devices can be put into low-power or deep sleep states when they are not actively sending data.
- **Integration of renewable energy:** IoT devices can be powered by solar panels, windmills, and kinetic energy to minimize electricity usage.

E-Waste Generation from IoT Devices

Due to short product lifetimes and fast technological progress, IoT devices are being discarded at a high rate, generating electronic waste (e-waste). This is having severe environmental and health implications

The Scale of E-Waste Problem

According to the *Global E-Waste Monitor 2022* report by the United Nations, more than 53.6 million metric tons of e-waste were generated globally in 2022, and IoT devices account for a substantial and rapidly growing portion of this waste. This figure is projected to surpass 74 million metric tons by 2030 if sustainable recycling and disposal measures are not implemented.

Environmental and Health Impacts

- **Toxic waste in landfills:** IoT devices are filled with lead, mercury, and cadmium, which can pollute soil and water resources.
- **Air and water pollution:** Burning of electronic parts due to improper disposal of IoT components results in emission of toxic chemicals into the atmosphere.
- **Health risks:** Employees in e-waste recycling factories are exposed to carcinogenic substances.

Green IoT Strategies to Minimize E-Waste

- **Modular and upgradable IoT devices:** Building devices for effortless upgrade rather than full replacement.
- **Eco-friendly manufacturing:** Implementing biodegradable materials and recyclable plastics in the manufacturing of IoT.
- **E-waste recycling initiatives:** Take-back programs are being used by companies to recycle obsolete devices in an environmentally friendly manner.

Carbon Emissions from IoT Infrastructure

IoT ecosystems produce enormous amounts of data, which are being processed in cloud data centers. The data centers use massive amounts of electricity, producing carbon dioxide (CO_2) emissions.

Carbon Footprint of IoT and Data Centers

- Continuous energy is needed by IoT-enabled cloud storage and processing, with data centers taking up to 1% of the world's energy demand.
- 5G and IoT networks need massive infrastructure, using more power compared to the previous communication technology.

The Greenhouse Effect and Climate Change

- Rising levels of CO_2 cause global temperatures to rise, leading to climate change.
- Severe weather conditions, like hurricanes and heatwaves, are made worse by higher carbon emissions due to industrial and technological expansion.

Green IoT Measures to Reduce Carbon Emissions

- **Energy-efficient edge computing:** Local processing of IoT data rather than pushing all to the cloud saves energy.
- **Renewable data centers:** Carbon-neutral cloud computing adoption through the use of renewable power sources.
- **Energy optimization through AI:** Machine learning algorithms can forecast energy consumption habits and optimize IoT use to minimize energy use.

Finite Natural Resources and Raw Material Depletion

IoT hardware components, including sensors, circuit boards, and batteries, require materials such as rare earth metals, lithium, and copper. Mining and extraction of these materials contribute to resource depletion and environmental degradation.

The Demand for Rare Earth Metals

- IoT devices rely on elements like neodymium, indium, and lithium, which are finite and expensive to extract.
- Mining processes lead to deforestation, water pollution, and destruction of natural habitats. habitats. Nano-biotechnology is an emerging area in IoT, where nano-scale sensors integrated with AI enable advanced sensing and intelligent applications, while many of these technologies rely on rare earth metals for efficient electronic and sensing components.

Consequences of Resource Overuse

- **Soil and water contamination:** Mining sites generate toxic waste, contaminating rivers and agricultural lands.
- **Rising costs of IoT production:** Limited availability of metals leads to increased production costs and affects supply chains.
- **Dependency on non-renewable resources:** Many IoT systems still rely on petroleum-based plastics and non-renewable energy sources.

Sustainable Alternatives in Green IoT

- **Biodegradable electronics:** Research is advancing on organic semiconductors and eco-friendly PCB (printed circuit board) materials.
- **Circular economy in IoT:** Encouraging reuse and refurbishment of old IoT devices instead of manufacturing new ones.

- **Efficient material recycling:** Recovering metals and materials from discarded devices through advanced e-waste processing technologies.

The Need for Sustainable Development in IoT

Green IoT is essential for achieving the United Nations Sustainable Development Goals (SDGs), particularly in the areas of affordable clean energy (SDG 7), responsible consumption (SDG 12), and climate action (SDG 13).

Balancing Technological Growth with Sustainability

- IoT enables smart cities, automated industries, and intelligent healthcare, but without sustainability measures, its benefits are overshadowed by its environmental impact.
- Companies need to implement corporate social responsibility (CSR) initiatives to ensure sustainable IoT development.

Government Regulations and Policies

- Many countries have introduced strict regulations on e-waste disposal and energy efficiency in electronic devices.

- Policies such as extended producer responsibility (EPR) require IoT manufacturers to manage product end-of-life waste.

The Future of Green IoT

- The future of IoT relies on smart, sustainable solutions that incorporate AI-powered energy management, blockchain-based carbon tracking, and IoT-driven renewable energy grids.
- Green IoT will be a key enabler in reducing emissions and creating a low-carbon economy through smart, sustainable infrastructure.

In conclusion, Green IoT is not just a technological advancement but a necessity to ensure that IoT continues to expand without causing environmental harm. By addressing energy consumption, e-waste management, carbon emissions, and resource depletion, Green IoT enables a sustainable future where smart devices enhance human life without compromising ecological balance.

By adopting renewable energy sources, low-power communication protocols, sustainable manufacturing practices, and AI-driven energy management, industries can ensure that IoT remains an enabler of positive change rather than a contributor to environmental challenges.

Core Concepts of Green IoT

This section discusses the core concepts of Green IoT, as illustrated in Figure 9-2.

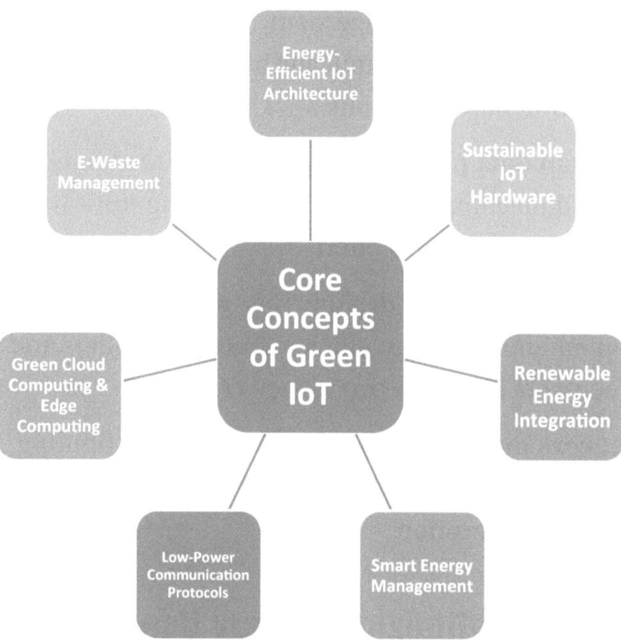

Figure 9-2. *The core concepts of Green IoT*

Energy-Efficient IoT Architecture

Energy efficiency is a fundamental goal of Green IoT. Designing an energy-efficient IoT architecture involves optimizing every layer of the system, from hardware components to network communication and data processing strategies.

Key Principles of Energy-Efficient IoT Architecture

- **Minimal power consumption:** IoT devices should consume the least amount of power while maintaining optimal performance.

- **Adaptive power management:** Devices should adjust energy use dynamically based on workload and environmental conditions.
- **Efficient data processing:** This involves reducing redundant computations and optimizing software to lower energy consumption.
- **Low-energy circuit design:** This involves implementing energy-efficient microcontrollers and processors to reduce overall power use.
- **Network load balancing:** This involves distributing workload efficiently across network nodes to optimize power consumption.

Techniques for Optimizing Energy Use in IoT Architectures

- **Duty cycling:** IoT devices switch between active and sleep states to conserve power.
- **Energy-aware routing protocols:** Networks use intelligent algorithms to minimize energy drain in communication paths.
- **Data compression and optimization:** Compressing data before transmission reduces energy use in communication.
- **Wake-up radio mechanisms:** Reducing unnecessary signal transmissions by activating devices only when required.
- **Low-power IoT gateways:** Utilizing energy-efficient gateways that aggregate data before forwarding it to the cloud.

Sustainable IoT Hardware

Sustainable IoT hardware focuses on designing and manufacturing devices that minimize their environmental footprint by using eco-friendly materials, recyclable components, and biodegradable alternatives.

Features of Sustainable IoT Hardware

- **Low power consumption:** IoT devices should consume minimal power for an extended battery life.
- **Eco-friendly materials:** Devices should use biodegradable plastics, organic semiconductors, and recyclable metals.
- **Extended lifecycle:** Durable hardware reduces the frequency of replacements, minimizing e-waste.
- **Energy-harvesting techniques:** Implementing kinetic, solar, or thermal energy harvesting to power devices.
- **RoHS compliance:** Restricting hazardous substances in IoT device manufacturing.

Green Materials in IoT Device Manufacturing

- **Biodegradable circuit boards (PCBs):** Made from natural fibers instead of traditional plastics.
- **Lead-free soldering:** Reducing toxic heavy metals in circuit board manufacturing.

- **Solar-powered IoT sensors:** Using photovoltaic cells to power sensors reduces dependency on conventional batteries.
- **Recyclable packaging:** Using minimal and eco-friendly packaging materials for IoT devices.

Renewable Energy Integration

IoT devices and networks can be powered using solar, wind, kinetic, and thermal energy to reduce reliance on traditional electricity sources.

Benefits of Renewable Energy in IoT

- **Reduces carbon footprint:** IoT networks powered by renewables contribute less to greenhouse gas emissions.
- **Energy independence:** IoT systems can function in remote areas without relying on power grids.
- **Cost savings:** Once deployed, renewable energy sources reduce electricity expenses.
- **Sustainable power storage:** Using advanced battery technologies such as solid-state and lithium-sulfur are better for energy storage.

Types of Renewable Energy Sources for IoT

- **Solar energy:** IoT sensors with solar panels can enjoy self-sustaining operation.
- **Wind energy:** Small-scale wind turbines can power IoT applications in agricultural fields.

- **Kinetic energy:** Wearable IoT devices can harvest energy from body movement.
- **Thermal energy:** Heat-powered IoT sensors can utilize thermoelectric generators.

Smart Energy Management

Smart energy management involves using AI-driven algorithms and power-optimization techniques to reduce unnecessary energy consumption in IoT devices.

Strategies for Smart Energy Management

- **Demand-based power use:** IoT devices consume energy only when needed.
- **Dynamic voltage scaling:** Adjusting power supply to match workload demand.
- **Battery optimization techniques:** Using energy-harvesting methods and low-power standby modes.
- **Predictive maintenance:** AI-driven energy monitoring predicts failures and reduces unnecessary energy use.

AI and Machine Learning in Energy Management

- AI-based systems predict device usage patterns and adjust energy consumption accordingly.
- Machine learning helps optimize HVAC (heating, ventilation, and air conditioning) systems in smart buildings.
- Edge AI processing reduces cloud communications to save energy.

Low-Power Communication Protocols

IoT networks require efficient communication protocols that consume minimal power while maintaining reliable data transfer.

Energy-Efficient IoT Communication Technologies

- **LPWAN (Low-Power Wide-Area Network):** Used for long-range, low-energy IoT applications.
- **Zigbee and Bluetooth Low Energy (BLE):** Short-range wireless protocols for smart homes and healthcare devices.
- **Narrowband IoT (NB-IoT):** A cellular-based solution for wide-area IoT connectivity with low energy use.

Power-Saving Techniques in IoT Networking

- **Adaptive transmission power control:** Adjusting signal strength based on network conditions.
- **Data aggregation:** Combining multiple sensor readings to reduce redundant data transmissions.
- **Asynchronous communication:** Devices send data only when necessary instead of using continuous streaming.

Green Cloud Computing and Edge Computing

Cloud and edge computing play a crucial role in reducing the energy consumption of IoT systems by optimizing data processing.

Green Cloud Computing

- Uses energy-efficient data centers to minimize carbon emissions.
- Employs virtualization and resource sharing to optimize power usage.
- Uses green AI algorithms, which consume less computational power.

Edge Computing for Energy Savings

- **Reduces latency:** Data is processed closer to the device, avoiding long-distance transmission to cloud servers.
- **Minimizes bandwidth use:** Less data is sent to cloud servers, reducing network energy consumption.
- **Edge analytics:** Data is processed locally, reducing cloud dependency.

E-Waste Management

Managing electronic waste (e-waste) is essential for making IoT more sustainable and reducing its negative environmental impact.

Challenges of IoT-Generated E-Waste

- Short device lifespan leads to massive electronic waste accumulation.
- Toxic materials in IoT devices pose environmental hazards.
- Difficulties in recycling miniaturized electronics.

Strategies for Reducing IoT E-Waste

- **Modular hardware design:** Allows individual components to be upgraded or replaced.
- **Device recycling programs:** Manufacturers take back old devices for recycling.
- **Biodegradable electronics:** Use of organic materials that decompose naturally.
- **Extended manufacturer responsibility:** Ensuring companies track and recycle their products responsibly.

In summary, Green IoT is an innovative approach that focuses on energy efficiency, renewable energy integration, low-power communication, and responsible e-waste management. By implementing these core concepts, IoT can continue to grow without compromising environmental sustainability. Future advancements in AI-driven optimizations, renewable energy adoption, and efficient hardware designs will further enhance Green IoT solutions.

Applications of Green IoT

Green IoT aims to marry the rapid innovation of connected devices with environmentally sustainable practices. Its applications span multiple sectors, where it not only improves operational efficiency but also minimizes energy consumption, reduces carbon emissions, and lessens environmental degradation (see Figure 9-3). The following sections take an in-depth look at the various applications of Green IoT.

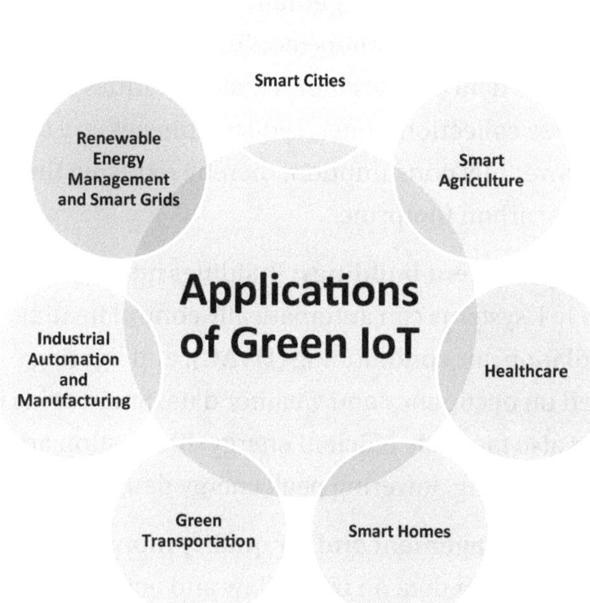

Figure 9-3. *The applications of Green IoT*

Smart Cities

Optimizing Urban Resource Use

Smart cities leverage Green IoT to create urban environments that are more efficient and environmentally friendly. The following are key applications in this sector:

- **Smart lighting:** IoT-enabled streetlights equipped with sensors can detect ambient light and pedestrian or vehicular movement. This allows for dynamic adjustment of brightness—reducing energy consumption during low-traffic periods while maintaining safety and security at night.

- **Intelligent waste management:** IoT sensors installed in public waste containers monitor fill levels in real time. This data enables municipal authorities to optimize collection routes, reduce unnecessary trips, and lower fuel consumption, thereby reducing the overall carbon footprint.
- **Energy-efficient buildings:** Buildings integrated with IoT systems can automatically control heating, ventilation, air conditioning (HVAC), and lighting based on occupancy and weather data. Smart grids in cities also facilitate efficient energy distribution and load balancing, lowering peak energy demands.
- **Traffic management and air quality monitoring:** IoT devices collect data on traffic flow and environmental pollutants. This information can be used to adjust traffic signals to reduce congestion (and hence vehicle emissions) and to inform policies for air quality improvements.

Smart Agriculture

Enhancing Resource Efficiency in Farming

Agriculture is one of the sectors that stands to gain significantly from IoT-enabled sustainability practices:

- **Precision farming:** By deploying IoT sensors across fields, farmers can obtain real-time data on soil moisture, nutrient levels, and weather conditions. This allows for the precise application of water, fertilizers, and pesticides only when and where needed, reducing waste and environmental runoff.

- **Automated irrigation systems:** IoT-based irrigation systems use data from moisture sensors to regulate water flow. This not only conserves water but also optimizes crop growth by ensuring that plants receive the exact amount of water necessary for healthy development.
- **Livestock monitoring:** Wearable IoT devices can monitor the health and location of livestock, ensuring timely interventions if an animal falls ill. Healthier animals and optimized feeding practices lead to a reduction in resource waste and more humane conditions.
- **Greenhouse management:** In controlled environments like greenhouses, IoT sensors adjust temperature, humidity, and CO_2 levels, optimizing plant growth while minimizing energy use. This dynamic adjustment contributes to lower energy bills and sustainable farming practices.

Healthcare

Driving Energy Efficiency in Medical Systems

Green IoT is transforming healthcare by reducing energy consumption and improving patient care through smart, connected devices:

- **Low-power wearable devices:** Wearable health monitors such as fitness trackers, heart rate monitors, and glucose sensors are designed for low energy consumption. Extended battery life means fewer battery replacements and less electronic waste, which is crucial for both patient convenience and environmental sustainability.

- **Remote patient monitoring:** IoT enables telemedicine solutions where patient data is continuously monitored and transmitted to healthcare providers. This reduces the frequency of hospital visits, cutting down on travel-related emissions and allowing healthcare facilities to operate more efficiently.
- **Smart hospital infrastructure:** Hospitals equipped with IoT systems can monitor and control their energy use—optimizing lighting, HVAC, and medical equipment based on real-time occupancy and usage patterns. This not only reduces operating costs but also minimizes the hospital's carbon footprint.
- **Cold chain management:** For vaccines and other temperature-sensitive medications, IoT sensors ensure that storage conditions remain optimal during transport and storage, reducing energy waste and ensuring product efficacy.

Smart Homes

Creating Energy-Efficient Living Environments

At the residential level, Green IoT is fundamental in promoting sustainable living by integrating technology into everyday appliances and systems:

- **Smart appliances:** Modern appliances, including refrigerators, washing machines, and dishwashers, are now equipped with sensors that optimize their energy consumption based on usage patterns. This not only lowers electricity bills but also extends the lifespan of these appliances.

- **Automated climate control:** Smart thermostats and HVAC systems use data from temperature and occupancy sensors to adjust the home's climate automatically. This ensures that energy is not wasted heating or cooling empty spaces.
- **Energy monitoring systems:** Home energy management systems provide real-time feedback on electricity use, empowering homeowners to adjust their consumption habits. Integration with renewable energy sources, like rooftop solar panels, further enhances sustainability.
- **Smart power strips and lighting:** These devices can detect when appliances are idle and cut off power automatically. Additionally, lighting systems that adjust brightness based on ambient conditions help reduce unnecessary energy consumption.

Green Transportation

Enabling Sustainable Mobility Through IoT

Transportation systems are one of the largest contributors to carbon emissions. Green IoT is at the forefront of transforming mobility with smart solutions:

- **Smart traffic management:** IoT sensors collect data on vehicle density and traffic flows, enabling the dynamic adjustment of traffic signals. This optimization reduces congestion, minimizes idling times, and cuts down on fuel consumption and emissions.

- **Electric vehicle (EV) optimization:** Green IoT technologies manage EV charging stations and monitor battery performance in real time. Smart charging infrastructure can balance the load on the grid and ensure that EVs are charged during off-peak hours, increasing efficiency and reducing environmental impact.
- **Fleet management:** Logistics companies use IoT devices to track fleet performance, optimize routes, and monitor fuel consumption. This leads to improved fuel efficiency, lower operational costs, and reduced greenhouse gas emissions.
- **Public transportation systems:** Real-time monitoring of buses and trains helps in scheduling and route optimization. Improved efficiency in public transport not only makes it more attractive to commuters but also reduces the reliance on private vehicles, thereby cutting urban emissions.

Industrial Automation and Manufacturing

Sustainable Industrial Processes with IoT

Industries are increasingly leveraging IoT to enhance operational efficiency and reduce their environmental footprint:

- **Smart energy monitoring in factories:** Industrial IoT systems continuously track energy consumption across various production lines. This enables factory managers to identify energy waste and implement corrective measures such as adjusting production schedules or upgrading inefficient machinery.

- **Predictive maintenance:** IoT sensors monitor the performance of industrial equipment in real time, detecting anomalies that could indicate potential failures. Early detection allows for timely maintenance, reducing unexpected downtime and minimizing the energy costs associated with equipment inefficiencies.
- **Process optimization:** By analyzing sensor data, manufacturers can fine-tune production processes to reduce material waste and energy consumption. Automated adjustments in production lines help maintain optimal performance without overusing resources.
- **Sustainable supply chain management:** IoT-enabled tracking of raw materials and finished goods ensures that supply chains are optimized for efficiency. This reduces transportation-related emissions and promotes the use of sustainable logistics practices.

Renewable Energy Management and Smart Grids

Integrating IoT in Energy Distribution Systems

Green IoT also plays a vital role in managing renewable energy sources and modernizing power grids:

- **Smart grids:** IoT technologies enable the creation of smart grids that can balance electricity supply and demand in real time. Smart meters and sensors monitor energy flows, allowing for better integration of renewable energy sources and reducing waste.

- **Renewable energy forecasting:** IoT devices collect meteorological and environmental data to predict renewable energy generation (e.g., solar and wind). This information is crucial for adjusting grid operations and ensuring a stable power supply from intermittent renewable sources.
- **Distributed energy resources (DERs):** IoT systems manage a network of distributed energy resources such as solar panels, wind turbines, and energy storage systems. This decentralized approach increases grid resilience and reduces reliance on fossil fuels.
- **Demand response programs:** By communicating with smart appliances and industrial systems, IoT can enable demand-response programs where energy use is adjusted during peak times. This helps balance the load on the grid and reduces the need for additional fossil-fuel-based power generation.

Green IoT represents a transformative approach to harnessing the benefits of connectivity and automation while ensuring that technological progress does not come at the expense of our environment. By integrating energy-efficient architectures, sustainable hardware, intelligent energy management, low-power communication protocols, and renewable energy systems, Green IoT paves the way for a more sustainable future.

From smart cities and agriculture to healthcare, smart homes, transportation, industrial automation, and renewable energy management, the applications of Green IoT are diverse and impactful. Each sector benefits from reduced energy consumption, lower operational costs, and a minimized environmental footprint. As the global community increasingly prioritizes sustainability, the role of Green IoT will only grow in importance, driving innovation that supports both economic growth and ecological preservation.

Challenges and Future Trends of Green IoT

As GIoT continues to evolve, it faces several challenges that hinder its widespread adoption. At the same time, emerging trends are shaping its future, driving innovation toward a more sustainable and energy-efficient IoT.

Challenges of Green IoT

This section outlines some of the challenges associated with Green IoT, as illustrated in Figure 9-4.

Figure 9-4. *The challenges of IoT*

High Energy Consumption of IoT Devices

- IoT devices require continuous power to operate, making energy efficiency a major concern.
- Many IoT sensors and actuators rely on batteries, which need frequent replacement, leading to electronic waste.
- Solution efforts include low-power IoT protocols (e.g., Zigbee, LoRaWAN) and energy-harvesting technologies.

Limited Battery Life and Energy-Harvesting Issues

- Energy harvesting (solar, thermal, or RF-based charging) is still not efficient enough for all IoT devices.
- Many IoT networks rely on non-rechargeable batteries, which contradict the sustainability goal of Green IoT.
- There is a need for self-sustaining energy solutions for IoT sensors and devices.

Data Processing and Storage Challenges

- IoT generates huge amounts of data, leading to high computational power consumption in cloud data centers.
- Traditional cloud computing infrastructures are energy-intensive, increasing the carbon footprint.
- Solutions like edge and fog computing are being explored to reduce energy use.

Scalability and Network Efficiency Issues

- As the number of IoT devices grows, network traffic increases, consuming more bandwidth and power.
- Managing millions of interconnected devices without energy waste is a major challenge.
- Optimized network protocols and energy-efficient 5G technologies are required.

E-Waste and Environmental Concerns

- The rapid growth of IoT leads to increased e-waste from discarded sensors and devices.
- Lack of proper recycling strategies for outdated IoT components poses sustainability challenges.
- Biodegradable electronic components and modular IoT devices are potential solutions.

Security and Privacy Issues

- Many Green IoT devices use low-power networks, making them vulnerable to cyberattacks.
- Data privacy concerns arise due to real-time monitoring in smart cities, homes, and industrial applications.
- There is a need for secure communication protocols with minimal energy consumption.

High Initial Deployment Costs

- Implementing Green IoT solutions requires investment in energy-efficient hardware and sustainable infrastructure.
- Many industries hesitate due to the high upfront costs and uncertain return on investment (ROI).
- Government incentives and standardization of Green IoT technologies can encourage adoption.

Future Trends of Green IoT

This section outlines the furture trends associated with Green IoT, as illustrated in Figure 9-5.

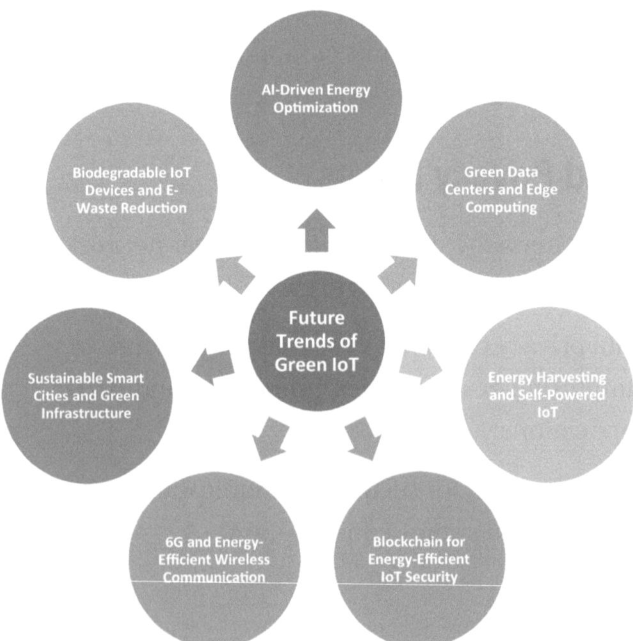

Figure 9-5. *The future trends of Green IoT*

AI-Driven Energy Optimization

- AI and ML are being integrated into IoT systems to optimize energy use.
- AI-based predictive analytics helps in smart power management and reduces unnecessary energy consumption.

Green Data Centers and Edge Computing

- Shifting from traditional cloud computing to edge computing reduces data transmission energy costs.
- Green AI-powered data centers use renewable energy and efficient cooling techniques.

Energy Harvesting and Self-Powered IoT

Development of self-powered IoT sensors using energy-harvesting techniques such as the following will reduce dependency on batteries and enhance sustainability:

- Solar energy
- Kinetic energy (motion-based charging)
- RF energy harvesting

Blockchain for Energy-Efficient IoT Security

- Blockchain is emerging as a low-power, decentralized security solution for IoT networks.
- Lightweight consensus mechanisms are being developed to ensure secure, energy-efficient transactions.

6G and Energy-Efficient Wireless Communication

- 6G networks (expected by 2030) will bring ultra-low latency and energy-efficient communication.
- Energy-aware IoT routing protocols will enable smart, sustainable connectivity.

Sustainable Smart Cities and Green Infrastructure

IoT will play a key role in:

- Smart grids for optimized energy distribution
- Smart transportation reducing carbon emissions
- Smart buildings with automated energy-saving systems

Governments worldwide are investing in eco-friendly smart city projects powered by Green IoT.

Biodegradable IoT Devices and E-Waste Reduction

- Researchers are working on biodegradable electronics to reduce e-waste.
- Eco-friendly materials like organic semiconductors and sustainable plastics will replace traditional components.

Green IoT is a crucial technology for creating a sustainable and energy-efficient digital future. While it faces challenges like energy consumption, security risks, and e-waste, innovative trends such as AI-driven energy optimization, self-powered IoT, and blockchain security are shaping its future. With advancements in 6G, edge computing, and biodegradable devices, Green IoT will play a transformative role in reducing the environmental impact of digital systems.

Advantages of Green IoT

Green IoT focuses on minimizing energy consumption, reducing e-waste, and integrating sustainable practices into IoT systems (see Figure 9-6). The following sections discuss some of its key advantages.

Figure 9-6. *The advantages of Green IoT*

Energy Efficiency

Green IoT solutions prioritize energy-efficient hardware and software designs.

- **Optimized power consumption:** IoT devices are designed to use minimal energy while maintaining optimal performance.

- **Smart power management:** Techniques like duty cycling, dynamic voltage scaling, and AI-based power control improve energy utilization.
- **Efficient data processing:** Edge computing and lightweight algorithms reduce processing power requirements, thereby saving energy.

Reduced Carbon Footprint

By adopting energy-saving practices and renewable energy sources, Green IoT helps lower greenhouse gas emissions.

- **Solar, wind, and kinetic energy use:** IoT devices powered by renewables cut down reliance on fossil fuels.
- **Smart grids and energy monitoring:** IoT-based smart meters help industries and households optimize energy consumption, reducing carbon emissions.

Cost Savings

Implementing Green IoT solutions leads to long-term cost reductions in the form of:

- **Lower energy bills:** Energy-efficient IoT devices consume less electricity, reducing operational costs.
- **Extended hardware lifespan:** Sustainable materials and efficient power usage increase device longevity, reducing maintenance and replacement costs.
- **Lower data transmission costs:** Compression techniques and edge computing reduce bandwidth and cloud storage expenses.

Sustainable Manufacturing and Reduced E-Waste

Green IoT promotes eco-friendly manufacturing and responsible disposal of electronic components.

- **Eco-friendly materials:** Biodegradable circuit boards and lead-free soldering reduce environmental pollution.
- **Modular hardware design:** Components can be upgraded individually, extending the device lifecycle and minimizing e-waste.
- **Recycling and circular economy:** Companies adopt take-back programs to refurbish or recycle old IoT devices.

Improved Environmental Monitoring and Conservation

IoT technology helps track environmental conditions and reduce resource waste.

- **Smart agriculture:** IoT-based sensors monitor soil moisture, preventing water waste in farming.
- **Air and water quality monitoring:** IoT devices analyze pollution levels in real time, enabling quick responses to environmental hazards.
- **Wildlife conservation:** IoT-enabled tracking devices help monitor endangered species and combat illegal poaching.

Better Performance in Remote Areas

Green IoT solutions help provide sustainable services in regions with limited electricity access.

- **Off-grid operations:** Solar-powered IoT devices can function without grid connectivity.
- **Disaster management:** IoT sensors deployed in disaster-prone areas work on renewable energy to provide real-time alerts.

Regulatory Compliance and Corporate Responsibility

Governments and organizations encourage Green IoT adoption through policies and incentives.

- **Green certifications and tax benefits:** Companies using sustainable IoT solutions can benefit from tax credits and regulatory advantages.
- **Corporate social responsibility (CSR):** Businesses adopting Green IoT align with global sustainability goals, improving brand reputation.

Disadvantages of Green IoT

Despite its benefits, Green IoT also presents challenges that must be addressed. The disadvantages of Green IoT, shown in Figure 9-7, are outlined in this section.

Figure 9-7. *The disadvantages of Green IoT*

High Initial Costs

The adoption of energy-efficient IoT hardware and renewable energy solutions can be expensive.

- **Cost of development:** Designing energy-efficient hardware with eco-friendly materials requires a higher initial investment.
- **Installation costs:** Deploying solar panels, wind turbines, and other renewable energy sources for IoT devices is costly.
- **Research and innovation costs:** Continuous advancements in low-power IoT technology require significant R&D funding.

Complexity in Implementation

Green IoT requires a multi-layered approach to optimizing power consumption and sustainability.

- **Energy-efficient protocol integration:** Implementing low-power communication protocols like LPWAN, Zigbee, and NB-IoT demands expertise.
- **Adaptive power management complexity:** Managing energy use dynamically based on real-time conditions is challenging.
- **Sustainability compliance challenges:** Ensuring compliance with green manufacturing standards across global supply chains is difficult.

Limited Power Supply in Certain Conditions

Renewable energy sources are not always reliable.

- **Weather dependency:** Solar-powered IoT devices may struggle in areas with minimal sunlight, and wind-powered IoT systems require sufficient wind speeds.
- **Energy storage limitations:** Batteries for storing renewable energy have limited capacities and can degrade over time.
- **High latency in power transition:** Switching between grid power and renewable sources can cause temporary disruptions.

Security and Privacy Concerns

Green IoT networks must balance low-power consumption with strong security measures.

- **Limited processing power for encryption:** Energy-efficient devices may not support complex encryption, making them vulnerable to cyber threats.
- **Data transmission risks:** Wireless IoT networks can be exploited by hackers if security measures are weak.
- **Smart grid vulnerabilities:** Cyberattacks on IoT-based energy management systems can lead to widespread power failures.

Limited Availability of Eco-Friendly Materials

While Green IoT promotes sustainable manufacturing, some eco-friendly materials are not widely accessible.

- **High cost of biodegradable components:** Sustainable alternatives for PCBs and semiconductors are expensive.
- **Limited production and supply chain issues:** Sourcing eco-friendly raw materials in large quantities can be difficult.
- **Performance trade-offs:** Some biodegradable materials may not match the durability of traditional electronics.

Compatibility Issues with Legacy Systems

Transitioning to Green IoT can be challenging for organizations with older infrastructures.

- **Integration challenges:** Upgrading existing IoT systems to incorporate energy-efficient hardware and software is complex.
- **Interoperability issues:** Different vendors use varying sustainability standards, causing compatibility problems.
- **Software and firmware upgrades:** Legacy devices may not support the latest energy-saving protocols, requiring costly updates.

Potential Reduction in Performance

Some energy-saving techniques can affect IoT device performance.

- **Lower processing power:** Ultra-low-power processors may struggle with complex computations.
- **Reduced communication range:** Low-power communication protocols (e.g., Zigbee, BLE) have limited range compared to traditional networks.
- **Latency issues in data processing:** Edge computing optimizes energy use but may introduce slight delays in real-time processing.

Green IoT presents a transformative approach to sustainability by optimizing energy use, reducing e-waste, and integrating renewable energy sources. However, high initial costs, implementation challenges, and security concerns must be addressed for large-scale adoption.

By advancing research in energy-efficient hardware, eco-friendly materials, and smart power management, Green IoT can help create a sustainable and environmentally responsible digital future.

Case Studies on Modular and Recyclable IoT Devices

With the rapid growth of IoT devices across industries, the challenge of e-waste has become a critical concern. Modular and recyclable IoT devices have emerged as a solution to reduce e-waste by promoting sustainable manufacturing and extending the lifespan of IoT products. This section explores various case studies demonstrating the effectiveness of modular and recyclable IoT devices in different industries.

Case Study 1: Fairphone – A Modular Smartphone with IoT Capabilities

Fairphone, a Dutch company, is a pioneer in creating sustainable electronic devices. Their modular smartphone is designed to be repairable, upgradable, and recyclable, setting an example for Green IoT applications in consumer electronics.

Implementation

Fairphone developed a smartphone with interchangeable modules, including:

- **Removable batteries:** Unlike most modern smartphones with sealed batteries, Fairphone's battery can be replaced easily, extending the phone's usability.

- **Camera and processor upgrades:** Users can upgrade individual components like the camera module or processor instead of replacing the entire phone.
- **Recyclable materials:** The device is made from ethically sourced materials, including recycled plastics and Fairtrade-certified gold.

Impact on Green IoT

By adopting a modular approach, Fairphone significantly reduces e-waste and energy consumption. Users can keep their devices functional for longer periods, and old modules can be recycled or repurposed, reducing landfill contributions.

Case Study 2: Google's Project Ara – A Vision for Modular IoT Devices

Google's Project Ara aimed to create a fully modular smartphone where users could customize and upgrade each component. Although the project was ultimately discontinued, it provided valuable insights into the feasibility of modular IoT devices.

Implementation

Project Ara introduced:

- **Interchangeable hardware components:** Users could swap out displays, batteries, and processors depending on their needs.
- **IoT sensor expansion:** Additional sensors could be added to enhance functionalities, such as environmental monitoring and health tracking.

- **Eco-friendly manufacturing:** The modular nature reduced the need for full-device replacements, minimizing electronic waste.

Challenges and Lessons Learned

Despite its promising concept, Project Ara faced production challenges, including:

- **High manufacturing costs:** Developing a fully modular system increased complexity and costs.
- **Market readiness:** Consumers were accustomed to non-modular designs, limiting adoption rates.
- **Durability issues:** Frequent module swapping introduced mechanical wear-and-tear concerns.

Although discontinued, Project Ara inspired further research into modular IoT solutions for sustainability.

Case Study 3: Circular Economy in Industrial IoT (IIoT) – Siemens' Sustainable Sensors

Siemens, a leader in industrial automation, has integrated circular economy principles into its IoT sensor manufacturing to reduce e-waste and improve sustainability.

Implementation

Siemens developed industrial IoT sensors with:

- **Modular design:** Sensors can be repaired or upgraded without replacing the entire unit.

- **Recyclable components:** Devices are built using materials that can be reprocessed and reused.
- **Energy-efficient processing:** Low-power processors optimize energy consumption, extending battery life and reducing carbon footprint.

Impact on Industrial Sustainability

By embracing modularity, Siemens has reduced electronic waste in industrial settings. Factories using these sensors can replace individual parts rather than discarding entire systems, aligning with green manufacturing initiatives.

Case Study 4: Modular Smart Home Devices – IKEA's TRÅDFRI Smart Lighting

IKEA introduced TRÅDFRI, a modular smart lighting system that aligns with Green IoT principles.

Implementation

The system includes:

- **Interchangeable LED components:** Instead of replacing entire bulbs, users can swap out individual LED drivers or control modules.
- **Recyclable housing materials:** Lamps and control units are made with sustainable materials.
- **Low-energy wireless communication:** The system uses Zigbee, an energy-efficient wireless protocol, to minimize power consumption.

Impact on Green IoT

TRÅDFRI reduces e-waste and enhances energy efficiency in smart homes. By allowing upgrades and replacements at the module level, IKEA ensures that smart lighting remains sustainable and cost-effective for consumers.

These case studies highlight the potential of modular and recyclable IoT devices in addressing environmental concerns. While challenges exist, such as cost and market readiness, the long-term benefits of reducing e-waste and improving sustainability outweigh the drawbacks. As technology advances, modular IoT solutions will play a crucial role in promoting a greener, more circular economy in the IoT ecosystem.

Reducing Energy Waste in IoT Supply Chains with Smart Contracts

The integration of blockchain technology with IoT has revolutionized supply chain management. Smart contracts—self-executing agreements stored on a blockchain—enable automated, transparent, and energy-efficient supply chains. A key advantage of using smart contracts in IoT supply chains is the reduction of energy waste, as they facilitate real-time data tracking, automated decision-making, and optimized resource utilization. This section explores the role of smart contracts in improving energy efficiency across IoT-driven supply chains and presents case studies demonstrating their practical applications.

How Smart Contracts Reduce Energy Waste in IoT Supply Chains

Automated energy-efficient logistics:

- Traditional supply chains involve multiple intermediaries and inefficient communication channels, leading to delays, redundant processes, and excess energy consumption.
- Smart contracts streamline logistics by automatically executing agreements based on real-time IoT sensor data, reducing energy-intensive processes.
- For example, when an IoT-enabled shipment reaches a specific location, a smart contract can trigger an optimized delivery schedule, reducing idle time and fuel consumption.

Optimized inventory management:

- Smart contracts integrated with IoT sensors help monitor warehouse conditions such as temperature, humidity, and stock levels.
- They automatically adjust storage settings or trigger restocking processes to minimize energy waste.
- Companies can reduce energy-intensive overstocking and prevent spoilage in temperature-sensitive products, such as pharmaceuticals or perishable goods.

Real-time energy tracking and optimization:

- IoT devices collect data on energy consumption across supply chain operations, which smart contracts use to optimize energy distribution.

- For example, if a factory's energy consumption exceeds a set threshold, a smart contract can initiate load-balancing measures, reducing unnecessary power usage.
- Renewable energy sources, such as solar or wind, can be integrated into supply chains more efficiently with blockchain-based tracking.

Waste reduction in manufacturing and transportation:

- Smart contracts enforce sustainability policies by ensuring compliance with energy-efficient production methods.
- In transportation, they automate fuel-efficient route planning and prevent unnecessary engine idling, reducing carbon emissions.
- Manufacturers can track energy waste in real-time and receive automated recommendations to improve efficiency.

Case Studies on Smart Contracts in Energy-Efficient IoT Supply Chains

Case Study 1: Walmart's Blockchain-Based Food Supply Chain

Walmart implemented blockchain-powered smart contracts to improve food safety and energy efficiency in its supply chain.

Implementation:

- IoT sensors track temperature and humidity levels in food storage and transportation.

- Smart contracts automatically adjust refrigeration settings to prevent spoilage and reduce energy consumption.
- Blockchain records ensure transparency and energy-efficient handling of perishable goods.

Impact:

- Reduced energy waste in refrigeration by dynamically adjusting cooling levels.
- Minimized food waste due to real-time monitoring and automated decision-making.
- Improved operational efficiency, cutting down transportation energy costs.

Case Study 2: IBM and Maersk's TradeLens Blockchain for Shipping

Maersk, in collaboration with IBM, introduced TradeLens, a blockchain-based solution using smart contracts to optimize global shipping logistics.

Implementation:

- Smart contracts automate customs clearance and cargo tracking using IoT data.
- AI-driven energy management systems optimize fuel consumption based on real-time shipping data.
- Automated tracking eliminates unnecessary delays, reducing energy consumption at ports.

Impact:

- A forty percent reduction in paperwork-related delays, lowering fuel consumption.
- Improved fleet efficiency, saving millions of liters of fuel annually.
- Enhanced sustainability through data-driven decision-making.

Case Study 3: Siemens and Blockchain in Energy Distribution

Siemens integrated blockchain with smart contracts for optimizing energy distribution in industrial supply chains.

Implementation:

- IoT sensors monitor real-time energy use in factories.
- Smart contracts automatically switch between renewable and grid energy based on efficiency levels.
- AI-driven analytics predict energy demand and automate adjustments.

Impact:

- A thirty percent reduction in energy waste through optimized power allocation.
- Lower operational costs due to dynamic energy sourcing.
- Enhanced sustainability by prioritizing renewable energy consumption.

Challenges and Future Outlook

Challenges:

- High initial costs for integrating blockchain and IoT.
- Data privacy concerns in decentralized supply chains.
- Scalability issues for large-scale IoT blockchain networks.

Future trends:

- AI-driven smart contracts for predictive energy optimization.
- Cross-industry collaboration to develop standardized blockchain supply chain solutions.
- Increased adoption of carbon-neutral blockchain solutions to further enhance sustainability.

Smart contracts integrated with IoT are revolutionizing supply chains by reducing energy waste, enhancing transparency, and improving operational efficiency. Case studies from Walmart, Maersk, and Siemens illustrate the real-world impact of this technology in optimizing logistics, reducing fuel consumption, and minimizing energy waste in industrial operations. As blockchain adoption grows, its role in creating sustainable IoT supply chains will become increasingly significant, contributing to a more energy-efficient and environmentally responsible future.

Green IoT for Disaster Management

Disaster management has become a crucial global concern due to the increasing frequency and intensity of natural and man-made calamities. Traditional disaster management systems often rely on manual interventions and inefficient communication mechanisms, leading to delayed responses and higher casualties. The integration of IoT into disaster management has revolutionized the way authorities monitor, predict, and respond to disasters. Green IoT ensures that these systems remain energy-efficient, sustainable, and environmentally friendly while maintaining high reliability. This section explores the role of Green IoT in disaster management, detailing its applications, benefits, challenges, and real-world case studies.

The Role of Green IoT in Disaster Management

Green IoT employs energy-efficient sensors, renewable energy sources, and smart analytics to enhance disaster preparedness, response, and recovery. The following key areas illustrate how Green IoT contributes to disaster management.

Early warning systems:

- IoT-enabled sensors monitor environmental parameters such as temperature, humidity, seismic activity, and water levels to detect potential disasters.
- Energy-efficient communication protocols like LPWAN (Low-Power Wide-Area Network) ensure continuous data transmission with minimal power consumption.
- AI-driven analytics predict disasters in advance, allowing authorities to take preventive measures.
- Integration of satellite imagery with IoT systems enhances accuracy in disaster predictions and response planning.

Real-time disaster monitoring:

- Green IoT solutions provide real-time data on disaster-affected areas using drones, satellite-based sensors, and GPS tracking.
- Low-power, long-range networks enable uninterrupted data flow, even in remote locations.
- Smart cameras and motion detectors help assess damage and monitor rescue operations efficiently.
- Sensor fusion techniques combine data from multiple sources to improve decision-making accuracy.

Energy-efficient communication networks:

- Traditional disaster response relies heavily on energy-intensive communication systems that may fail during crises.
- Green IoT integrates solar-powered communication towers and energy-efficient networking protocols to ensure seamless connectivity.
- Mesh networking and ad hoc networks allow disaster responders to establish communication even in regions where traditional networks are down.
- AI-driven network optimization minimizes energy consumption and prioritizes critical communications.

Smart resource allocation:

- IoT-enabled logistics systems optimize the distribution of relief materials using AI-driven demand forecasting.
- Energy-efficient RFID tracking ensures that food, medical supplies, and shelter materials reach affected populations in a timely manner.

- Blockchain integration ensures transparency and prevents fraud in disaster relief efforts.
- Dynamic routing of rescue teams based on real-time data reduces response times and improves operational efficiency.

Post-disaster recovery and sustainability:

- IoT-based waste management systems help in cleaning up debris and toxic materials in an eco-friendly manner.
- Renewable energy-powered shelters ensure continued operation of rescue centers without overloading conventional power grids.
- IoT-assisted environmental monitoring helps assess long-term ecological impacts and aids in rebuilding efforts.
- Data analytics from past disasters help improve future disaster-management strategies.

Case Studies on Green IoT in Disaster Management

Case Study 1: IoT-Based Flood Monitoring in the Netherlands

The Netherlands, being a low-lying country, is prone to severe flooding. Traditional flood management systems faced challenges in providing timely alerts and efficient responses.

Implementation:

- IoT-enabled water level sensors were deployed across rivers and canals to monitor real-time flood risks.
- AI-driven predictive analytics analyzed historical data to anticipate flood patterns.
- Low-power, wide-area network (LPWAN) technology ensured continuous data transmission with minimal energy consumption.
- Integration of climate modeling tools enhanced forecasting accuracy.

Impact:

- Early warnings allowed authorities to take proactive measures, reducing economic and human losses.
- Smart water management reduced unnecessary drainage operations, optimizing resource use.
- Citizens received real-time updates through mobile applications powered by energy-efficient communication networks.
- Reduced reliance on fossil-fuel-powered flood response measures.

Case Study 2: Smart Wildfire Detection in California

California experiences frequent wildfires due to its dry climate and vast forest areas. Detecting and controlling wildfires early is critical to minimizing damage.

Implementation:

- Solar-powered IoT sensors were placed in fire-prone zones to detect temperature, humidity, and smoke levels.
- AI algorithms processed data to differentiate between harmless temperature fluctuations and real wildfire risks.
- Drone surveillance with real-time image processing monitored wildfire progression.
- Machine learning models predicted fire spread based on wind patterns and topographical data.

Impact:

- Early detection reduced response time, preventing wildfires from spreading.
- Firefighting resources were optimally allocated, reducing environmental and financial costs.
- Energy-efficient sensors ensured 24/7 monitoring without overloading power grids.
- Coordination among emergency responders improved due to real-time IoT data.

Case Study 3: Earthquake Early Warning System in Japan

Due to its location on the Pacific Ring of Fire, Japan is highly susceptible to earthquakes. Traditional early warning systems often lacked real-time accuracy and consumed excessive energy.

Implementation:

- Seismic activity sensors powered by renewable energy sources were installed across fault lines.
- AI-driven analytics provided real-time predictions, reducing false alarms.
- IoT-enabled building monitoring systems detected structural integrity after earthquakes.
- Public alert systems were integrated with IoT networks to ensure timely dissemination of warnings.

Impact:

- Reduced casualties due to timely warnings.
- Smart evacuation plans minimized chaos during earthquakes.
- Green IoT reduced energy consumption compared to conventional warning systems.
- Data collected from past earthquakes enhanced future response strategies.

Future Trends in Green IoT for Disaster Management

AI-powered predictive analytics:

- Machine learning models will improve disaster prediction accuracy, reducing false alarms.
- AI-driven decision-making will enhance resource allocation and response strategies.

- Predictive maintenance of disaster response equipment will ensure readiness at all times.

5G-enabled smart disaster response:

- Ultra-low latency 5G networks will improve real-time disaster monitoring.
- Energy-efficient communication protocols will ensure low power consumption in IoT networks.
- Edge computing will process disaster data locally, reducing reliance on cloud-based systems.

Blockchain for transparent disaster relief distribution:

- Blockchain will provide immutable records of disaster aid distribution, ensuring accountability.
- Smart contracts will automate and optimize relief supply chains.
- Decentralized identity management for victims will facilitate efficient aid distribution.

Autonomous drones for disaster surveillance:

- AI-integrated drones will assess damage, deliver medical aid, and locate survivors efficiently.
- Solar-powered drones will enable continuous operation without relying on external power sources.
- Swarm intelligence in drone networks will improve coordination in large-scale disasters.

Smart wearable IoT for disaster survivors:

- IoT-enabled wearables will track the health status of survivors and transmit real-time data to emergency responders.
- Energy-efficient biometric monitoring will ensure prolonged operation in crisis scenarios.
- GPS-enabled smart wristbands will help locate missing persons quickly.

In conclusion, Green IoT is transforming disaster management by enabling energy-efficient, real-time monitoring, prediction, and response mechanisms. Case studies from the Netherlands, California, and Japan demonstrate its effectiveness in minimizing disaster impact while ensuring sustainability. Despite challenges such as deployment costs and security risks, emerging technologies like AI, blockchain, and 5G are set to revolutionize the field. As the frequency of disasters increases due to climate change, Green IoT will play a vital role in building resilient and sustainable disaster management systems worldwide.

Quantum Computing and Green IoT: A Sustainable Technological Synergy

The integration of quantum computing with GIoT represents a transformative shift toward energy-efficient and sustainable digital ecosystems. As IoT networks expand exponentially, concerns about energy consumption, data security, and computational inefficiencies have become more pressing. Traditional computing architectures struggle to handle the massive volumes of data generated by IoT devices while maintaining sustainability goals. Quantum computing, with its ability to perform complex computations at unprecedented speeds, offers a promising solution to optimize energy use, enhance security, and improve the efficiency of Green IoT systems. This section explores the intersection of quantum computing and Green IoT, detailing its benefits, challenges, applications, and future potential.

The Role of Quantum Computing in Green IoT

Quantum computing leverages the principles of quantum mechanics to process information in fundamentally new ways, using quantum bits (*qubits*) rather than classical binary bits. The following key attributes of quantum computing contribute to the advancement of Green IoT.

Enhanced computational efficiency:

- Quantum algorithms significantly reduce the computational power required to analyze IoT-generated data, leading to lower energy consumption.
- Traditional IoT data processing requires high-performance cloud computing centers that consume vast amounts of electricity. Quantum computing minimizes this demand by performing computations more efficiently.

Optimized energy management:

- Quantum computing enables real-time optimization of energy grids and IoT-powered smart buildings.
- By rapidly processing sensor data, quantum algorithms can dynamically adjust power consumption, reducing waste and ensuring sustainable energy use.

Advanced encryption for secure IoT networks:

- Security concerns in IoT are growing as billions of interconnected devices create vulnerabilities for cyberattacks.
- Quantum cryptography, particularly Quantum Key Distribution (QKD), offers an unbreakable encryption method to secure IoT networks.

Efficient data transmission and storage:

- Quantum algorithms optimize data compression and retrieval, minimizing energy-intensive cloud storage requirements.
- Quantum entanglement can enable ultra-fast data transfer, reducing latency in IoT networks while lowering energy use.

Improved machine learning and AI for IoT:

- Quantum machine learning can accelerate AI-driven optimizations in Green IoT, improving predictive analytics and anomaly detection.
- AI-powered IoT devices can use quantum-enhanced algorithms to reduce redundant computations, further decreasing energy consumption.

Applications of Quantum Computing in Green IoT

Quantum computing is paving the way for innovative Green IoT applications across multiple industries. The following list discusses the key use cases demonstrating its impact:

1. Smart energy management in smart cities
    - Quantum algorithms optimize energy distribution in smart grids, ensuring efficient power allocation to IoT-enabled infrastructure.
    - Quantum-enhanced sensors monitor real-time electricity use, reducing waste and preventing energy overload.
    - AI-powered smart thermostats, integrated with quantum computing, predict energy demand fluctuations and adjust settings accordingly.
2. **Green transportation and traffic optimization**
    - Quantum computing improves real-time traffic management by processing large-scale IoT sensor data faster than classical computers.
    - Quantum-enhanced route optimization helps reduce fuel consumption in electric and hybrid vehicles.
    - Public transportation systems leverage quantum algorithms to predict passenger demand, optimizing energy use in buses and trains.
3. **Secure and sustainable industrial IoT (IIoT)**
    - Industrial automation benefits from quantum computing through predictive maintenance and operational efficiency.
    - Energy-efficient manufacturing processes use quantum-driven optimizations to minimize resource waste.

- Quantum-safe cryptographic protocols protect industrial IoT networks from cyber threats while ensuring data privacy.

4. **Sustainable agriculture with quantum IoT**

    - Quantum sensors analyze soil conditions, moisture levels, and climate patterns to optimize irrigation and fertilizer use.
    - Quantum-enhanced weather predictions enable farmers to make data-driven decisions, minimizing agricultural energy consumption.
    - IoT-powered vertical farming utilizes quantum algorithms to balance light, water, and nutrients efficiently.

5. **Quantum AI for disaster prediction and management**

    - Quantum computing accelerates AI-driven disaster forecasting, improving the accuracy of early warning systems.
    - IoT devices in disaster-prone areas leverage quantum processing to detect seismic, meteorological, and environmental anomalies faster.
    - Quantum-enhanced emergency response coordination reduces the time required to allocate resources efficiently during crises.

Challenges in Implementing Quantum Computing for Green IoT

While the potential of quantum computing in Green IoT is immense, several challenges need to be addressed before widespread adoption.

Hardware and scalability limitations:

- Quantum computers require extremely low temperatures and specialized infrastructure, making large-scale deployment challenging.
- Current quantum processors have limited qubits, affecting computational stability and accuracy.

High development and implementation costs:

- The cost of developing and maintaining quantum computing technology remains high, limiting accessibility to enterprises and governments.
- Transitioning from classical to quantum computing requires substantial investment in research and development.

Algorithm complexity and integration issues:

- Quantum algorithms must be tailored for Green IoT applications, requiring expertise in quantum mechanics and in IoT development.
- Integrating quantum computing with existing IoT infrastructure poses compatibility challenges.

Security and ethical concerns:

- While quantum cryptography enhances security, it also poses a risk to current encryption methods, necessitating a transition to quantum-resistant security protocols.
- Ethical considerations arise regarding the impact of quantum computing on data privacy and surveillance.

Future Trends and Prospects

The convergence of quantum computing and Green IoT is set to redefine sustainability in technology. Key future trends include the following;

Quantum-classical hybrid computing for IoT:

- Hybrid computing models will combine classical and quantum computing to optimize IoT operations efficiently.
- Quantum cloud services will offer computational power on demand, reducing the need for localized quantum hardware.

Quantum-enhanced AI for IoT optimization:

- Quantum AI will improve decision-making in IoT applications, from smart city planning to climate monitoring.
- Self-learning Green IoT systems will leverage quantum processing for dynamic energy conservation.

Advancements in quantum sensors for IoT:

- Quantum sensors will offer ultra-precise environmental monitoring for climate change adaptation.
- Quantum-enhanced biomedical sensors will revolutionize IoT-based healthcare monitoring systems.

Expansion of quantum-secure IoT networks:

- Governments and enterprises will increasingly adopt quantum-resistant cryptographic solutions for IoT security.
- The deployment of QKD in smart infrastructure will establish secure and tamper-proof IoT communication.

Commercialization and standardization of quantum IoT:

- Industry leaders, research institutions, and governments will work toward standardizing quantum computing for IoT applications.
- Commercial quantum computing services will become accessible to businesses and startups, accelerating Green IoT adoption.

In conclusion, the integration of quantum computing with Green IoT represents a groundbreaking advancement in sustainable technology. By optimizing energy consumption, enhancing security, and enabling real-time data processing, quantum computing addresses critical challenges in IoT ecosystems. While challenges such as scalability, cost, and implementation complexities remain, ongoing research and development efforts will pave the way for practical applications. The future of Green IoT lies in leveraging quantum computing to create more efficient, secure, and environmentally sustainable digital infrastructures. As quantum technology matures, its role in driving sustainable IoT innovation will become increasingly vital, fostering a greener and smarter future for industries worldwide.

Future Opportunities in Green IoT

As industries and societies shift toward sustainability, Green IoT is expected to evolve in several ways, focusing on energy efficiency, eco-friendly hardware, and smart resource management. The following key developments highlight how IoT will contribute to a greener future:

- **Self-sustaining IoT devices with energy harvesting:** IoT devices traditionally rely on batteries or wired power sources, but advancements in energy-harvesting technologies are enabling self-sustaining IoT devices. Future IoT systems will harness power from:
    - *Solar energy:* Small-scale solar panels integrated into IoT sensors for continuous energy supply.
    - *Kinetic energy:* Devices generating power from motion (e.g., wearables powered by body movement).
    - *Thermal energy:* Heat-based energy harvesting, where temperature differences generate electricity for sensors.

These innovations will significantly reduce electronic waste and extend the lifespan of IoT devices without frequent battery replacements.

- **AI-driven energy optimization in IoT systems:** AI will enhance energy efficiency by analyzing real-time data and making automated decisions to optimize energy use. For example:

- Smart lighting and HVAC systems can adjust power use based on occupancy patterns.
- Predictive maintenance can reduce energy waste by ensuring devices operate at peak efficiency.
- Adaptive data transmission is when IoT devices intelligently adjust how often they send data to save energy.

By integrating AI into IoT ecosystems, power consumption can be minimized without sacrificing performance.

- **Advancing biodegradable electronics for sustainable IoT hardware:** Electronic waste is a growing environmental concern, and biodegradable electronics offer a sustainable alternative. Future IoT devices will be built with:
    - Organic semiconductors that naturally decompose after use.
    - Biodegradable circuit boards made from eco-friendly materials instead of toxic metals.
    - Dissolvable sensors for temporary IoT applications, such as environmental monitoring.

These innovations will significantly reduce e-waste pollution and make IoT systems more environmentally friendly.

- **Implementing circular economy principles in IoT design:** A shift toward a circular economy means IoT devices will be designed for reuse, refurbishment, and recycling instead of being discarded. This includes:
    - Modular IoT devices that allow easy part replacements instead of replacing entire systems.

- Recyclable components that reduce reliance on rare and hazardous materials.
- Refurbishment programs where old IoT devices are upgraded and resold, reducing manufacturing waste.

These practices will help extend the life of IoT devices while reducing electronic waste.

- **Green IoT in smart cities for sustainable urban development:** IoT will play a crucial role in smart city initiatives focused on sustainability. Future applications include:
  - Smart grids that balance energy supply and demand efficiently.
  - Intelligent waste management with IoT-enabled bins that optimize waste collection routes.
  - Eco-friendly public transportation where IoT sensors monitor and reduce vehicle emissions.

With IoT-driven urban planning, cities can reduce carbon footprints and improve quality of life for residents.

- **Low-power and energy-efficient communication protocols:** Future IoT networks will rely on low-power communication protocols such as:
  - *LoRaWAN (Long Range Wide Area Network):* Allows devices to transmit data over long distances with minimal power consumption.
  - *BLE (Bluetooth Low Energy):* Ideal for short-range, low-energy IoT applications.

- *5G and beyond:* Future networks will introduce energy-efficient architectures for IoT connectivity.

These protocols will extend device battery life and reduce energy use in large-scale IoT deployments.

- **Edge computing for reduced energy consumption:** Instead of relying solely on cloud computing, edge computing processes data closer to the source (on local IoT devices), which:
    - Reduces energy-intensive cloud transmissions by processing only essential data.
    - Improves real-time decision-making without sending all data to remote servers.
    - Lowers overall power consumption of IoT networks.

This shift will make IoT more efficient and environmentally friendly by reducing energy costs associated with cloud-based operations.

The Way Forward

Green IoT is set to revolutionize industries, smart cities, and environmental management by making IoT more energy-efficient and sustainable. As technology advances, the focus will be on self-sustaining devices, AI-driven optimizations, biodegradable hardware, and circular economy models. These innovations will reduce the environmental impact of IoT while ensuring long-term sustainability.

CHAPTER 10

Future Trends in Energy Efficient IOT Networking

The rapid expansion of IoT has driven the need for energy-efficient networking solutions to support the growing number of connected devices. As IoT applications continue to evolve across industries such as smart cities, healthcare, industrial automation, and agriculture, optimizing energy consumption has become a critical focus. Future trends in energy-efficient IoT networking emphasize advancements in edge computing, AI-driven optimization, energy-harvesting technologies, and low-power communication protocols. These innovations aim to extend device lifespan, reduce power consumption, and enhance network performance without compromising reliability. Additionally, intelligent data processing techniques, adaptive transmission mechanisms, and resource-efficient network architectures are being developed to create sustainable IoT ecosystems. This chapter explores the key strategies and emerging technologies that will shape the future of energy-efficient IoT networking, ensuring scalability, cost-effectiveness, and environmental sustainability.

Dr. D. Sharma and Dr. B. Pandey, *Eco-Networking for IoT*,
https://doi.org/10.1007/979-8-8688-2317-6_10

Introduction

Global advancements in telecommunication systems have consistently driven wireless infrastructure to become more robust and scalable.[1] The Internet's applications and usage are vast and constantly evolving. Advancements like IoT, the Internet of Everything (IoE), and the Internet of Nano-Things (IoNT) introduce innovative ways to incorporate the Internet into different aspects of daily life, work, and society. Moreover, these technologies enhance connectivity by integrating the Internet with inanimate and semi-intelligent devices.[4]

Recent advancements in low-power communication and signal-processing technologies have significantly contributed to the widespread adoption of wireless sensor networks (WSNs).[2] Applications of IoT are increasingly being integrated into smart buildings and smart cities to enhance energy efficiency.[3] Among the different LPWAN (low-power wide-area network) technologies, Long-Range Wide-Area Network (LoRaWAN) has received significant interest from the industry and research sectors due to its self-managing networking setup and open standard specification.[5]

IoT has revolutionized the way devices interact with each other, allowing for vast applications across healthcare, agriculture, transportation, and smart cities, among others. However, as IoT networks continue to grow, energy efficiency has become a major challenge. Many IoT devices operate in places where power access is limited. It is important to create solutions that reduce energy use while keeping performance high.

Future trends in energy-efficient IoT networking emphasize designing sustainable solutions that extend device lifespans, lower power use, and improve network efficiency. Researchers and industry leaders are pursuing new methods like edge computing, energy harvesting, AI-driven optimization, and low-power communication protocols. These developments aim to keep IoT networks operational and adaptable without demanding too much energy.

One significant area of focus is using artificial intelligence and machine learning to boost network performance, adjust energy use in real time, and predict system failures before they happen. Furthermore, energy-harvesting technologies, such as solar and kinetic energy, are being studied to create self-sustaining IoT devices that need little outside power. Low-power communication technologies are improving to support efficient data transfer and reduce energy consumption.

With the increasing adoption of IoT in critical applications such as smart grids, environmental monitoring, and industrial automation, future energy-efficient networking strategies will play a vital role in ensuring long-term sustainability. The focus is on creating intelligent, adaptive, and power-conscious IoT systems that can operate efficiently in various environments while reducing overall energy consumption. These advancements will pave the way for more sustainable, cost-effective, and high-performing IoT ecosystems in the years to come.

Literature Review

A survey on recent trends and issues in energy efficiency in 5G wireless communication systems highlights the increasing need for energy-saving solutions. This demand arises from the growing number of connected devices and related power consumption challenges. The study by Muhammad, Usama, and Erol-Kantarci, Melike (2019)[1]examines various energy-saving techniques, including dynamic power allocation, network densification, and AI-based optimization methods, to improve energy efficiency in 5G networks. It also discusses trade-offs between energy efficiency and performance metrics and identifies research gaps and potential areas for future development.[1]

The exploration of energy-efficient routing protocols for wireless sensor networks focuses on different architectures, strategies, and performance evaluations. The study by Behera, Trupti Mayee, et al.

(2022)[2] analyzes various energy-efficient routing methods, including clustering-based, hierarchical, and multi-hop routing, discussing their pros and cons. The impact of these methods on network longevity and data transmission efficiency is emphasized, along with their applications in environmental monitoring, industrial automation, and healthcare systems.[2]

A review by Al-Obaidi, Karam M., et al. (2022)[3]on the use of IoT for energy-efficient buildings and smart cities looks at IoT-enabled energy management systems. These systems aim to reduce energy consumption and improve sustainability in urban areas. Intelligent automation, sensor-based energy monitoring, and data analytics play key roles in optimizing energy use. The study also discusses the integration of renewable energy sources and smart grid technologies, along with challenges in cybersecurity, interoperability, and large-scale implementation.[3]

The development of IoT, the Internet of Nano-Things (IoNT), and the Internet of Everything (IoE) has also been investigated, focusing on how nanotechnology-based devices interact with traditional IoT infrastructure. Applications in healthcare, industrial automation, and environmental monitoring are explored, along with integration challenges such as security risks, energy constraints, and data processing complexities.[4]

A survey by Almuhaya, Mukarram AM, et al. (2022)[5]on Long Range Wide Area Network (LoRaWAN) technology analyzes its trends, emerging opportunities, simulation tools, and future directions. It evaluates performance metrics such as scalability, security, and energy efficiency across application scenarios, including smart agriculture, industrial automation, and urban infrastructure. Simulation tools for network modeling and key research challenges like interference management and QoS improvements are also discussed.[5]

In the work by Malik, Usman Mahmood, et al.(2021)[6], fog computing is identified as a key technology for future 6G networks, providing storage and computational services to support massive IoT applications. Given energy limitations in IoT devices and fog nodes, energy-efficient solutions are crucial. This overview categorizes energy-related challenges and recent advancements while highlighting future opportunities and open issues in designing energy-efficient fog computing architectures for 6G-enabled IoT.[6]

Cellular networks are expected to play a pivotal role in industrial IoT (IIoT) connectivity by addressing industrial requirements such as coverage, capacity, robustness, and timeliness. This vision has led to vertical-centric 5G architectures, integrating AI and edge computing while tackling privacy and security concerns. Recent design trends and challenges for beyond-5G industrial wireless networks are also reviewed.[7]

The rapid growth of global population and urbanization has driven the need for smart technologies powered by IoT to ensure secure, sustainable urban environments. A review by Alahi, Md Eshrat E., et al. (2023)[8]of smart city concepts, wireless communication technologies, and AI algorithms emphasizes the integration of IoT and AI with 5G to enhance sustainability and quality of life.

LPWAN technologies have become essential for IoT applications due to their low cost, energy efficiency, and long-range capabilities. Among LPWANs, LoRaWAN and SigFox have been noted for their device lifetime and scalability, while NB-IoT is highlighted for its latency and QoS. Simulation tools and recent advancements in energy efficiency, scalability, and security are also reviewed.[9]

Emerging technologies such as 5G, IoT, blockchain, and AI are transforming global business. 5G is poised to support massive IoT ecosystems with high data rates and low latency. Research by Li, Shan, et al. (2024)[10] explores zero-trust security architectures and blockchain-based authentication models (BasIoT) for secure device access in future IoT (FIoT) applications.

Food security challenges driven by environmental conditions and population growth are addressed in the paper by Quy, Vu Khanh, et al. (2022)[11], which suggests transitioning to smart agriculture through

IoT and big data. Wireless sensor networks, cloud computing, and cognitive radio networks enable more efficient farming. The study highlights ecosystem architecture, use cases, and open issues in smart agriculture.[11]

The Internet of Everything (IoE) drives the demand for next-generation networks. While 5G supports many IoE services, it falls short of fully meeting emerging smart application needs. The development of 6G systems integrating AI, THz, and quantum communication is explored by Qadir, Zakria, et al. (2023)[12], along with enabling technologies like holographic beamforming and backscatter communications.

The integration of IoT in precision agriculture and smart greenhouses is supported by AI, sensors, UAVs, and big data analytics. Barriers such as high installation costs, energy demands, and electronic waste (*e-waste*) are discussed by Maraveas, Chrysanthos, et al. (2022)[13], with suggestions for broader adoption through 5G deployment and satellite broadband.

Healthcare 4.0, inspired by Industry 4.0, is an emerging paradigm enabling telemedicine, precision medicine, and disease prediction. Driven by technologies such as IoMT, AI, and edge computing, the review by Osama, Manar, et al. (2023)[14] highlights design challenges and the requirements of next-generation healthcare networks.

A systematic review of healthcare IoT (HIoT) systems by Kashani, Mostafa Haghi, et al. (2021)[15] categorizes literature into sensor-based, resource-based, communication-based, application-based, and security-based approaches. This paper highlights power management, fog computing, and privacy as key open issues, while identifying trends such as SDN/NFV, big data, and blockchain.[15]

The development of energy-harvesting (EH) technologies aims to address power limitations in IoT by enabling long-term, battery-free operation of wireless sensors. The paper by Sanislav, Teodora, et al. (2021) [16] reviews EH techniques and presents case studies while discussing future deployment challenges.

Green IoT (GIoT) applications address concerns around energy use, e-waste, and emissions in the ICT sector. Strategies such as energy-efficient hardware, data management techniques, and AI integration are examined in the paper by Albreem, Mahmoud A., et al. (2021)[17], with a call for sustainable hardware design and policy-maker collaboration.

Disruptive IoT applications such as AR/VR and autonomous driving require communication beyond 5G capabilities. 6G networks are expected to deliver Tbps data rates and sub-ms latency. A novel 6G architecture integrating space-air-ground-underwater networks is proposed by Guo, Fengxian, et al. (2021)[18] to support massive IoT applications.

The COVID-19 pandemic has emphasized the need for IoT-powered wearable technologies for health monitoring. In the paper by Li, Wei, et al. (2021)[19], big data analytics and machine learning techniques are explored for managing the large volume of health data generated by wearables, identifying strengths and future research directions.

The rise of IoT devices under 5G/6G connectivity generates significant privacy and storage concerns. Federated learning (FL) offers a privacy-preserving solution for collaborative learning. The paper by Zhang, Tuo, et al. (2021)[20] includes discussions on its challenges such as data heterogeneity and communication efficiency.

The Internet of Vehicles (IoV) integrates VANET and IoT to enable safe, multisensory vehicle communication while managing dynamic topologies and heterogeneous network architectures.[21]

Wireless technology enhances real-time applications and communication, especially in remote areas. Its benefits include flexibility, accessibility, and support for innovations such as autonomous systems and smart environments.[22]

The issue of overpopulation in India is analyzed in the paper by Chadha, Anmol, et al. (2024)[23] using predictive models, with increased adoption rates proposed as a sustainable intervention. The study projects future demographic impacts by 2050.

Hybrid optimization algorithms—including Ant Colony Optimization (ACO), Moth Flame Optimization (MFO), and Whale Optimization Algorithm (WOA)—are proposed by Aggarwal, Vaishali, et al. (2024)[24] to improve energy efficiency and packet delivery in WSNs.

Blockchain, introduced in 2008, enables secure digital transactions and smart contracts. Its applications in insurance and real-time solutions are explored in the paper by Sharma, Vandana, et al. (2024)[25], along with its evolution as a decentralized ledger technology.

Consumer shopping behavior is analyzed in the research by Garg, Sheena, et al. (2023)[26] using machine learning algorithms such as Apriori, KNN, ensemble learning, Naive Bayes, and NLP, with a comparison of their accuracy in processing e-commerce data.

A hybrid deep learning model combining LLM, CNN, and RNN is proposed in the paper by Gupta, Kartavya, et al. (2024)[27] to enhance crop yield prediction for wheat, maize, millet, rice, and barley, outperforming traditional models in accuracy and recall.

KubeEdge is explored in the paper by Saini, Lalit Mohan, et al. (2024) [28] as an edge computing solution for IoT applications. The framework reduces latency, improves resource utilization, and addresses scalability and infrastructure integration challenges.

Energy-Efficient and Sustainable IoT Solutions

The rapid proliferation of IoT devices worldwide has raised significant concerns regarding energy consumption, sustainability, and environmental impact. As IoT technology continues to evolve and expand, billions of interconnected devices are being deployed across various sectors such as agriculture, healthcare, industrial automation, transportation, smart cities, and environmental monitoring.

While these devices are changing how we collect, analyze, and use data, they also bring challenges related to energy efficiency, battery life, and environmental sustainability. The number of IoT devices is constantly growing, and this surge in demand for power has led to higher energy use and increased carbon emissions. Many IoT systems still depend on traditional batteries, which not only last for a limited time but also add to e-waste and harm the environment. Therefore, finding sustainable and energy-efficient IoT solutions is more important than ever.

To tackle these challenges, researchers and developers are working on energy-saving methods and sustainable practices. They aim to reduce power consumption while keeping device performance and network reliability intact. Some of the most promising methods include using LPWANs, energy-harvesting technologies, edge computing, AI-driven power management, and sleep mode/duty cycling mechanisms. These solutions extend battery life, lower maintenance costs, and improve the overall efficiency of IoT networks.

Additionally, energy-efficient communication protocols like Bluetooth Low Energy (BLE), Zigbee, and IPv6 over Low-Power Wireless Personal Area Networks (6LoWPAN) are in development to make data transmission more efficient while saving power. Blockchain technology is also being looked at to boost IoT security, lower energy use, promote decentralized management, and ensure secure transactions.

By adopting these smart strategies and new technologies, businesses and industries can greatly cut down the power needs of their IoT systems. They can also lessen the environmental impact linked to traditional power sources and battery replacements, supporting sustainable development and global efforts to lower carbon footprints.

The future of IoT hinges on finding a balance between technology and caring for the environment. As IoT networks become more complex and widespread, incorporating energy-efficient solutions, like the ones outlined in Figure 10-1 and discussed in the following sections, will be crucial for ensuring the long-term sustainability of this rapidly changing ecosystem.

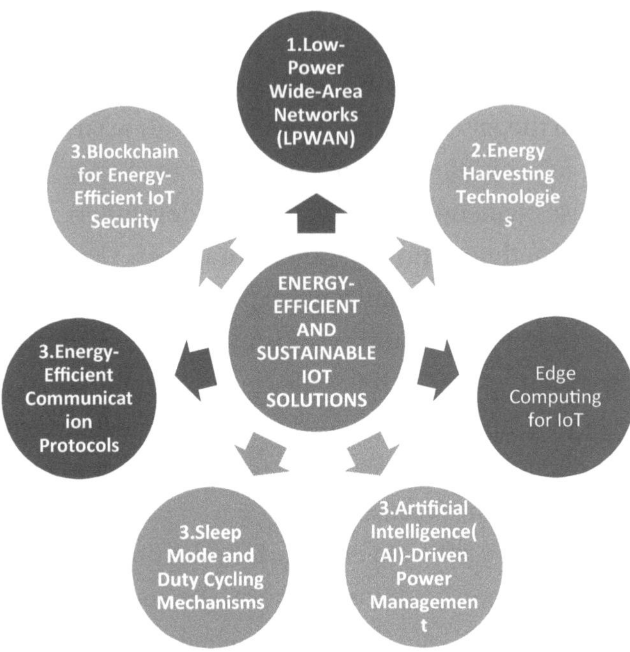

Figure 10-1. *Energy-efficient and sustainable IoT solutions*

Figure 10-1 shows the many sustainable and energy-efficient IoT solutions that form the foundation of next-generation networks. It includes technologies like energy-harvesting techniques, LPWANs, and edge computing for IoT. These solutions aim to support scalable IoT deployments and extend device lifespan. They also focus on improving power consumption and promoting environmental sustainability.

Low-Power Wide-Area Networks (LPWANs)

LPWAN technologies, like LoRaWAN and Sigfox, are designed to support strong and long-range wireless communications while using little power. They play a critical role in modern IoT ecosystems. These networks work well in situations where devices need to communicate over large distances without needing frequent battery changes. This ensures cost-effective and energy-saving operation.

LPWAN technologies are suitable for many IoT applications. Smart agriculture is one example. They allow for continuous monitoring of soil moisture, crop health, and environmental conditions. In environmental monitoring, LPWANs enable real-time data collection from sensors placed in remote and hard-to-reach areas, such as forests, mountains, and coastlines. They help track air quality, water levels, and wildlife movements effectively. Additionally, in industrial automation, LPWAN networks support smooth communication between sensors and control systems. This optimizes processes, improves safety, and lowers operational costs.

Furthermore, LPWAN's ability to keep a connection over long distances with minimal energy use makes it appealing for applications that need long-lasting battery life and low maintenance. By allowing efficient data transmission with low power consumption, LPWAN technologies are paving the way for scalable and sustainable IoT deployments across different industries.

Advantages:

- **Low power consumption:** Devices can run for years on small batteries.
- **Wide coverage:** Supports connectivity in remote areas.
- **Cost-effective:** Lowers infrastructure and operational costs.

Disadvantages:

- **Limited data rate:** Not suitable for applications that need high bandwidth.
- **Latency issues:** Not ideal for real-time applications.
- **Network congestion:** More devices connecting can cause interference.

Energy-Harvesting Technologies

IoT devices are increasingly using energy-harvesting techniques that draw on various natural and ambient energy sources, such as solar, thermal, radio frequency (RF), and kinetic energy, to power themselves. These methods greatly reduce dependence on traditional batteries, encouraging sustainable and long-lasting IoT setups. By capturing renewable energy, IoT devices can run independently for long periods without frequent battery changes or manual help.

Solar energy harvesting involves collecting sunlight through photovoltaic cells to generate electricity. This method works best for outdoor systems like solar-powered surveillance, environmental monitoring, and smart agriculture. In contrast, thermal energy harvesting turns temperature differences into electrical energy, making it useful in industrial settings where machinery produces a lot of heat.

RF energy harvesting collects electromagnetic waves from radio signals, Wi-Fi, or cellular networks to power low-energy IoT devices. This allows them to operate even in places where other energy sources are limited. Kinetic energy harvesting uses motion or vibrations to create power, making it perfect for wearable devices and mobile applications.

By incorporating energy-harvesting technologies, IoT devices can operate on their own, which lowers maintenance needs, cuts operational costs, and supports eco-friendly solutions. This method is especially beneficial for remote and hard-to-reach areas where changing batteries often is not practical or affordable. Consequently, energy harvesting not only extends the lifespan of IoT networks but also supports the larger goal of sustainable and resilient smart systems.

Advantages:

- **Sustainable power source:** Reduces reliance on traditional batteries.
- **Longer device lifespan:** Minimizes the need for frequent replacements.
- **Cuts maintenance costs:** Ideal for remote and hard-to-reach locations.

Disadvantages:

- **Unstable energy supply:** Depends on environmental factors, like sunlight and motion.
- **Higher initial cost:** Integrating harvesting components can be costly.
- **Limited power output:** Might not be suitable for high-energy applications.

Edge Computing for IoT

Edge computing processes data locally on IoT devices or nearby gateways instead of sending it to centralized cloud servers. This approach significantly cuts down on energy consumption, network traffic, and latency. By analyzing and processing data closer to the source, it minimizes the amount of data sent to the cloud and helps save bandwidth while improving response times.

By moving data processing to the edge of the network, edge computing facilitates faster real-time decision-making, which is especially useful in applications where an instant response is needed, including autonomous vehicles, industrial automation, and medical monitoring systems. This method also enhances data privacy and security by keeping sensitive information near its source, which reduces exposure to potential cyber threats during transmission.

Moreover, edge computing allows machine learning algorithms and AI models to run directly on edge devices. This capability enables faster data analysis and useful insights, which is crucial for applications like smart surveillance, predictive maintenance, and intelligent traffic management, where quick decisions are necessary.

Another benefit of edge computing is its ability to keep services running even when cloud connectivity is shaky or lost. This fault tolerance means that critical IoT applications, such as industrial control systems and healthcare monitoring, can continue to function smoothly without interruptions.

Overall, edge computing supports the growth of strong, scalable, and efficient IoT systems by enabling local data processing, reducing reliance on the cloud, and optimizing resource use. It plays an essential role in advancing next-generation IoT applications that require low latency, high efficiency, and better data security.

Advantages:

- **Lower energy use:** It reduces the need for constant cloud communication.
- **Improved latency:** It allows real-time data processing.
- **Bandwidth optimization:** It cuts down data transmission and improves network efficiency.

Disadvantages:

- **Higher hardware costs:** Edge devices need advanced processing capabilities.
- **Limited storage and processing:** They are not as powerful as cloud computing.
- **Security concerns:** These devices need strong security measures to stop local breaches.

AI-Driven Power Management

IoT networks are incorporating AI seamlessly to optimize power consumption dynamically. This is achieved by monitoring device activity, forecasting usage patterns, and modifying energy distribution accordingly. AI-driven power management systems can analyze real-time data from networked IoT devices, find opportunities for energy savings, and apply effective power control strategies by utilizing sophisticated machine learning algorithms.

The ability of AI to make data-driven, intelligent decisions that minimize energy waste while preserving optimal performance is one of the main advantages of incorporating AI into IoT power management. AI can, for example, forecast when devices will be in high or low demand and modify power distribution to account for varying workloads. Especially in large-scale IoT deployments, this dynamic approach lowers operational costs and unnecessary energy consumption.

Additionally, by continuously tracking device health and performance metrics, AI-driven systems can automate predictive maintenance. By preventing possible malfunctions before they happen, this proactive strategy lowers downtime and increases device lifespan. Furthermore, AI models can create more precise power-saving plans by learning from historical energy usage trends, guaranteeing that IoT networks run effectively over time.

The improved capacity to balance energy distribution in intricate networks, like smart grids and industrial automation systems, is another noteworthy benefit. AI can forecast times of peak usage and balance the load to avoid energy spikes and reduce system stress by evaluating the massive volumes of data produced by sensors, actuators, and connected devices.

Furthermore, by lowering the carbon footprint linked to energy use, AI-driven power management also promotes environmental sustainability. These intelligent systems support eco-friendly practices and reduce greenhouse gas emissions in smart cities and industrial settings by continuously optimizing energy use.

Ultimately, integrating AI into IoT networks improves operational efficiency, lowers energy costs, and supports green initiatives by optimizing power consumption and fostering a more resilient, sustainable, and intelligent IoT ecosystem.

Advantages:

- **Optimized energy use:** Reduces unnecessary power consumption.
- **Predictive maintenance:** Improves device longevity.
- **Improved network efficiency:** Ensures smart resource allocation.

Disadvantages:

- **High computational requirements:** AI algorithms may need extra processing power.
- **Data privacy issues:** AI-based power management needs access to usage data.
- **Implementation complexity:** Requires specialized infrastructure and expertise.

Sleep Mode and Duty Cycling Mechanisms

IoT devices can switch to low-power sleep modes when not in use, waking up only when needed. This process greatly reduces energy use and extends battery life. This power-management method is especially helpful in situations where devices are often idle, such as in environmental monitoring, smart agriculture, and remote sensing.

During sleep mode, non-essential functions are turned off, while essential parts stay in a low-energy state to keep basic monitoring or communication running. This cuts down power consumption drastically, allowing devices to last a long time without needing new batteries or recharging.

One major benefit of sleep mode and duty cycling is that they can significantly extend the lifespan of battery-powered IoT devices. By reducing active time and increasing low-power states, these devices can run for months or even years on a single battery charge.

Additionally, these methods help lower heat production, which is important for keeping devices safe and avoiding thermal problems that could affect performance. By keeping energy use low and stopping excessive heat from building up, IoT devices stay reliable and efficient over time.

Beyond saving power, sleep mode techniques also help improve network scalability. As more devices connect to an IoT network, lowering their power use decreases the overall energy demand and helps avoid network congestion from constant data transmission. This makes sleep mode mechanisms especially useful in large-scale IoT applications, like smart city systems and industrial IoT setups.

However, using sleep modes requires careful coordination among connected devices. Making sure devices wake up at the same time to share data without delays or losses can be difficult. Also, some real-time applications may experience delays if devices take too long to wake up.

In summary, using low-power sleep modes and duty cycling techniques is a smart and effective way to optimize energy use, increase device lifespan, and support the scalability of IoT networks, all while ensuring reliable performance across various applications.

Advantages:

- Significant power savings; this greatly increases battery life.
- Minimizes heat generation; this prevents IoT devices from overheating.
- Improves network scalability; it allows for more devices to be deployed while using less power.

Disadvantages:

- Potential latency problems could cause delays in devices waking up.
- Managing several devices in sleep mode can be difficult.
- Limited suitability; it is not suitable for real-time applications that need to run continuously.

Energy-Efficient Communication Protocols

New communication protocols, such as Bluetooth Low Energy (BLE), Zigbee, and IPv6 over Low-Power Wireless Personal Area Networks (6LoWPAN), are designed to reduce power use while ensuring strong and dependable connectivity in IoT ecosystems. These protocols are crucial for the smooth operation of IoT devices that need long battery lives and effective data transmission, especially in situations where constant communication is important. Their low energy consumption allows IoT devices to work for a longer time without frequent battery replacements or recharging, which makes them ideal for battery-powered sensors and remote monitoring systems.

Additionally, they provide low data rate transmission, saving power by sending small amounts of data at slow rates. This is particularly useful in applications that don't need high-bandwidth communication, such as environmental monitoring and smart metering. Even with their low power use, these protocols ensure reliable communication, so data is transmitted and received accurately without interruptions.

Furthermore, they support interoperability among different IoT devices, allowing easy integration into varied networks and ecosystems. For example, protocols like Zigbee enable mesh networking, where devices act as relays to expand network coverage without using extra power. Because of their low energy needs, these protocols can support large-scale setups with hundreds or thousands of devices. This makes them suitable for smart homes, wearable devices, industrial automation, and smart agriculture.

However, some challenges persist. Protocols like BLE have a shorter communication range, and their lower data transfer rates may not meet the demands of high-speed applications. Also, older devices or legacy systems may face compatibility issues. Still, by using these low-power communication protocols, IoT devices can improve energy efficiency and longevity while providing reliable connectivity. This plays a significant role in the sustainable deployment of IoT networks.

Advantages:

- **Optimized power use:** Made for applications requiring little energy.
- **Interoperability:** Facilitate a variety of IoT ecosystems and devices.
- Scalable solutions are perfect for industrial and smart home applications.

Disadvantages:

- **Shorter range:** For larger deployments, extra infrastructure might be needed.
- **Lower data rate:** Unsuitable for applications requiring a lot of bandwidth.
- **Compatibility problems:** New protocols might not be supported by certain older devices.

Blockchain for Energy-Efficient IoT Security

Blockchain technology plays an important role in providing secure, decentralized, and energy-efficient authentication and data management within IoT networks. As the number of connected IoT devices grows rapidly, maintaining data integrity, privacy, and security becomes more challenging. Blockchain tackles these issues by using its decentralized ledger system, where data is stored in a sequence of cryptographically secured blocks. This decentralized method removes the need for a central authority, lowering the risk of a single point of failure and boosting the resilience of IoT systems.

One major advantage of integrating blockchain with IoT is its ability to offer tamper-proof data management. Each block in the blockchain has a unique cryptographic hash that links it to the previous block, making data alteration nearly impossible without being detected. This feature is critical for applications that require high data authenticity and integrity, such as supply chain monitoring, healthcare data management, and smart contracts.

Beyond its strong security features, blockchain technology also promotes energy-efficient data management by cutting down on the need for high-energy central servers. With decentralized data validation and consensus methods, blockchain reduces the need to constantly send data to a centralized cloud, thus minimizing communication overhead and saving power. Furthermore, combining blockchain with lightweight consensus algorithms, like Proof-of-Stake (PoS) and Practical Byzantine Fault Tolerance (PBFT), can greatly improve the energy efficiency of IoT networks.

Blockchain also encourages transparency and traceability in IoT ecosystems, as each transaction is recorded immutably and can be audited without putting data security at risk. This level of traceability is useful in situations like asset tracking, environmental monitoring, and automated billing systems.

However, blockchain technology in IoT comes with some challenges. Implementing blockchain on resource-limited IoT devices can be tough due to limitations in computing power and storage. Moreover, traditional consensus algorithms like Proof-of-Work (PoW) can use too much energy, making them unsuitable for many IoT applications. Therefore, it is important to develop lightweight blockchain solutions specifically designed for IoT environments to overcome these challenges and maximize the technology's potential.

By using blockchain technology, IoT networks can improve data security, allow for decentralized control, manage data more efficiently, and increase transparency. This enables secure and scalable applications in sectors like healthcare, finance, logistics, and industrial automation.

Advantages:

- **Improved security:** Stops unauthorized access and cyber threats.
- **Decentralized management:** Removes the need for energy-consuming central servers.
- **Trust and transparency:** Guarantees secure transactions and data integrity.

Disadvantages:

- **Computational overhead:** Blockchain processing might need extra energy.
- **Storage limitations:** Handling blockchain data can be complicated for small devices.
- **Implementation costs:** Needs technical skill and infrastructure investment.

Challenges Faced with Future Trends in Energy-Efficient IoT Networking

The rapid growth of IoT has led to a rising need for energy-efficient networking solutions. These solutions support the increasing number of connected devices and applications. As IoT continues to spread across industries like healthcare, agriculture, smart cities, and industrial automation, energy efficiency has become crucial for the long-term success of IoT ecosystems. Improving energy efficiency is important for extending device life, lowering operational costs, and minimizing environmental harm. However, creating energy-efficient IoT networks comes with several challenges that must be tackled to allow for effective, scalable, and sustainable IoT implementations.

One major challenge is optimizing energy use in large-scale deployments. As the number of IoT devices rises, keeping energy efficient while handling different connectivity needs gets more complicated. Traditional networking solutions often fall short of supporting modern IoT applications. This calls for the creation of specialized protocols and designs focused on low-power operation.

Another significant challenge is data transmission efficiency. Frequent communication between devices and centralized servers can result in high energy use and network congestion. To lower energy consumption without sacrificing data integrity and real-time responsiveness, it is vital to implement effective data aggregation, compression, and communication protocols. Technologies like LPWAN and energy-efficient communication protocols such as BLE and Zigbee have proven to be good solutions.

Managing and maintaining devices also present considerable hurdles, especially in remote or difficult-to-access areas. IoT devices used in industrial automation, environmental monitoring, or agriculture may function in challenging environments, requiring strong energy management solutions to ensure that they run continuously. Approaches like adaptive power management, duty cycling, and sleep mode functions can greatly extend device life and reduce maintenance needs.

Sustainable energy use is another essential part of energy-efficient IoT networks. Using renewable energy sources like solar power and thermal energy harvesting can decrease reliance on conventional batteries. However, the variability and unpredictability of harvested energy make it hard to keep a steady power supply, leading to the need for innovative energy storage and management strategies.

In conclusion, tackling the challenges of energy-efficient IoT networking demands a broad approach that mixes effective communication protocols, energy-harvesting technologies, edge computing, and AI-driven power management methods. By overcoming these obstacles, IoT networks can achieve greater scalability, lower operational costs, and improved sustainability, setting the stage for more resilient and environmentally friendly IoT solutions.

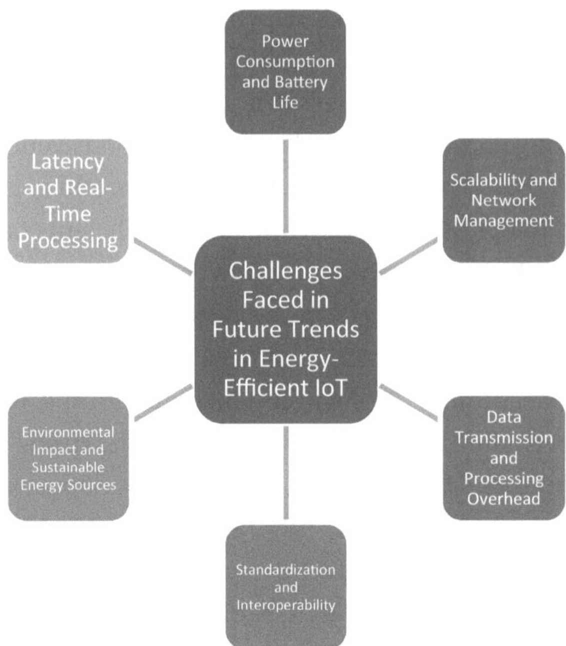

Figure 10-2. *Future challenges of energy-efficient IoT*

Figure 10-2 shows the main challenges related to future developments in energy-efficient IoT networks. To ensure reliable and efficient IoT systems at scale, these challenges need to be addressed, as explained in the following sections.

Power Consumption and Battery Life

Numerous IoT devices, including industrial monitors, wearables, and sensors, run on batteries. Reducing maintenance requirements, increasing device longevity, and guaranteeing continuous operation all require optimizing energy consumption. Still, striking a balance between performance and power efficiency is a significant challenge.

- While wireless communication protocols like LoRaWAN, Zigbee, and BLE help save energy, they also restrict coverage and data transmission speeds.
- Long battery life is necessary for devices in harsh environments or remote areas, but frequent data transmission and communication use up power more quickly.
- Adaptive data transmission and duty cycling are two power-optimization strategies that increase energy efficiency but may also cause delays and impair real-time responsiveness.
- Frequent battery replacements raise operating complexity and maintenance costs, particularly in large-scale IIoT deployments.

Energy-efficient hardware, firmware optimization, and intelligent power-management techniques that can dynamically balance energy consumption in response to network conditions and application requirements are all necessary to address these power consumption issues.

Scalability and Network Management

With deployments spanning smart cities, industrial automation, and agriculture, it is anticipated that the number of IoT devices will rise sharply. One of the biggest challenges is effectively managing these devices while preserving energy conservation.

- IoT networks need to be able to support thousands or even millions of devices while maintaining low power consumption and seamless data transfer.

- Urban areas with high device densities experience network congestion, interference, and higher power consumption as a result of frequent communication attempts.
- Advanced coordination and resource allocation strategies are necessary for managing heterogeneous networks, which comprise various wireless communication protocols, including Zigbee, BLE, and LoRaWAN.
- Energy-efficient mechanisms are necessary for remote diagnostics, device monitoring, and firmware updates in order to reduce needless power consumption.

To overcome these scalability issues and optimize power consumption in extensive IoT deployments, intelligent network architectures with effective routing, adaptive scheduling, and load balancing can be developed.

Data Transmission and Processing Overhead

IoT devices constantly produce large amounts of data, including environmental measurements and real-time analytics in industrial settings. Transmitting and processing this data efficiently while using less energy is a significant challenge.

- Traditional cloud-based data processing requires continuous data transmission, which increases energy use in battery-operated IoT devices.
- Edge computing reduces reliance on centralized cloud services by processing data closer to where it is generated. However, edge devices need to be designed to run on low power while handling complex calculations.

- Unnecessary data transmissions use up bandwidth and drain battery life, making it important to implement smart data filtering and aggregation processes.
- Wireless sensor networks must find a balance between energy efficiency and latency, ensuring that data is sent optimally without delays that impact real-time decision-making.

Techniques like data compression, adaptive sampling, and machine learning-based data reduction can help address these transmission and processing issues, allowing for more energy-efficient IoT networks.

Standardization and Interoperability

The lack of universal standards across IoT ecosystems creates compatibility issues. This makes it hard to develop smooth, energy-efficient networking solutions. IoT devices from different manufacturers often use different communication methods and data formats, resulting in interoperability challenges.

- Energy-efficient networking protocols like Zigbee, BLE, and 6LoWPAN are widely used, but they don't always work well together.
- The absence of standard guidelines makes it tough to create networks that communicate effectively across different platforms. This leads to higher energy use because of protocol conversions and repeated transmissions.
- Proprietary hardware and software solutions further divide the IoT ecosystem. They limit compatibility between networks and force businesses to spend on expensive integration solutions.

- Upgrading legacy IoT systems to newer, energy-efficient protocols requires significant changes to infrastructure, making large-scale transitions difficult.

Developing industry-wide standards for communication, security, and energy management will lead to more connected and energy-efficient IoT networks. These networks will work better across different applications and environments.

Environmental Impact and Sustainable Energy Sources

IoT networks rely on a large number of electronic devices. Many of these devices contribute to power consumption and e-waste. Sustainable energy solutions are necessary to reduce environmental impact, but several challenges make it hard for them to be widely used.

- Solar-powered IoT devices provide a renewable energy option, but their efficiency drops in low-light settings. This makes them unsuitable for indoor or underground use.
- Energy-harvesting technologies, like piezoelectric and radio frequency (RF) energy harvesting, need specific conditions to work well. This limits their reliability in certain IoT setups.
- Battery disposal and replacement add to e-waste, raising environmental concerns and maintenance costs.
- Sustainable materials for IoT devices are still being developed. Integrating biodegradable or recyclable parts into energy-efficient hardware is also a challenge.

Improvements in energy harvesting, low-power circuit design, and alternative power sources will be vital in reducing the environmental impact of IoT networks while keeping energy efficiency intact.

Latency and Real-Time Processing

Many IoT applications, such as smart healthcare, industrial automation, and autonomous systems, need real-time data processing with minimal delays. Achieving this responsiveness while staying energy efficient is a tough challenge.

- Wireless sensor networks often face latency because of power-saving methods that cut transmission frequency, which affects real-time decision-making.
- Edge computing processes data closer to the source, reducing reliance on the cloud, but edge devices must function well without using too much power.
- Delays in data transmission and response times can impact applications like medical monitoring, where quick action is crucial.
- Low-power communication protocols naturally lead to trade-offs between speed and efficiency, making it hard to build high-performing, energy-efficient real-time IoT networks.

To improve real-time responsiveness in energy-efficient IoT applications, we need to develop better processing algorithms, more efficient network setups, and low-latency communication methods.

In conclusion, as IoT networks develop, it's important to tackle issues related to power use, scalability, data transmission efficiency, standardization, environmental sustainability, and latency. Energy-efficient IoT networking needs progress in hardware design, optimized software algorithms, and new power management techniques to ensure long-term performance across different applications. Overcoming these challenges will lead to more efficient, scalable, and reliable IoT networks that balance energy savings with high performance.

Advantages of Future Trends in Energy-Efficient IoT Networking

Future developments in energy-efficient IoT networking will result in major advancements that will increase the sustainability, dependability, and scalability of IoT systems. New methods and technologies are being developed to solve energy efficiency issues and improve the general functionality of IoT networks as the demand for connected devices keeps growing. One of the most significant developments is the creation of sophisticated energy-harvesting methods that incorporate cutting-edge solutions like radio frequency (RF) energy harvesting and piezoelectric systems, going beyond conventional approaches like solar and thermal energy. With the help of these developments, IoT devices can now run independently by using ambient energy sources, greatly lowering their dependency on batteries and requiring less maintenance. Furthermore, hybrid energy-harvesting systems give energy collection more flexibility, allowing devices to adjust to changing environmental conditions and guarantee continuous operation.

The other significant trend is the integration of AI and ML to enable intelligent power management, in which algorithms based on AI anticipate usage patterns and allocate energy resources optimally, thereby dynamically managing power consumption in real time. This promotes sustainable IoT deployments by reducing waste and improving automated energy distribution and predictive maintenance. Additionally, LPWANs like Sigfox, LoRaWAN, and NB-IoT are essential because they provide long-range connectivity at low power consumption, which makes them perfect for applications like industrial automation, smart agriculture, and environmental monitoring. By ensuring that devices can run for extended periods of time on little power, these networks lower energy consumption and keep connectivity even in remote locations.

Additionally, by processing data locally at the edge instead of sending it to centralized cloud servers, edge computing has shown promise in lowering latency and energy consumption. Because it reduces data transmission, network congestion, and bandwidth use, this method is especially advantageous for applications that need real-time data processing and analysis. Alongside edge computing, energy-efficient communication protocols like 6LoWPAN, BLE, and Zigbee are crucial for wearable technology, smart home applications, and industrial monitoring because they minimize power consumption while maintaining dependable connectivity.

In order to provide safe, decentralized, and energy-efficient authentication and data management, blockchain technology is also being integrated into IoT systems. Resource-constrained IoT devices can engage in safe and transparent transactions without consuming a lot of power, thanks to lightweight blockchain algorithms. Utilizing duty cycling and sleep modes, which enable devices to switch to low-power states when not actively transmitting data, is another energy-saving strategy that significantly lowers energy consumption without sacrificing network functionality.

Furthermore, federated and collaborative learning models are becoming more popular because they allow devices to train models together without exchanging raw data, greatly lowering communication overhead while protecting user privacy. In distributed IoT environments, this decentralized method facilitates scalable, secure data processing while improving energy efficiency. In conclusion, by combining low-power communication protocols, intelligent management algorithms, sustainable energy sources, and decentralized data processing, future developments in energy-efficient IoT networking have the potential to completely transform the way IoT systems function and make IoT networks more robust, economical, and ecologically friendly.

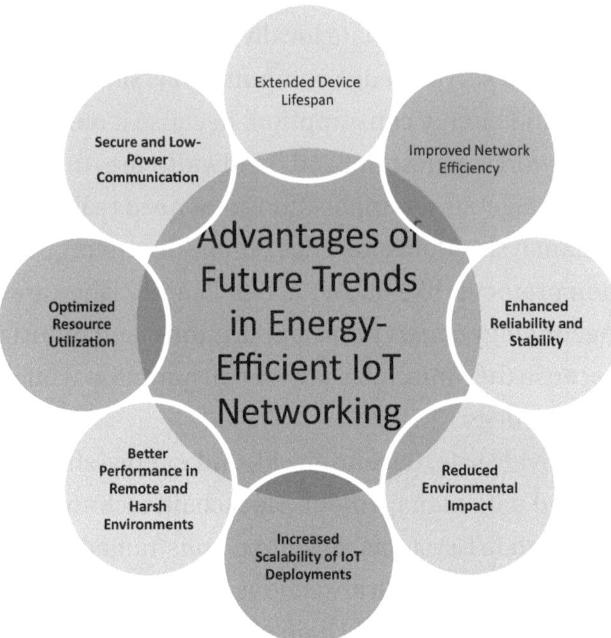

***Figure 10-3.** Benefits of future IoT trends*

Figure 10-3 depicts the advantages of implementing energy-efficient IoT networking in upcoming technologies. These advantages contribute to the development of strong, long-lasting, and extremely efficient IoT ecosystems, as discussed in the following sections.

Extended Device Lifespan

Energy-efficient devices can use less power thanks to IoT networks, which prolong their useful lives. Devices can operate for years without frequent battery replacements, thanks to technologies like LoRaWAN, BLE, and Zigbee, which lower energy consumption.

This is especially advantageous for these IoT applications:

- Industrial monitoring, which lowers maintenance in remote locations
- Smart agriculture, where sensors track soil moisture and climate conditions
- Environmental sensing, which guarantees ongoing data collection without the need for human intervention

Improved Network Efficiency

Optimizing data transfer and cutting down on pointless communication are the main goals of advanced IoT networking techniques. By ensuring that IoT devices only transmit data when necessary, technologies like Zigbee and 6LoWPAN help to reduce energy consumption. Benefits of improved network efficiency include:

- Reduced energy consumption per transmission by reducing redundant data
- Efficient data routing to prevent congestion in large-scale IoT deployments
- Optimized bandwidth utilization that permits more devices to connect without overloading the network

This ensures smooth IoT operation without excessive infrastructure expansion.

Enhanced Reliability and Stability

Low-power networking protocols such as LoRaWAN and Zigbee ensure consistent and stable connections, even in remote areas. These protocols are optimized to operate in low-signal environments, making them ideal for applications such as:

- Smart cities, which require reliable communication between thousands of sensors
- Healthcare monitoring, to ensure medical devices don't have connectivity problems
- Industrial automation without downtimes, which can result in substantial operational losses

IoT systems can operate without frequent interruptions by improving reliability.

Reduced Environmental Impact

Energy-efficient IoT technologies contribute to environmental sustainability by:

- Reducing battery waste by extending device lifespans
- Lowering power consumption and reducing dependency on non-renewable energy sources
- Minimizing e-waste by using biodegradable sensors

Smart cities and industries will become more sustainable as industries adopt more eco-friendly IoT solutions.

Increased Scalability of IoT Deployments

Efficient networking allows organizations to deploy thousands of IoT devices without excessive power consumption. Technologies such as 6LoWPAN and Zigbee are designed for large-scale networks, supporting high-density IoT ecosystems such as:

- Smart homes, where multiple devices interact seamlessly
- Industrial automation, optimizing manufacturing processes
- Smart agriculture, enabling large-scale sensor deployments across farmlands

With better scalability, businesses and governments can expand IoT networks efficiently.

Better Performance in Remote and Harsh Environments

Energy-efficient IoT networking ensures that devices operate reliably even in extreme conditions, such as underground, in the ocean, or in deserts. Technologies like LoRaWAN and RF energy-harvesting allow devices to function without a stable infrastructure.

This is especially useful for:

- Monitoring conditions in remote regions during mining and oil exploration
- Environmental monitoring by gathering information from forests and oceans
- Communication during emergencies and disaster response

By leveraging energy-efficient solutions, IoT devices can operate autonomously in harsh environments.

Optimized Resource Utilization

Energy-efficient smart resource management is made possible by IoT networking, guaranteeing that little energy, bandwidth, or processing power is wasted. By processing data locally rather than relying on the cloud, AI and Edge Computing further optimize operations. Benefits include these conditions:

- In smart homes, gadgets modify energy use according to current circumstances.
- In healthcare, only vital patient data is transmitted by medical sensors.
- In industrial automation, devices dynamically modify power to cut down on waste.

This ensures efficient and sustainable IoT operations.

Secure and Low-Power Communication

Modern IoT networks prioritize security while maintaining low power consumption. Low-power communication technologies like LoRaWAN and Zigbee integrate encryption and authentication mechanisms to protect data.

Benefits include:

- Secure transmission for delicate applications, such as smart infrastructure
- Defense against online attacks without depleting device batteries
- Effective cryptographic methods that guarantee data integrity while using little power

IoT networks can function effectively and safely for extended periods of time thanks to built-in security features.

In summary, longer device lifespans, better resource use, greater scalability, and less environmental impact are key components of future trends in energy-efficient IoT networking. IoT solutions that are sustainable and scalable are being propelled by technologies like LoRaWAN, Zigbee, 6LoWPAN, and BLE. These developments will be essential to building smart, safe, and environmentally responsible IoT ecosystems while lowering overall power consumption as IoT adoption increases.

Disadvantages of the Future Trends in Energy-Efficient IoT Networking

Future developments in energy-efficient IoT networking have many benefits, but they also come with a lot of hurdles. These difficulties hinder smooth deployment and broad use by affecting adoption, functionality, and scalability. The difficulty and expense of incorporating cutting-edge, energy-efficient technologies into current IoT infrastructures are two of the main obstacles. For small and medium-sized businesses (SMEs), upgrading or retrofitting legacy systems to support contemporary power management and energy-harvesting techniques can be costly and time-consuming.

Additionally, even though energy-harvesting methods like solar, thermal, and radiofrequency energy collection provide sustainable power solutions, environmental factors frequently cause their energy supply to fluctuate. Device reliability may be jeopardized by this unpredictability, particularly in crucial applications that require constant operation. Even though hybrid energy-harvesting systems are more adaptable, optimizing energy use from various sources remains a challenge.

The computational overhead of AI-driven power management systems is yet another important drawback. It takes strong processing power to integrate AI and ML algorithms into IoT networks, which can make devices more complex and use more energy instead of less. Furthermore, balancing computational demands with power-saving goals is challenging when training AI models on devices with limited resources.

Despite being built for long-range connectivity and energy efficiency, LPWANs like Sigfox and LoRaWAN are frequently constrained by high latency and low data rates. Because of this, they are not appropriate for applications that need high-bandwidth communication or real-time data transmission. When many devices are connected in the same coverage area, network congestion can also be an issue, which can lead to interference and signal deterioration.

Although processing data locally lowers latency and energy consumption, edge computing has drawbacks of its own, such as higher hardware costs and less processing power than centralized cloud servers. Additionally, since compromised edge devices could endanger the entire network, maintaining strong security at the edge is essential to preventing local breaches.

Despite being energy-efficient, communication protocols like BLE, Zigbee, and 6LoWPAN frequently have low data throughput and a limited communication range. Because of this, these protocols might not work well in settings that need constant high-speed data transfer or in large-scale industrial applications. Network integration can also be hampered by incompatibilities between new and old protocols.

Blockchain technology presents computational overhead and energy demands that can be difficult for IoT devices with limited resources, despite its potential for safe and decentralized data management. While some of these problems might be resolved by lightweight blockchain solutions, they frequently sacrifice security and data integrity, which makes them unreliable for important applications.

Finally, federated learning still has issues with data heterogeneity, model convergence, and resource allocation even though it addresses data privacy and lowers communication costs. It's still difficult to ensure efficient coordination between devices with different computational capacities.

In conclusion, even though performance and sustainability will be improved by future developments in energy-efficient IoT networking, resolving these issues is essential to finding scalable and dependable solutions. The key to achieving the full potential of energy-efficient IoT networks will be striking a balance among innovation, practicality, and cost-effectiveness.

Figure 10-4. *Disadvantages of energy-efficient IoT*

Figure 10-4 depicts the possible disadvantages of upcoming energy-efficient IoT networking techniques. When designing and implementing IoT networks, these drawbacks, which are discussed in the following sections, must be carefully taken into account.

Limited Data Transmission and Processing Capabilities

Reducing power consumption is a top priority for energy-efficient IoT networks, frequently at the expense of processing speed and data transmission.

- Applications that require real-time data, like industrial automation or video surveillance, cannot use LPWANs like LoRaWAN, because they transmit small data packets at low bit rates.
- Devices that use edge computing to lessen reliance on the cloud might not have as much processing power, which limits their capacity to perform intricate calculations locally.
- IoT sensors that run on batteries have to restrict their communication frequency in order to save energy, which causes delays in data transfer and decision-making.

This restriction primarily impacts sectors like manufacturing, healthcare, and autonomous vehicles that need to transmit large amounts of data quickly.

High Initial Deployment Costs

Implementing energy-efficient IoT networks requires significant investment in infrastructure and technology.

- Upgrading networks to support low-power communication protocols such as 6LoWPAN, Zigbee, or BLE requires purchasing new devices and gateways.
- Energy-harvesting solutions (e.g., solar, radio frequency, and piezoelectric harvesting) increase initial setup costs due to specialized hardware requirements.
- Edge computing integration demands high-performance microcontrollers and optimized software, leading to additional development costs.

While these technologies reduce long-term operational costs, the high upfront expenses can be a barrier for small businesses and developing regions.

Complexity in Network Management and Maintenance

Future energy-efficient IoT networks involve complex structures that require specialized management.

- Multiple communication protocols (e.g., LoRaWAN, Zigbee, and 6LoWPAN) need to be integrated, increasing network complexity.
- Dynamic power optimization algorithms must adjust energy consumption and data transmission rates, requiring continuous monitoring.

- Firmware and software updates are difficult for low-power, battery-operated devices, as frequent updates can drain power.

Managing thousands of interconnected devices while maintaining efficiency is a significant challenge for enterprises and administrators.

Security Risks Due to Low-Power Constraints

Energy-efficient IoT devices often lack strong security mechanisms due to power limitations, making them vulnerable to cyber threats.

- The use of sophisticated encryption techniques is limited by limited processing power, which raises the possibility of data breaches.
- If not adequately secured, LoRaWAN devices are vulnerable to replay and man-in-the-middle attacks.
- Distributed Denial-of-Service (DDoS) attacks are more likely to occur in decentralized IoT networks because they give hackers multiple points of entry.

Preventing unwanted access and data breaches requires the implementation of simple yet powerful security measures.

Scalability Challenges in Large-Scale Deployments

Scalability problems still exist even though energy-efficient IoT networking seeks to accommodate extensive deployments.

- Large-scale deployments are challenging for low-power devices due to their limited processing power.

- In dense environments with thousands of devices transmitting data at once, network congestion occurs.
- When integrating various 6LoWPAN, Zigbee, and BLE devices into a single network, interoperability issues can arise.

IoT deployments may encounter latency, inefficiency, and unreliable communication if network planning is not optimized.

Dependence on Environmental Conditions for Energy Harvesting

Energy-harvesting methods like solar power, radio frequency, and piezoelectric generation are the foundation of many energy-efficient IoT solutions. These remedies, however, rely on the surrounding environment.

- Indoor and low-light conditions are ineffective for solar-powered sensors.
- Wireless signals are necessary for radio frequency energy harvesting, but they might not always be present.
- Not all applications can benefit from thermal and piezoelectric energy harvesting because they require particular conditions, like temperature differentials or mechanical vibrations.

Reliability may be impacted by inconsistent performance from devices that use environmental energy sources.

Limited Standardization and Compatibility Issues

Due to the absence of common standards, the quick development of energy-efficient IoT networking technologies has caused compatibility problems.

- Devices made by various manufacturers have different power management strategies and communication protocols, which makes integration difficult.
- Multi-network integration is challenging because interoperability between various networks (such as Zigbee and the Long Range Wide Area Network (LoRaWAN)) is still being improved.
- Long-term compatibility problems arise from the fact that not all IoT devices support the same security patches and firmware updates.
- Lack of standardization makes network administration more difficult and delays broad adoption.

In summary, although energy-efficient IoT networking has advantages for sustainability, it also has drawbacks, including low data transfer rates, expensive deployment costs, complicated administration, security flaws, scalability problems, reliance on external factors, and a lack of standardization.

Continuous improvements in low-power communication protocols, network optimization techniques, and security measures are necessary to get past these challenges. IoT networks will become more secure, scalable, and efficient while preserving energy efficiency as technology advances.

Applications of Future Trends in Energy-Efficient IoT Networking

Future developments in energy-efficient IoT networking are enabling low-power, high-efficiency, and sustainable IoT solutions, which are revolutionizing a number of industries. Numerous applications in smart infrastructure, healthcare, industrial automation, and environmental monitoring are supported by these developments.

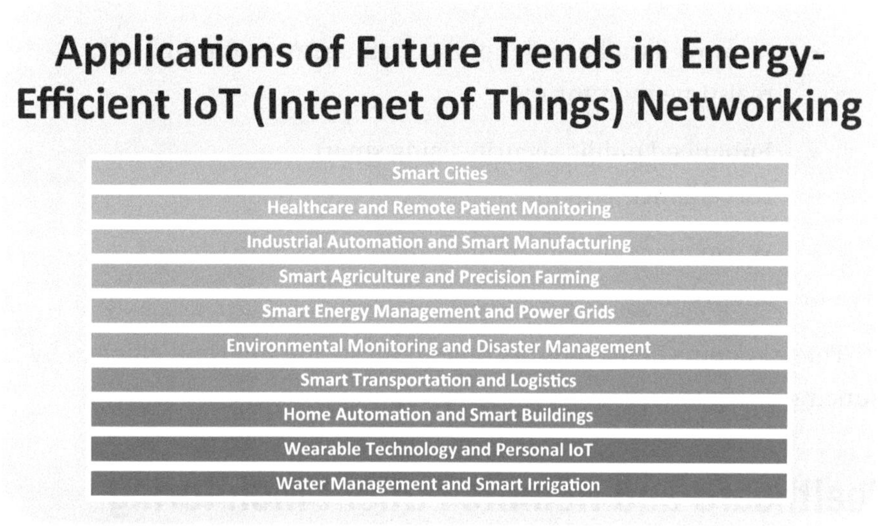

Figure 10-5. *Future uses of energy-efficient IoT*

Real-world instances of energy-efficient IoT networking across multiple domains are displayed in Figure 10-5 and are discussed in detail in the following sections. These use cases demonstrate how, in practical situations, efficient energy use can improve output, security, and service quality.

Smart Cities

Energy-efficient IoT networking is essential in developing intelligent urban infrastructure. It enables efficient management of resources, improves traffic control, and enhances public safety by utilizing low-power sensor networks.

Key functionalities:

- Optimized energy consumption in urban lighting and utilities
- Improved traffic and mobility management through real-time monitoring
- Enhanced public security using smart surveillance systems
- Waste management optimization through IoT-based smart bins

These systems help cities become more sustainable and efficient by reducing energy waste and improving urban planning.

Healthcare and Remote Patient Monitoring

Medical device connectivity and healthcare monitoring depend heavily on energy-efficient IoT networking. The effectiveness of remote healthcare is increased by these networks' ability to support continuous health tracking while using little power.

Key functionalities:

- Continuous health monitoring for chronic disease management
- Low-power medical equipment for monitoring patient vitals

- Intelligent medical systems to maximize resources
- Critical care emergency response aided by IoT

Better patient care, real-time diagnoses, and efficient use of hospital resources are the results of these advancements.

Industrial Automation and Smart Manufacturing

Energy-efficient IoT networking is used in smart manufacturing and industrial automation to improve predictive maintenance and operational efficiency. Low-power sensors enhance production quality while lowering maintenance expenses and downtime.

Key functionalities:

- Predictive maintenance that uses less energy to monitor the health of machinery
- Low-power industrial IoT networks for automated production control
- Supply chain optimization with real-time monitoring
- Smart wearables used to monitor worker safety

In industrial settings, these developments improve cost-effective production, increase efficiency, and contribute to worker safety.

Smart Agriculture and Precision Farming

Energy-efficient IoT networking is revolutionizing agriculture by enabling automated monitoring and data-driven farming techniques. These networks help optimize resource usage, leading to higher productivity and sustainability.

Key functionalities:

- Low-power soil and climate monitoring for better crop yield
- Automated irrigation systems based on sensor data
- Livestock tracking and health monitoring
- Smart greenhouse management for energy-efficient cultivation

These applications contribute to increased agricultural efficiency and environmental sustainability.

Smart Energy Management and Power Grids

In energy management, future trends in energy-efficient IoT networking improve power distribution, demand response, and grid stability. These solutions help reduce energy waste and optimize consumption.

Key functionalities:

- Automated demand-response management in energy grids
- Low-power smart meters for real-time energy usage monitoring
- IoT-based predictive maintenance for power infrastructure
- Integration of renewable energy sources into smart grids

These advancements enable sustainable energy use and improved grid reliability.

Environmental Monitoring and Disaster Management

Energy-efficient IoT networking plays a vital role in environmental monitoring and disaster prevention by deploying low-power sensors for real-time data collection and early warning systems.

Key functionalities:

- Air and water quality monitoring using low-energy sensors
- IoT-based early warning systems for natural disasters
- Deforestation and wildlife monitoring for environmental conservation
- Sustainable resource management through real-time environmental data

These applications help governments and organizations respond quickly to environmental challenges.

Smart Transportation and Logistics

Future trends in energy-efficient IoT networking support smart transportation systems, improving efficiency in fleet management, public transit, and supply chain logistics.

Key functionalities:

- IoT-enabled route optimization for fuel-efficient transport
- Energy-efficient vehicle tracking systems

- Low-power cargo-monitoring solutions for supply chains
- Smart parking-management systems to reduce congestion

These advancements lead to better transport efficiency, reduced energy consumption, and optimized logistics management.

Home Automation and Smart Buildings

Energy-efficient IoT networking is transforming smart home automation by integrating low-power devices for enhanced convenience, energy savings, and security.

Key functionalities:

- Smart lighting and climate control for energy-efficient homes
- IoT-powered security and access control systems
- Automated appliance management based on user preferences
- Energy-efficient building monitoring for resource optimization

These applications improve living conditions and reduce energy costs in smart homes and buildings.

Wearable Technology and Personal IoT

By allowing for continuous monitoring without frequent recharging, low-power IoT networking is propelling the development of wearable technology and personal IoT solutions.

Key functionalities:

- Energy-efficient wearable health monitoring devices and fitness trackers
- Apps for augmented reality and smart glasses
- Low-power connectivity for personal safety devices
- Smart clothes with IoT capabilities to track biometrics

These innovations improve lifestyle convenience and individual well-being.

Water Management and Smart Irrigation

Through waste reduction and water distribution monitoring, energy-efficient IoT networking is advancing water management and conservation initiatives.

Key functionalities:

- Smart irrigation controllers for efficient water use
- Low-power leak detection sensors in water supply systems
- Real-time water quality monitoring for safety compliance
- IoT-based flood prevention systems

These applications support better management of water infrastructure and sustainable water use.

By increasing automation, optimizing energy use, and boosting real-time data monitoring, emerging trends in energy-efficient IoT networking are influencing a number of industries. These applications facilitate intelligent and sustainable solutions in a variety of fields, including energy management, smart cities, healthcare, industrial automation, and agriculture.

Organizations can improve overall system performance, cut operating expenses, and boost efficiency by utilizing low-power networking technologies.

Conclusion

An essential component of smart technology's future is energy-efficient IoT networking, which guarantees sustainability and longer device lifespans. Long-range and low-energy communication is made possible by trends like 6LoWPAN and LPWANs. While AI and ML dynamically optimize energy consumption, energy-harvesting techniques lessen reliance on conventional batteries. Smart grid integration improves the efficiency of energy distribution, and the drive for recyclable and sustainable IoT hardware promotes environmental sustainability. Energy-efficient communication protocols allow for scalable and low-power IoT networking, while sleep mode and duty cycling mechanisms further minimize energy waste. Lastly, blockchain integration preserves energy efficiency while improving security.

The adoption of these energy-efficient IoT networking solutions will be crucial for the future of IoT, despite obstacles like higher initial costs, network congestion, and computational complexity. Industries can guarantee a more secure, economical, and sustainable IoT ecosystem that promotes global digital transformation while reducing environmental impact by tackling these constraints.

CHAPTER 11

Security and Privacy in Green IoT Systems

The fast-growing deployment of IoT technologies has already provided many sectors (such as healthcare, agriculture, transportation, and smart cities) with operational improvements and new applications. As a result, we have reached a breakpoint in the way we collect, process, and act on data in order to increase efficiencies, automate tasks, and better support decision-making. Increased adoption of IoT devices brings with it worries about large-scale deployment, including the energy used by the devices, the creation of electronic waste (e-waste), and the carbon footprint of all the wires and data centers in between. As IoT networks grow larger, and the demand for energy and resources increases, it will become more difficult to support sustainability goals.

Green IoT systems attempt to address these problems through sustainability, in the way of energy-efficient protocols and greener solutions with a smaller carbon footprint. In Green IoT, energy consumption is minimized. Green IoT employs lightweight communication protocols, uses methods of energy consumption harvesting, and incorporates energy-saving strategies with negligible or zero degradation to all systems. Green IoT also includes using hardware that is less environmentally damaging, being either recyclable or containing less harmful materials. Green IoT contributes to the world mission of combating climate change and protecting the environment.

Dr. D. Sharma and Dr. B. Pandey, *Eco-Networking for IoT*,
https://doi.org/10.1007/979-8-8688-2317-6_11

While Green IoT systems have many benefits, because of their inherently resource-constrained and heterogeneous network environment, they potentially create significant security and privacy challenges. Such limitations prevent resource-constrained IoT systems from implementing common security paradigms in traditional IT systems. As with traditional IT systems, security and alteration of operational protocols using so-called "suicide devices" increases the likelihood of compromise to Green IoT networks. Cyberthreats include unauthorized access or exploitation through data breaches and system infiltration. Furthermore, Green IoT systems are more likely to consist of autonomous or semi-autonomous devices, which introduce complexity that can complicate security mechanisms and result in additional security risks.

Consistent with IoT systems, privacy is also a serious issue because they can collect sensitive information about user behavior, environmental conditions, and operational measures. Privacy violations can result from acquiring data that data can then be misused or misappropriated. The potential for significant privacy violations includes surveillance and technology-mediated identity theft. Each application has to process data in real time and in multiple platforms, so privacy issues are complicated by inherent issues regarding authorization, consent, ownership, and control of data.

This chapter is a thorough analysis of these security and privacy issues found in Green IoT systems. Based on case studies in real-world settings, it demonstrates how the integrity and trustworthiness of Green IoT applications can be compromised and how the capability of Green IoT deployments to realize sustainability goals can be compromised by cyberattacks. In addition, this chapter articulates advanced mitigation strategies for addressing these issues, such as lightweight encryption methods, secure data aggregation methods, and blockchain-based authentication methods.

To improve security, this chapter addresses the use of AI and ML for continual malicious threat assessments, threat and malicious action (proactive) detection, and adaptive defense mechanisms. The chapter also highlights the effectiveness of data stewardship practices related to privacy, analytics, and data science—including active consent/semi-consent options, anonymized data, and secure data-handling practices. The chapter also provides real-world examples and case studies to demonstrate how combining secure and robust security frameworks with compliance to data protection, guidelines, and regulations can safeguard sensitive information without sacrificing functionality, user experience, and usability.

The more interconnected the environment becomes with IoT devices, the higher the cost of energy consumption. With IoT systems using large amounts of power, they have an increased carbon footprint and contribute to growing global environmental impact. E-waste from IoT devices are an environmental concern, as many IoT devices become obsolete quickly. Green IoT can reduce power consumption, e-waste, and create sustainability by using energy-efficient communication protocols, sustainable materials, and intelligent power management.

Green IoT systems are concerned not only with conserving energy use, but also enabling a more efficient lifecycle for IoT devices (from manufacture to disposal). This can be achieved through the use of sustainable materials, promoting the life of devices by developing modular designs to allow for reuse and maintenance, and reducing the overall amount of e-waste in the environment. Additionally, relying on energy-harvesting methods, such as solar and kinetic energy, lessens the dependence on non-renewable energy sources and facilitates a green ecosystem.

Although Green IoT solutions offer tremendous benefits related to sustainability and conservation, they have new security and privacy problems. Energy-efficient IoT devices are resource constrained. Therefore, threats to the Green IoT system cannot be mitigated with conventional security mechanisms. This limitation leaves Green IoT systems vulnerable to cyberattacks and data breaches like unauthorized access, data manipulation, denial-of-service attacks, and device hijacking. Due to the exponential increase in the scope and complexity of Green IoT solutions, exposing a Green IoT system to threats is seemingly easier than mitigating threats to them. The development of connected devices in conjunction with the diversity of the IoT ecosystem makes it increasingly challenging for application and device developers to enforce identical security protocols consistently across the multiplied number of connected devices.

One of the greatest security challenges of Green IoT systems is to design solutions that preserve data integrity and confidentiality while reducing energy consumption. However, encryption and authentication systems often consume considerable resources, which may not be available to low-power devices. Thus, protecting sensitive data efficiently has created a demand for lightweight cryptographic implementations that are specific to Green IoT. In addition, the availability and reliability of services is also important to maintain security of Green IoT devices (especially in a critical application like smart grids, telehealth monitoring, etc.).

In Green IoT systems, privacy considerations are equally important. The nature of IoT technologies, which involve constant monitoring and the collection of data, can expose users' privacy. Any sensitive information, such as location, personal habits, and environmental conditions, may become vulnerable if left unprotected from malicious users. Protecting data privacy involves anonymization, secure data aggregation, and data minimization, reducing the chances of access to personally identifiable information (PII).

This chapter reviews the major security and privacy threats that face Green IoT systems, the risks that arise when adopting Green IoT, and the principles for building secure and sustainable IoT spaces. It covers the basic principles, current problems, practical applications, and future directions of security and privacy in Green IoT. It includes a thorough discussion of vulnerabilities associated with Green IoT and networks, including weak authentication methods, no encryption for data obfuscation, and vulnerabilities associated with networking protocols such as ZigBee, Bluetooth, and so on.

Literature Review

In Kaur, Manjit, et al. (2021)[1], a secure and energy-efficient IoT model for e-health was proposed, focusing on the secure transmission and retrieval of biomedical images. The model employs compressive sensing and a five-dimensional hyper-chaotic map for encryption, and addresses hyper-parameter tuning using a θ-non-dominated sorting genetic algorithm III. Experimental results show improved performance in speed and efficiency, making the model well-suited for Green IoT networks [1].

A cognitive ambient backscatter communication (C-AmBC) framework has been developed by Li, Xingwang, et al. (2021)[2] to facilitate large-scale connections and green communication for future 6G networks. The C-AmBC framework permits the utilization of shared spectrum and RF resources, but it can be subject to eavesdropping. Along with communication reliability and security, the outage and intercept probabilities are examined under different SNR and MER scenarios to demonstrate that optimizing system parameters can improve both reliability and security.[2]

A hybrid AI, IoT, and blockchain conceptual framework has been created to model smart cities. The hybrid model utilizes cloud computing through decentralized data storage to support sustainable intelligent IoT applications. Ahmed, Imran, et al. (2022)[3] pointed out the necessity of secure and efficient data analytic solutions for next-generation urban environments.

IoT adoption continues to grow rapidly, with an estimated 500 billion devices predicted to be connected by 2030. Numerous new challenges will also arise rapidly, including quality of service, spectrum efficiency, and data analysis. New approaches to support dynamic macroscale IoT systems through an AI perspective are under exploration across numerous domains, including healthcare, agriculture, and industries.[4]

A comprehensive survey is presented by Singh, Prashant, et al. (2022) [5] on IoT technologies for railway systems, highlighting applications in operations, video surveillance, maintenance, and safety. The paper discusses the role of 5G, LTE, and LPWAN technologies in enabling real-time decision-making and enhancing sustainability in railway transportation.[5]

The Internet of Healthcare Things (IoHT) is transforming healthcare through smart devices for monitoring, storing, and transmitting sensitive data. However, this raises concerns about data privacy and compliance with regulations. A regulatory framework is proposed by Shahid, Jahanzeb, et al. (2022)[6] to mitigate risks and strengthen healthcare data protection.

Blockchain technology has been identified as a powerful solution to enhance IoT security. A comprehensive survey by Saxena, Shivam, et al. (2021)[7] of blockchain-integrated IoT systems outlines improvements in privacy, integrity, and decentralization, while addressing interoperability, scalability, and performance concerns.

An extensive tutorial and performance evaluation of blockchain-based security systems in IoT networks by Ferrag, Mohamed Amine & Lei Shu (2021)[8] covers 17 different application domains. Various consensus mechanisms and security analysis tools are compared to guide the development of efficient, scalable, and secure systems.

A foundational review of IoT architecture and communication protocols was conducted by Gerodimos, Apostolos, et al. (2023)[9], identifying implementation challenges and key vulnerabilities. The study emphasizes the importance of a secure deployment framework for IoT expansion.

IoT in healthcare has enabled remote patient monitoring, smart environments, and wearable sensors. A comparative study by Abdulmalek, Suliman, et al. (2022)[10] on IoT healthcare systems analyzes factors such as privacy, security, efficiency, and quality of service, offering recommendations for future enhancements.

The impact of IoT on sectors such as smart homes, traffic systems, and power grids calls for enhancements in data security. There are numerous cryptographic algorithms available for securing IoT communication, such as block ciphers and hybrid models.[11]

Security concerns in 6G edge networks are examined in the paper by Mao, Bomin, et al. (2023)[12], focusing on edge computing, caching, and intelligence. Federated learning and blockchain are explored as defenses against vulnerabilities in decentralized systems.

Security and privacy challenges in 6G wireless networks are discussed in the study by Porambage, Pawani, et al. (2021)[13], addressing vulnerabilities in enabling technologies like physical layer security, quantum computing, and DLT. The study also explores standardization efforts and research gaps.

A detailed review of security mechanisms for the Internet of Medical Things (IoMT) is provided in the paper by Hireche, Rachida, et al. (2022) [14], categorizing techniques based on performance, and recommending robust solutions to mitigate risks in healthcare environments.

The study by Ruan, Zhengping (2023)[15] proposes blockchain as a solution to enhance IoT security by decentralizing data storage and reducing single points of failure. The integration of blockchain with IoT improves security but introduces challenges in scalability and complexity.

AI-based medical imaging techniques are explored by Ajmani, Prerna, et al. (2024)[16] for early detection and classification of breast cancer, using machine learning and deep learning algorithms to improve diagnostic accuracy.

A decentralized platform for secure digital transactions is discussed by Sharma, Vandana, et al. (2024)[17] through blockchain applications, especially in smart contracts and the insurance domain, showcasing its transformative impact on trustless ecosystems.

In the paper by Garg, Sheena, et al. (2023)[18], consumer shopping behavior is analyzed using machine learning algorithms such as Apriori, KNN, Naive Bayes, and ensemble methods to evaluate their effectiveness in e-commerce data processing.

A hybrid deep learning model combining LLM, CNN, and RNN architectures is proposed in the study by Gupta, Kartavya, et al. (2024) [19] for precision agriculture, achieving improved crop yield prediction for staple crops like wheat and maize.

KubeEdge is demonstrated in the study by Saini, Lalit Mohan, et al. (2024)[20] as an efficient edge computing framework for IoT, reducing latency and optimizing resources, while also addressing challenges in scalability and integration with cloud-native applications.

Understanding Green IoT Systems

Green IoT systems are characterized by their focus on sustainability through energy-efficient designs and eco-friendly practices. To minimize environmental impact, these systems use low-power communication protocols, sustainable energy sources, and efficient data processing. Green IoT focuses on resource efficiency and aims to mitigate the increased demands for connected devices while having a minimal impact on the environment. Green IoT is not simply about reducing energy consumption; it also applies to the use of eco-materials, longevity, and reducing e-waste. As IoT networks continue to proliferate across industries and disciplines, it will become increasingly important to incorporate practices of Green IoT in order to provide innovative technologies in a sustainable manner. A fundamental element of Green IoT is the use of low-power communication protocols (e.g., ZigBee, BLE, and LoRaWAN) that can reduce the energy used to transmit data reliably. Many times, Green IoT also utilizes renewable energy sources (for example, solar panels, or kinetic energy harvesting) to power IoT devices and to limit or eliminate use of non-renewable sources. Data processing techniques like edge computing and data compression mitigate energy use by limiting and/or compressing the amount of data that needs to be sent to central servers.

Key Applications of Green IoT

With various uses in several industries, Green IoT advances sustainable development by conserving energy, reducing waste, and managing resources more effectively. All these uses play an important role in creating a smarter future while incorporating up-to-date technology into sustainable practices. One of the most highly regarded uses of Green IoT is through smart grids, which can dramatically improve energy management by monitoring energy use data in real time and automating energy distribution and pre-assessment of faults. When utility companies use IoT-enabled devices and sensors, they can determine energy use patterns using an incredible amount of data, which allows them to generate the energy their customers need, while wasting comparatively little. This not only conserves energy but also greatly reduces carbon emissions, leading to a smaller impact on the environment. Smart grids also help integrate renewable energy sources like solar and wind more effectively, which increases the odds that clean energy will be successfully and competently used. Through predictive maintenance and automation of fault diagnosis in their systems, Green IoT can maximize the lifespan of critical infrastructures, reduce downtime, lower costs, and lessen negative impact on the environment.

Green IoT has yet another important application—smart homes and smart buildings, which use technology and energy-use features to automate lighting, heating, ventilation, and air conditioning (HVAC) systems. Environmental controls, enabled by IoT with thermostats and occupancy sensors, dynamically adjust based on current use to lower energy consumption and carbon footprint. Energy monitoring reports from smart appliances can allow the household occupant to make better decisions about their energy use. Integrating energy use and renewable energy supply data into IoT connected devices and energy storage units, in the home or building, can enable partial or fully self-sufficient buildings and reduced engagement with the utility company's electrical grid. As an added bonus, creative energy management systems could adopt the information to flag peak usage and suggest energy efficient alternatives, resulting in energy-efficient homes and buildings.

Green IoT also operates at a very important level in the health sector by providing sustainable solutions and a better experience for patients. Wearable health devices and IoT-enabled medical devices are designed with and for energy efficiency. These design processes consider the battery life of the medical devices or wearables in combination with continually assessing vital signs and sharing relevant data with their providers. The telemedicine that Green IoT creates limits the need for in-person visits, therefore limiting travel emissions. This remote patient monitoring option also reduces the health service's carbon footprint and makes accessibility more inclusive and sustainable. Intelligent health structures are established through Green IoT to use automated light and HVAC systems that enable proactive energy management of healthcare environments based on occupant use, the number of the people in a space, or the study hours.

In the agricultural sector, Green IoT systems are connecting traditional agriculture to innumerable sustainable options that create even greater efficiencies, largely in terms of precision agriculture and smart farming solutions. For example, IoT-capable sensors can monitor moisture and nutrient levels in the soil, as well as weather conditions. The sensors allows farmers to determine when to irrigate their fields—a key method for optimizing water use and reducing resource use. Drones with sensors and imaging capabilities enable farmers to assess the condition of their crops and determine what needs attention. Farmers can use this information to tackle specific problems and use fewer chemicals. At the same time, the approach leads to more yield, and as water and energy are optimized, it positively contributes to the environment. Real-time monitoring of animal health and behavior means farmers can minimize energy use in large-scale operations, while ensuring animal welfare is maintained during various farming animal activities.

In the case of intelligent transportation systems, Green IoT can improve fuel efficiency and reduce emissions in part by providing real-time traffic management and directing traffic appropriately through route optimization. Connected vehicles outfitted with IoT devices communicate information regarding road conditions, levels of congestion, and emission metrics so that traffic management systems can adjust dynamically by modifying traffic signals or directing traffic in another way. Public transportation networks may also utilize IoT to optimize routes to reduce idle time and improve fuel consumption. EV charging stations coupled with Green IoT technology allow for efficient energy use, furthering the goal of adoption for a more sustainable transportation option.

The utilization of data-driven insights in sectors like transportation can allow for efficiencies in various industries while reducing their environmental footprint. Furthermore, as Green IoT systems become more widely accepted and adopted, attention must be focused on security and privacy policies to help protect sensitive data and keep the public trust. With ongoing advances in technology, innovation, and collaboration between stakeholders, Green IoT's potential to deliver sustainable development and a cleaner, greener environment for future generations can become a reality.

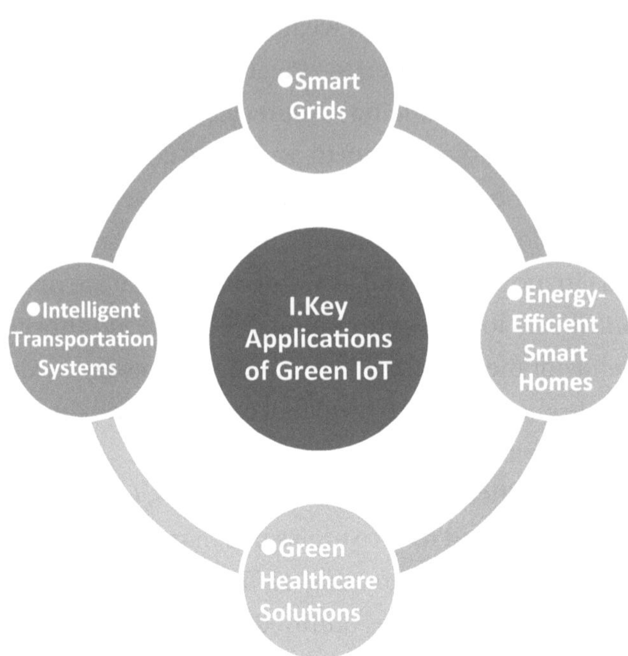

Figure 11-1. *Key applications of Green IoT*

Figure 11-1 shows the main practical applications of Green IoT technologies. These consist of energy-efficient smart homes with automated control, smart grids for efficient energy delivery, healthcare applications for remote monitoring and diagnostic, and intelligent transport with reduced fuel use and traffic, all discussed in the following sections. Combined, these applications represent energy optimization and sustainability.

Smart Grids

Green IoT allow utilities to monitor energy consumption in real time and optimize their energy management. This prevents energy waste and encourages utilities to distribute energy in a more efficient way. By combining IoT sensors and smart meters, utilities can analyze the patterns of power consumption and improve them. They have the ability to leverage data analytics for dynamic load balancing and demand response management. This can ultimately lead to energy grid resilience, more efficient use of energy resources, reduced carbon emissions, and the ability to use renewable sources proportionally, rather than intermittently.

- **Dynamic load balancing:** IoT smart grids can perform dynamic load balancing for energy loads to eliminate or reduce the pressure on the grid. This can minimize surges, maximize stability, and increase reliability.
- **Demand response management:** Smart metering capabilities with real-time data provide continuous information to utilities in terms of peak consumption and off-peak consumption. This can improve management and delivery of available energy and reduce waste of valuable resources.
- **Renewables integration:** All aspects of smart grids show significant potential for reliability in managing renewables, including solar and wind and intermittently powered sources with real-time data. They can manage power output generationally relative to demand.
- **Predictive maintenance:** Throughout any facility that needs to maintain power in the infrastructure, IoT devices constantly monitor the health and conditions of the equipment and its overall performance. The IoT devices can stream data for predictive analytics and predict faults via predictive maintenance interventions before defects occur and/or mitigate any failures.

- **Energy theft detection:** Analytics can help with anomaly detection, which can identify unauthorized energy use and theft of available energy resources.
- **Automatic fault detection:** Smart grid systems can automatically detect power outages and faults, thereby enabling rapid response and investigation, potentially causing less down time.
- **Decentralized energy management for resiliency:** Microgrids and local generation models help improve resilience by providing distributed energy management capabilities during a failure of the central power grid.
- **Energy forecasting:** Machine learning products and technologies help utilities predict future energy consumption based on historical data and external influences like weather patterns. This assists in grid planning and load management applications.
- **Energy storage optimization:** Monitoring battery storing systems with IoT can provide valuable evidence to ensure that energy is being used and stored appropriately.

Energy-Efficient Smart Homes

In smart homes, Green IoT devices work collaboratively to minimize energy use by automatically adjusting lighting, heating, and cooling systems based on occupancy and user preferences. Smart thermostats, motion-sensing lighting, and energy-monitoring plugs are just a few examples of how IoT enhances residential energy efficiency. These solutions not only reduce energy bills but also contribute to sustainable living by decreasing the household's carbon footprint. Here are just some of the Green IoT solutions found in smart homes:

- **Smart thermostats:** Automatically regulate temperature settings based on occupancy, the weather, and user habits, all of which can optimize energy use while maintaining comfort.
- **Motion-sensing lighting:** Detect human presence and turn the lights on or off. Reduces power use substantially when the lights are on but no one is occupying the room.
- **Energy monitoring plugs:** Monitor and analyze the power consumption of individual devices so homeowners can identify devices that are high energy users and develop plans for energy conservation.
- **Smart HVAC:** Optimize heating and cooling schedules using occupancy as well as weather forecasts and manage energy consumption while keeping homeowners comfortable.
- **Automated window shades:** Open and close based on sunlight coming into the home and the indoor temperature (a component of the sustainable solution).
- **Appliance scheduling:** Homeowners can schedule when energy-consuming appliances run, typically at non-peak times, so that they are lowering costs and the amount of energy required.
- **Renewable energy management systems:** Systems such as solar panels combined with battery storage work in conjunction; best practices provide a mix of their own self-generated green energy.

- **Voice activated automation:** Energy-efficient appliances/controls respond to voice commands seamlessly, and the concept of voice-controlled energy management must be explored.
- **Energy usage data:** Provides real-time analytics of power consumption behavior and actionable energy savings recommendations to homeowners.
- **Smart water heater systems:** Decrease standby energy loss, enhance water heater operation, and minimize utility bills by taking advantage of hot water usage prediction.

Green Healthcare Solutions

Green IoT solutions in healthcare seek to provide as much patient health monitoring as possible while minimizing energy use, all while ensuring data accuracy and reliability. They do this by using low-energy sensors and low-energy protocols. Wearable health devices leverage low-energy sensors and low-energy communications to enable continual vital sign monitoring. Further, remote patient monitoring solutions allow patients to avoid repeated trips to the hospital for monitoring by allowing patient healthcare visits through telemedicine and remote monitoring systems. Together, these Green IoT solutions create more sustainable health systems and improved patient care with equitable access.

- **Low-power wearable devices:** Use efficient sensors and communication methods (e.g., BLE, ZigBee) to monitor vital signs (e.g., heart rate, blood pressure, oxygen levels) with minimal battery usage.
- **Remote patient monitoring:** Provide continual monitoring of health in a patient's home, decreasing hospital admission and emissions related to travel.

- **Telehealth and virtual consultation:** Allow healthcare services remotely (IoT powered) and use less energy related to travel, while providing quality care to patients.
- **Smart medical equipment:** Use energy-efficient features and power management to reduce the energy use of diagnostic and therapeutic equipment.
- **Smart lighting and HVAC control:** In hospitals, automatic lighting and climate controls based on occupancy and activity levels reduce energy consumption.
- **Predictive maintenance of medical equipment:** Deploy IoT sensors to constantly check the health and performance of medical devices, thereby extending the life of a medical device and reducing e-waste.
- **Real-time aggregation of health data:** Aggregating patient data in real time reduces data use while maintaining data sensitivity. It also reduces the energy load on central servers through edge computing.
- **Integration of renewable energy:** Hospitals and healthcare facilities incorporate solar panels and wind turbines to power IoT-based healthcare systems, encouraging sustainability.
- **Automated inventory and waste management:** Smart inventory systems can track the use of medical supplies and waste disposal, thereby supporting resource use and responsiveness and minimizing environmental impacts.

- **Health data analytics for sustainability:** Analytics can be used to minimize resource use, such as energy consumption during non-peak hours and opportunities for energy-efficient improvements.

Intelligent Transportation Systems

Transportation is a significant contributor to greenhouse gas emissions, and Green IoT solutions aim to address this challenge by optimizing traffic flow, reducing fuel consumption, and promoting the use of electric and autonomous vehicles. IoT-enabled traffic monitoring and management systems can decrease road congestion, mitigate idle times, and improve trip routing. Furthermore, public transport systems, in combination with IoT, can improve scheduling and lower fuel consumption, thus reducing pollution levels and providing more sustainable modes of urban mobility.

- **IoT traffic monitoring:** Sensors and cameras combine real-time data from IoT technologies, enabling changing light patterns in response to detected traffic. This results in fewer congestion events.
- **IoT parking solutions:** Parking solutions based on IoT provide real-time updates to available parking spots, reducing time searching for parking and lowering emissions.
- **Route recommendation algorithms:** Because IoT collects traffic patterns over time and combines that with environmental conditions, IoT routing can continually recommend the most energy-efficient routes, thus reducing fuel consumption.

- **EV charging using IoT:** EV charging stations can monitor energy use in real time and identify potentially broken charging stations. This can ensure that EVs are charged adequately.
- **Connected and autonomous vehicles:** IoT communication uses V2V and V2I communication for energy savings and safety.
- **Smart public transport:** IoT technology can monitor passengers in buses and trains and optimize routes to reduce fuel consumption and idle time.
- **Emissions monitoring:** IoT dependent technology can used for real-time emissions monitoring and reporting to ensure regulatory compliance regarding the continuous and passive supply of emissions data from vehicle sensors.
- **Fleet monitoring:** IoT can alarm owners of fleet vehicles that have problems arising from wear/tear and enable them to prevent annoying breakdowns.
- **Integrated mobility solutions:** This involves using data from modes of transport, including public transport, ride-sharing, and cycling, to promote multi-modal and sustainable forms of mobility.
- **Green logistics and supply chain management:** This includes tracking the carbon footprints of transportation and delivery, optimizing route designs, and removing trips that are unnecessary in order to limit environmental disruption.

Notable Case Studies and Real-World Implementations

A great application of Green IoT and an intelligent smart city initiative is where smart street lighting systems automatically adjust their brightness levels based on vehicle and pedestrian motion. These smart energy-efficient lights promote increased energy efficiency and improve public safety. Instead of just dimming or brightening when motion is detected, the technological communication offered through live analytics can dim or brighten and continue to use the least amount of energy while also allowing for safely usable light. This is an example of how Green IoT is performing both environmental sustainability and social functions.

Another compelling example is the implementation of renewable energy-powered IoT sensors for environmental monitoring. These sensors can now be powered from renewable sources (solar or wind) which when placed in tight groupings, can control pollution levels, degree of temperature change, and climatic conditions while providing recent analytical data. The data collected was used to decrease pollution levels and to take action in famine situations addressing climate change. The combined systems, when used in the context of an environmental study, include important information on air and water quality in a timely fashion, so appropriate responses can be undertaken quickly.

Case Study 1: Smart City Lighting Systems

Another interesting example involves the use of Green IoT in a smart city development (e.g., smart street lighting systems). These technologies can monitor motion and automatically control street light luminosity according to pedestrian or vehicular movement and presence. These technologies save energy, while also providing public safety with adequate light. In this example, the motion sensor and data analytics recorded for the street lights sensors used motion to dim or brighten the overhead street lights. The project ultimately was able to reduce electricity consumption without compromising safety, highlighting an easy application that demonstrates how Green IoT can provide environmental and social benefits.

- **Motion sensors:** Street lights received motion sensors that generated light upon observing pedestrians, cyclists, and moving vehicles.
- **Real-time analytics:** Updated analytics determined night, time of day, amount of privacy, and environmental conditions that accounted for lighting, in order to limit excessive power consumption.
- **Energy-efficient LED street lights:** Smart street lighting with LED bulbs consumes a fraction of the energy of traditional lighting designs and provides twice or three times the brightness. They also have as triple the lifespan of the traditional light bulb.
- **Adaptive brightness:** Dynamic conditions are related to lighting intensity. Some dynamic conditions include the amount of traffic, severe weather events, and public events that would account for safety on the street while limiting energy uses.
- **Centralized monitoring and control:** A central IoT platform monitors the operating condition of each street light, allowing real-time fault monitoring and remote control, which helps reduce maintenance costs.
- **Solar-powered street lights:** Many street lights use solar panels, so they operate independent of main electric service and support the use of renewable energy.

- **Predictive maintenance:** Street lights with IoT sensors identify issues like bulb failure and power outages, send alerts when the times for maintenance are minimal, and facilitate faster repairs to ensure lights remain in service longer.
- **Data-centric urban planning:** Data on street light usage patterns and movement help city planners understand trends like pedestrians or vehicle use so the planners can design safer urban spaces.
- **Less light pollution:** Automated dimming in areas with low traffic reduces light pollution, which enhances the night time experience and supports natural ecosystems.
- **Cost and energy resiliency:** Smart street light systems can decrease energy use by as much as 60%, when the change in light levels and use of solar energy is considered, while simultaneously saving on costs and using less energy.

Case Study 2: Renewable Energy-Powered Environmental Monitoring Sensors

Another example is to implement renewable energy IoT sensors for environmental monitoring. They are typically powered by solar or wind energy and are deployed where they can monitor levels of pollutants, changes in temperature, or changes in climate in real time. This data can allow urban planners and environmental agencies to make informed policy decisions regarding pollution reduction and climate change mitigation. Most importantly, these systems can provide information about air and water quality that spurs timely intervention and addresses issues related to the environment.

- **Solar- and wind-powered sensors:** IoT devices can come equipped with solar panels and wind turbines, thus relying on independent power generation. They can run indefinitely without traditional electricity.
- **Air quality monitoring:** Sensors can measure pollutants, including carbon dioxide (CO_2), nitrogen oxides (NOx), particulate matter (PR2.5 and PM10), and volatile organic compounds, (VOCs) in real time.
- **Water quality monitoring:** Sensors that are placed inside bodies of water (rivers, lakes, ponds, etc.) monitor pollutants, pH level, temperature, and turbidity. This helps authorities set communities up with a safe place to obtain and use clean water.
- **Local climate condition monitoring:** Tracking local climate conditions using data, including temperature, humidity, wind and precipitation, can contribute to climate resilience, through adaptation to the local climate.
- **Data aggregation and fusion:** Data collected from several sensors can be aggregated and analyzed to get an overall assessment of environmental conditions across regions.
- **Integration with cloud and edge computing:** A hybrid system using edge computing and cloud computing can enhance data processing, thus optimizing for latencies and energy use.

- **Real-time alerts:** Automatic alerts when air or water quality exceeds thresholds can trigger immediate action from environmental agencies.
- **Long-term data archival and analysis:** The archival of historical data can contribute to trend analysis and evaluation of long-term changes in the environment.
- **Community engagement and awareness:** The public has open access to environmental data and can participate and be aware of air and water qualities, which leads to more responsible community action.
- **Policy support and decision-making:** Environmental data helps support policy decisions related to pollution (i.e. pollution abatement), waste management, and creating sustainable communities. It can help cities make better environmental choices and be more environmentally resilient.

Research Opportunities

Moving forward, this section covers designing quantum-resistant encryption algorithms to permit Green IoT systems to respond to the future threat of quantum computing. As quantum computing rapidly progresses, it is likely that existing cryptographic and security measures will also become vulnerable, adding to the need for advanced encryption schemes to secure devices from quantum computing attacks. Green IoT devices can employ lattice-based cryptography and other post-quantum algorithms to safeguard data integrity and confidentiality in the quantum technology age.

Drastic changes to federated learning provide fascinating opportunities for doing privacy-preserving data analysis without needing to release raw data from particular devices. Federated learning machine learning provides an alternative by collecting data from devices but keeping it there—rather than moving data to a single server. This also minimizes the energy costs associated with transferring data.

Improvements in federated learning are an exciting development for privacy-preserving data analysis. Researchers are now investigating federated learning related to resource-constrained IoT devices and attempting to minimize power consumption while maintaining accurate and secure data.

Applying AI that can monitor network traffic and detect anomalies in real time would help increase the resiliency of a Green IoT system. AI-based threat detection is capable of automatically recognizing patterns that might indicate a cyberattack, someone unauthorized accessing a device, or otherwise unusual behavior. When AI is used with edge computing, it can reduce latency and energy consumption by processing data closer to its source increases. Also, by incorporating self-learning algorithms, an IoT privacy preserving system could adapt to new threats autonomously.

To further enhance security and privacy, several researchers are investigating decentralized identity management alternatives based on blockchain. Blockchain technology can be used to provide secure, immutable records of device interactions, which can limit identity spoofing and data tampering. With the addition of lightweight consensus mechanisms, Green IoT systems can achieve high-security levels without overspending on energy.

In addition, edge intelligence is emerging as a disruptive technology for energy reduction while computational efficiency remains intact. With embedded AI at the edge, Green IoT devices have the ability to process data locally, therefore decreasing the amount of reporting. This would allow for real-time decisions and could also assist in improving security with sensitive information kept in the local domain, instead of provided to the public.

Another significant area of research is adaptive security frameworks that can scale their security controls context and device resources. This may include lightweight security protocols on low-power devices, while providing high-power nodes for heavier security controls. This would provide energy security while ensuring that critical data is protected on higher capability devices. Green IoT security embodies interdisciplinary engagement regarding the data that is collected and processed, while also addressing the ethical, legal, and social implications.

Researchers are looking for usable ways to take advantage of privacy impact assessments (PIAs) and data protection by design, both of which would add transparency and security while also working within laws such as the General Data Protection Regulation (GDPR) and promoting user trust.

Energy-harvesting methods are being considered to increase the longevity of IoT devices prior to battery replacement, because each new battery generates e-waste and negatively impacts sustainability. Energy harvesting allows IoT systems to utilize energy sources, in particular ambient energy sources from the sun, motion, or thermal energy, to function for longer periods of time. In this regard, the technology adheres to the principles of green technology because it makes it largely self-sustainable, further advancing environmental sustainability.

Most importantly, globally consistent mechanisms are needed to develop frameworks for Green IoT security and privacy. Standards are being developed worldwide through research and government policies and legislation, which in many cases are working together to develop these global standards for security and privacy through collaborative interoperability, data protection, and sustainable design. This collaborative approach will create a means for industry stakeholders to work with consensus, creating a set of guidelines to create secure and sustainable IoT to all developers, regardless of where they are in the world.

Through the proactive adoption of these innovative solutions and a holistic, organized approach, Green IoT systems should prove to be sustainable, reliable, and reliable solutions for today's society. If we work collaboratively and constantly innovate, it is possible to strike a healthy balance between ecological sustainability, associated with Green IoT, and cyber resilience, associated with IoT technologies, and create Green IoT technologies that benefit the environmental and digital ecosystems.

Security in Green IoT Systems

Green IoT systems provide comparable performance to conventional IoT systems with the added benefit of reducing energy use and environmental impacts. Security is a fundamental aspect of Green IoT systems, as proliferate in various applications, including smart cities, smart farming, and sustainable energy. The following section summarizes the various security issues and solutions related to Green IoT systems.

Key Security Challenges

Figure 11-2. *Key security challenges*

Figure 11-2 reveals many outstanding challenges in terms of security regarding Green IoT networks. These challenges involve resource-constrained devices and challenges brought about by lightweight communication protocols. These challenges internally generate weak security patterns for energy-efficient IoT devices, leaving them exposed to spoofing, data tampering, and eavesdropping.

Resource constraints:

- Energy-efficient Green IoT devices are not designed with high-security measures. Energy-efficient devices must preserve energy and provide strong security measures.

- Conservative use of energy represents a lifecycle of energy usage that is satisfactory for the use of minimal energy overall. It then picks up any strong cryptographic guarantees in terms of confidentiality.
- Limited memory and processing capabilities may result in advanced security measures not being implemented, exposing a period of risk.
- Finding that balance between energy efficiency and secure protocols is still a challenge, especially as the landscape accounts for any number of devices in motion.
- Due to battery life limitations, security checks and updates may not be performed frequently, which increases sustained vulnerabilities.

Data privacy:

- IoT systems produce large amounts of private data such as personal and environmental data.
- Unauthorized access can lead to significant violations of privacy.
- Processes of data aggregation can put sensitive data at risk, which may impact confidentiality of users.
- There is also a privacy risk from unintended data breaches resulting from bad anonymizations or data exfiltration during transmission.
- It is critical to use approaches such as end-to-end encryption of all data sent to and from devices and data minimization to protect users.

Network vulnerabilities:

- Green IoT systems leverage wireless communication protocols (e.g., ZigBee, Bluetooth, and Wi-Fi), which are susceptible to multiple attacks, including eavesdropping, jamming, and man-in-the-middle attacks (MITM).
- It is essential to mitigate protocol-based vulnerabilities to keep up with secure data transmission.
- Network congestion or interference can weaken data transfer integrity, which can expose the network to packet injection or spoofing attacks.
- Rogue device insertion and identity spoofing attacks can also compromise network security integrity and lead to unauthorized access.
- Without network segmentation, the attacker can leverage their access to move more laterally through the network and affect multiple devices at once.

Physical threats:

- Many Green IoT devices are often deployed in unattended or insecure outdoor, public, or exposed spaces and can be stolen, tampered with, or physically attacked.
- Tamper detection and device authentication are indispensable.
- If the attacker has physical access to the actual hardware, they may execute arbitrary code in the firmware or extract the cryptographic keys from the device.

- Without sufficient physical hardening, the device may suffer malicious damage or destruction, creating large gaps in data collection, communication, and so on.
- Devices that exist in exposed environments can leverage sealed enclosures or other anti-tamper measures available to devices that are intentionally secured.

Firmware and software vulnerabilities:

- Insufficient software configuration, updates, and patching can leave devices vulnerable to malware or exploits that would not ordinarily exist.
- Fast, efficient, and secure firmware updates are critical to the resilience of their respective devices and systems (including overall ecosystem resilience).
- If the firmware update is not authenticated, the attacker can exploit this to deliver their malicious software to devices or simply gain control of a given device.
- Firmware rollback attacks may leverage a software downgrade, restoring the older version of firmware that was originally vulnerable.
- Secure boot processes and integrity checking can mitigate the negative implications of a device with exploited firmware.

Security Requirements for Green IoT Systems

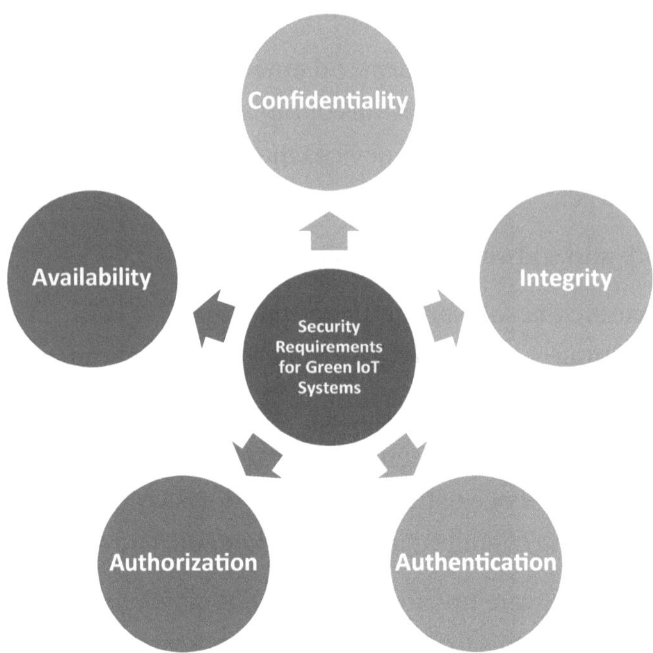

Figure 11-3. *Security requirements for Green IoT systems*

Figure 11-3 depicts the key security features necessary to protect Green IoT domains. These include access management authorization, integrity to prevent non-intended changes, and confidentiality to ensure data privacy. These attributes must be satisfied in order for Green IoT applications to protect sensitive operations and establish trust.

Confidentiality:

- Data is safeguarded from unauthorized access.
- Energy-efficient encryption methods are used, such as Elliptic Curve Cryptography (ECC).

- End-to-end encryption ensures that data is protected from the original device to the final destination, thereby limiting potential interception of data during transmission.

Integrity:

- Data is unchanged from generation until the time it is accessed or stored.
- Hash functions and digital signatures are used for data authenticity.
- The Message Authentication Codes (MACs) feature must be present in co-existing communications so that any changes post message generation can be detected and prevented.

Authentication:

- Validation of devices/users in receiving sensitive data to prevent unauthorized access.
- Lightweight authentication methods reduce energy consumption.
- Multi-Factor Authentication (MFA) adds another hurdle to overcome even though resource-constrained environmental considerations are the norm.

Authorization:

- Determining which individuals (users) access data using role and privilege management.
- Role Based Access Control (RBAC) provides a level of protection that can decrease and remove unnecessary data.

- Applying attribute-based access control (ABAC) for permission based on contextual information (e.g., location of the device or time of access).

Availability:

- Make sure that services are not interrupted through cyberattacks (e.g., DDoS) or hardware failures (e.g., transmission failures).
- Have redundancy and failover.
- Use load balancing and traffic filtering; for example, do-not-lift-distributed denial-of-service (DDoS) attack.

Security Solutions for Green IoT Systems

Figure 11-4. *Security solutions for Green IoT systems*

Figure 11-4 illustrates the contemporary techniques for enhancing the security of Green IoT. New distributed ledgers and blocking technologies are being used to make data exchange immutable. They offer secure routing protocols that provide energy-efficient mitigation against operational intrusions. The goal is to design a secure, decentralized, and energy-efficient IoT environment.

Lightweight cryptographic algorithms:

- Efficient and secure algorithms (e.g., elliptic curve cryptography—ECC) and advanced encryption standards (AES), assuming small key size, should be employed.
- Homomorphic cryptography can be performed to enable computation on encrypted data without first needing to decrypt it.
- Symmetric key algorithms, such as lightweight block ciphers (e.g., SPECK and SIMON), reduce computational overhead.
- Blended encryption protocols use symmetric and asymmetric cryptography to provide security, while decreasing resource costs.
- Always use optimized cryptographic libraries that are tailored for low-power IoT devices to achieve the best efficiency and performance.

Blockchain and distributed ledger technologies:

- Provide data integrity and transparency while allowing for decentralization of authentication.
- Lower the chances of single points of failure and interference.

- The blockchain will utilize lightweight protocols. The protocol will minimize computational requirements as much as possible while optimizing security and decentralization.
- The solution can implement consensus methods such as Proof of Authority (PoA) or Delegated Proof of Stake (DPoS) to lower energy consumption.
- Blockchain-based identity management will provide secure, decentralized authentication and authorization for IoT devices.

Secure routing protocols:

- Energy-efficient routing has built-in security (e.g., Secure and Energy Aware Routing Protocols—SEARP).
- Smart trust-based routing reduces the impact of malicious nodes on routing processes.
- Adaptive routing algorithms will intermittently reschedule routes depending on threat level and environmental conditions.
- Multi-hop communication will be utilized to minimize power while remaining encrypted.
- Cross-layered security will be more holistic as it takes into consideration the physical and network layer of IoT devices. Because both layers can be attacked, you want to provide a more solid defense.

Intrusion detection and prevention systems (IDPS):

- IDPS solutions capable of IoT environments can detect behavioral anomalies.

- Machine learning models compromise between accuracy and energy use.
- Federated learning uses smaller datasets to train IDS systems without sharing the raw dataset, which can protect user interest.
- IDPS capable of detecting real-time anomalous behavior can respond to instances without depleting device life.
- Collaborative IDPS systems across correlated devices can create broader support against adversaries attempting to coordinate attacks.

Data aggregation techniques:

- Less data being sent, along with fewer transmissions, saves energy. The data must be secure, including the following:
- Some type of secure data aggregation protocols that can deal with encrypted data
- In-network data aggregation for communication that minimizes energy consumption
- Compression on any aggregation before transmission to minimize bandwidth use
- Hierarchical aggregation methods that preserve data confidentiality and integrity during aggregation

Case Study: Smart Grids and Green IoT Security

In the case of smart grids, energy-efficient IoT devices communicate with one another to improve energy distribution. Security considerations include:

- **Data integrity:** Tampering with energy consumption data could mean that the wrong data is used to make decisions, which would be financially detrimental to consumers and could also facilitate billing fraud.
- **Authentication:** Without an authenticated device, the consumer might consent to using bad data, which is an issue the user or aggregator has to manage.

Future Trends and Research Directions

- **Quantum-resistant cryptography:** Planning for threats from quantum computing, when encrypted machine use is compromised by industry standards.
- **AI-enabled security:** Deployment of ML as part of the detection of and response to threats.
- **Development of green security models:** New models have to be developed that will address the trade-offs of security vs. energy efficiency.

As the demand for new solutions as well as sustainability through IoT increase, so will the pressure to develop new models that provide security.

Security Challenges in Green IoT Systems

The security issues surrounding Green IoT contexts are reliant on numerous issues related to computing limits, heterogeneous software use, and changing networking structures. There exist serious security challenges with Green IoT platforms, including:

- **Data integrity and confidentiality:** Unauthorized access and data tampering will lead to compromised information.
- **Authentication and authorization of devices:** Lightweight authentication protocols are vitally important when accessing lower power devices in Green IoT systems because they will either limit or deplete battery life. Authorization strategies that continuously maintain trustworthy access control must also be established when identifying a device.
- **Secure communication protocols:** While communication protocols like ZigBee and LoRaWAN are energy-efficient, they can be susceptible to techniques like eavesdropping and man-in-the-middle attacks. Establishing secure channels while conserving energy means integrating advanced cryptographic applications and protocol optimizations.
- **Firmware and software vulnerabilities:** Devices can be compromised if the firmware is not updated for vulnerabilities. Not all device owners carry out maintenance on their devices, so patch management and software updates are essential, especially since older firmware remains in production and can exhaust energy resources.

- **Physical security threats:** Numerous IoT devices are installed in open and unsecured environments, which can present physical threats. To minimize these threats, it's imperative to use tamper-proof hardware and incorporate physical access control.
- **Supply chain vulnerabilities:** Green IoT devices frequently contain parts from many manufacturers. Insecure supply chains can lead to compromised hardware and/or software, which may create a security deficit.

Privacy in Green IoT Systems

Green IoT systems have the main purpose of limiting energy consumption while providing innovative services in various domains, such as smart homes, smart cities, healthcare, and industry. To limit their environmental impact, Green IoT systems utilize low-power communication protocols, energy-efficient sensors, and intelligent data processing. By monitoring resource use and lowering carbon footprint, Green IoT supports sustainable development and helps promote environmental cleanliness.

However, there are many difficult privacy challenges related to the data that Green IoT collects, transmits, and processes over multiple connected devices. In smart homes, the data may contain information about an individual's habits and preferences, whereas in an industrial environment, it may contain operational metrics. The constant data flow creates an ever-present concern over unauthorized access to endpoints, data breaches, and potential exploitation of personal data and other sensitive data. The heterogeneous nature of IoT networks involves a variety of stakeholders, which creates new challenges for security and data privacy.

Data protection and energy-efficiency are arguably two of the most important facets of Green IoT services. While traditional security functions exhibit resiliency and become efficient, the computational power required by these functions means they are not feasible for resource-constrained devices in normal IoT use cases.

Additionally, standards for data protection such as GDPR and the California Consumer Privacy Act (CCPA) further complicate privacy-preserving practices. Another ongoing challenge is creating security frameworks that can adapt to threats as they emerge, while still minimizing power consumption. Colleagues in the industry, researchers, and regulators must collaborate to develop best practices for protecting data privacy in Green IoT applications.

As these Green IoT systems are developed and used, and as environmental sustainability and data privacy gain more prominence in their respective fields, it is vital to achieve public trust as part of building and facilitating acceptance and use. If these elements can be logically combined, Green IoT can radically transform how we develop ecologically responsible solutions without putting the safety of users or the protection of their data at risk.

Privacy Challenges in Green IoT Systems

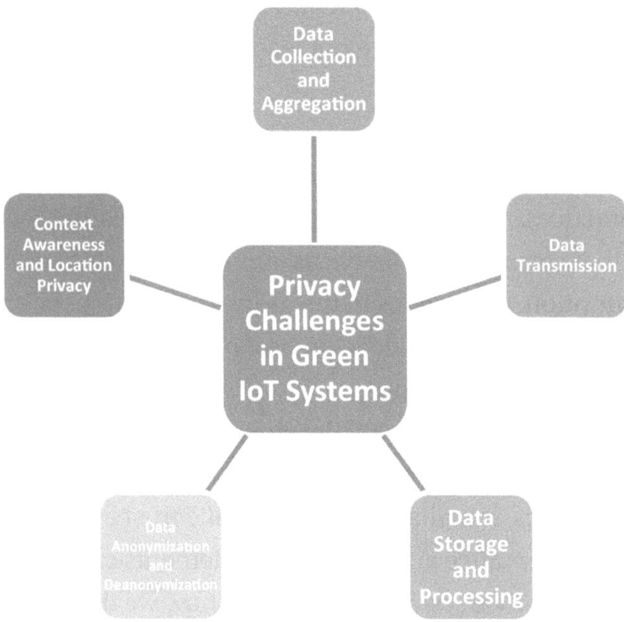

Figure 11-5. *Privacy challenges in Green IoT systems*

Figure 11-5 highlights to the main privacy issues related to Green IoT. The issues include areas of functionality such as data processing vulnerabilities, data storage vulnerabilities, and data transmission vulnerabilities, where networks allow transmission across open wireless channels. Potential solutions must be devised for these areas, especially because Green IoT is focused on securing sensitive and personal data.

Data collection and aggregation:

- Green IoT systems continuously collect vast amounts of data from sensors and devices, including personal and environmental data.

- Aggregating this data can reveal sensitive information about individuals or organizations.
- Lack of clear data ownership policies can lead to disputes over data control and misuse, especially when multiple stakeholders are involved.

Data transmission:

- Wireless communication protocols (e.g., ZigBee, Bluetooth, and LPWAN) transmit data over public and shared networks.
- Attackers can intercept transmissions and gain unauthorized access to personal or confidential information.
- Weak encryption or outdated protocols can make transmitted data vulnerable to eavesdropping and man-in-the-middle (MITM) attacks.

Data storage and processing:

- Collected data is often stored on centralized servers or cloud platforms.
- A single point of compromise can expose massive amounts of data.
- Insufficient access control measures can result in unauthorized data modification, deletion, or leakage.

Data anonymization and de-anonymization:

- Anonymizing data is essential to protect user identities.
- However, attackers can use advanced analytics or data correlation techniques to de-anonymize seemingly anonymized data.

- Inadequate anonymization practices can inadvertently leave data vulnerable to re-identification through cross-referencing with external data sources.

Context awareness and location privacy:

- Green IoT frequently collects contextual data, such as location data, usage habits, and environmental conditions.
- Inference attacks could exploit location or contextual data to develop insights about individual habits and routines.
- If location data from Green IoT is combined with timestamps and behavioral patterns, very dangerous daily routines can be exposed.

Privacy Requirements for Green IoT Systems

To keep users' trust intact and comply with privacy laws and regulations, the Green IoT system must meet the following requirements.

Data minimization:

- Collect only enough data required to ensure that the Green IoT system is working correctly.
- The less data that a Green IoT system collects in any format, the lower the risk to privacy.
- It is essential to have an automated way to delete all unnecessary or unwanted data at periods, including redundant data.
- Adopt edge computing to perform data processing locally, thus reducing the need to transmit raw data to centralized servers.

Consent and transparency:

- Users must be informed about what data is being collected, how it will be used, and for how long it will be retained.
- Providing clear and easily understandable privacy policies is essential.
- Regularly update users about any changes to data collection practices or policy updates.
- Offer users granular consent options to select which data they are willing to share and under what conditions.

Anonymization and pseudonymization:

- Remove or replace personal identifiers with pseudonyms before storing or processing the data.
- Use methods such as k-anonymity or differential privacy to make the data less linkable.
- Consider pseudonymization with multiple pillars, so that there are both dynamic and randomly changing pseudonyms.
- Consider multi-layer anonymization to protect the data while in different points of processing or transferring.

Data integrity and confidentiality:

- Protect the data against unauthorized access, modification, or disclosure by using encryption and digital signatures.
- Use encryption methods that are lightweight in order to promote energy efficiency.

- Implement secure key management practices to protect against unauthorized decryption.
- Continuously review data access logs to monitor for and respond to suspicious activity in real time.

User control:

- Empower users to manage their data, including viewing, editing, or deleting collected information.
- Implement privacy dashboards for users to configure their data preferences.
- Provide users with the ability to opt out of data collection or anonymize their data upon request.
- Allow users to export their data in a secure and standardized format, ensuring data portability.

Privacy-Preserving Techniques in Green IoT Systems

Differential privacy:

- Add manageable aggregate noise to data to protect against the identification of individual users while preserving aggregate information.
- Noise equipment can be used for smart city applications where statistical data analysis is critical.

Homomorphic encryption:

- Enable computation on encrypted data, while preserving data privacy even while processing data.
- Excellent for energy recourse in grids, as data can be processed in place.

Federated learning:

- All data stays on the devices it is produced on and models are trained collaboratively across the local devices without sending raw data. Just the model updates are sent.
- Reduces the exposure of data, as it never leaves the local device; also keeps network data low (and so, energy consumption low).

Blockchain and decentralization:

- Store data in a decentralized manner to avoid single points of failure.
- Blockchain ledgers can ensure data integrity while giving users more control over their information.

Secure multi-party computation (SMPC):

- Allows multiple parties to jointly compute a function over their inputs without revealing them.
- Useful for collaborative Green IoT applications like energy sharing among smart homes.

Privacy in Specific Green IoT Applications

Smart homes:

- Collecting data on energy consumption, occupancy, and device usage can infringe on personal privacy.
- Implementing anonymized data aggregation and local data processing can minimize risks.

Smart cities:

- Public data collection, such as traffic monitoring and pollution tracking, may inadvertently expose personal information.
- Differential privacy techniques can help mitigate these risks.

Smart agriculture:

- Data on soil conditions, crop health, and environmental factors may include sensitive business information.
- Where possible, it is critical to develop secure system communication channels that encrypt the channel, thereby limiting data sharing and at the same time keeping the data confidential.

Smart grids:

- Information about real-time energy use could imply something about household behavior.
- Encrypting the data over the communication channel, via way of residual energy consumption output (specifically, homomorphic encryption and secure data communication protocols) will protect user information.

Privacy Regulation Compliance

Green IoT systems must comply with international data protection regulations, such as:

- **General Data Protection Regulation (GDPR):** Mandates data minimization, user consent, and the right to access or delete personal data.
- **California Consumer Privacy Act (CCPA):** Grants users the right to know what data is collected and opt out of its sale.
- **Data privacy frameworks:** Including ISO/IEC 27701, which provides guidelines for data protection and privacy management.

Future Directions and Research

- **Privacy-aware energy management:** Developing models that would optimize energy consumption while still protecting user information.
- **AI-driven privacy enhancements:** Using ML to identify and deal with privacy breaches in "real" time.
- **Privacy-first architecture design:** Each of the preceding represents potential opportunities to ensure that privacy by design is embedded in Green IoT systems from the beginning, to mitigate risk from the start.

In summary, privacy and energy efficiency should be integral considerations in the design and management of Green IoT systems, and we have learned that bringing these two goals together is not an easy task and must be addressed from many different angles. Privacy-preserving approaches (e.g., differentially privacy, homomorphic encryption, federated learning, etc.) could address the privacy risk of a Green IoT application while keeping the same functionality and efficiency. In addition, if the user knows there is a regulatory framework around ethical and responsible data management practices, this will increase trust.

Privacy Concerns in Green IoT Systems

Here are a number of key privacy challenges associated with Green IoT applications:

- **Data breaches and accidental disclosure:** Compromised forms of communicating or not taking into account how the data can be stored can lead to disclosing personal information or usage patterns. Anonymizing data and using data encryption techniques effectively can mitigate privacy implications.
- **Data ownership and data control:** Typically, with Green IoT applications users don't always know if they have control over how their data is collected, stored, and shared. A trust mechanism that includes user consent and control, as well as allowing users to manage their data, is important.
- **Profiling and surveillance:** Once data is aggregated, it can often be used for profiling and surveillance purposes. This has the potential to violate privacy rights. Environment regulations, such as GDPR and others, are designed to protect user data.
- **Contextual privacy challenges:** Green IoT systems operate in various contexts, ranging from homes to industry. Privacy challenges depend on contextual aspects, necessitating newer or adaptive privacy policies and controls.

Mitigation Strategies

This section provides some suggested mitigation strategies for dealing with security and privacy risks in Green IoT systems. These strategies, outlined in Figure 11-6, can be utilized together, and if executed in a holistic manner, can strengthen the adaptability and resilience of a Green IoT system to new threats while still maintaining sustainability.

Figure 11-6. *Mitigation strategies*

The challenges pertaining to securing Green IoT and security for greener IoT systems are summarized in Figure 11-6. These methodologies, which are discussed in detail in the following sections, seek to achieve a balance between high security and success over the long-term.

Lightweight Cryptography

The challenges of using a reliable cryptographic method while conserving device resources in Green IoT systems is significant. Typical cryptographic methods, such as RSA, are very thorough but also computationally expensive, making them unsuitable for low-power IoT devices. To address these limitations, the following lightweight cryptographic technologies are suggested:

- **Elliptic curve cryptography (ECC):** ECC provides a higher level of security than RSA but with significantly smaller key sizes, which reduces computational complexity and energy consumption.
- **Lightweight block ciphers:** Lightweight block ciphers, such as PRESENT and SPECK, were specifically designed for low-power devices. LIGHTWEIGHT BLOCK CIPHERS provide efficient encrypted data while maintaining a sufficient level of security.
- **Homomorphic encryption:** Homomorphic encryption allows users to run computations on encrypted data without needing to decrypt it. This ensures that any data confidentiality is preserved, even while analyzing data in the post-collection process.
- **Efficient key management:** Hierarchical key distribution with renewal processes produce less computation and stronger security.

Privacy-Preserving Data Aggregation

Data aggregation will be required in any Green IoT system to minimize transmitted data and reduce energy use. Aggregating data without sufficient privacy measures risks exposing sensitive information. Therefore, privacy-preserving technologies will also need to be incorporated into the data aggregation process:

- **Differential privacy:** Insert some amount of calibrated noise into an aggregation of similar type data to protect individual input data from being exposed while making accurate overall conclusions.
- **Secure multi-party computation (SMPC):** SMPC allows parties to process data without revealing the raw data of any individual party so the individual level of privacy is protected even after sharing for collaborative analysis.
- **Data anonymization and pseudonymization:** Mask or replace personally identifiable information (PII) prior to collection. This will reduce the risk of exposing user privacy during data collection and aggregation.
- **Compressed sensing methods:** Reduce the amount of data while keeping the essential information, resulting in the reduction of the energy consumption and improving the protection of the data.

Adaptive authentication mechanisms

Static authentication methods are insufficient in dynamic IoT environments. Adaptive authentication mechanisms bolster security by continually assessing context and risk of use interactions:

- **Context-aware authentication:** Allow information from environmental and behavioral factors (e.g., device location, usage behaviors, your network state) to affect the authentication strength dynamically.

- **Multi-factor authentication (MFA):** Add any number of factors of authentication, including biometric verification, device authentication, and user credentials while accounting for energy capacity.
- **Biometric-based authentication:** A low-power method for identity verification through low-power biometric sensors. This provides quick access not only to the application, but is also good practice.
- **Risk-based authentication:** Alter and relax the authentication requirement based on the perceived levels of risk. The goal is to minimize computational burden during low risk interactions.

Decentralized Security Models

Centralized security methods use a single point of failure that could lead to tremendous risk should it be compromised. Decentralized security models using blockchain and distributed ledger technology (DLT) are another means of collective reliability. They improve data integrity and trust without subjectively determining a trusted base of data. There is no single entity:

- **Blockchain-based authentication:** Redundant and distributed spreadsheets storing credentials of authentication. Independent and redundant storage provides a double-edged sword and leads to data improved integrity.
- **Smart contracts:** Automate implementation of security policies, protocols, and authentication on blockchain to reduce reliance on humans, therefore reducing human errors.

- **Distributed trust models:** Again, instead of a centralized authentication, the use of a peer-to-peer chain of trust increases fault tolerance and builds a resilient chain of trust.
- **Consensus protocols:** Using energy-efficient blockchain consensus protocols (e.g., PoS, DPoS, etc.) can ensure security without additional energy use.

Security by Design

It is essential to incorporate security during the design phase of Green IoT systems to ensure that these architectures have built-in resilience when initially developed. Security by design helps the designer prevent potential future threats and allows for a comprehensive resilience strategy moving forward:

- **Threat models:** Identify attack vectors, threat vulnerabilities, and attack surfaces early on to incorporate security.
- **Secure coding standards:** Develop coding standards and guidelines to reduce or mitigate vulnerabilities pre-implementation. This limits the possibility of security issues.
- **Device hardening:** Reduce attack surfaces by disabling nonessential services and shutting down nonessential open ports.
- **End-to-end encryption:** Protect data confidentiality in transit and at rest by utilizing encryption protocols such as TLS or DTLS.

Dynamic Risk Assessment

Green IoT systems are designed to work in unstructured environments with a dynamic landscape of rapidly changing security risks. The use of continuous and ongoing risk assessment strategies to detect threats and vulnerabilities in real time provides significant value:

- **ML to detect threats:** Train ML models to detect abnormal patterns and potential intrusion with the use of real-time and historical data.
- **Anomaly detection systems:** Utilize complex algorithms to detect deviations in network behavior.
- **Real-time monitoring and analytics:** Continuously monitor and analyze device and network activity to identify and mitigate threats proactively.
- **Risk-scoring tools:** Score devices and activity in a way that creates an alternative risk path that allows mitigation to recookies when it is unclear what the threats are.

Automated Firmware Updates

It is vital to ensure that device firmware is always up to date in order to support ongoing security, which is implied in the patching of security vulnerabilities. Automated and secure update solutions help maintain your updates without human intervention:

- **Secure update protocols:** Using signed and encrypted update packages prevents and detects tampering.
- **Over-the-air (OTA) updates:** Offer OTA update capabilities to update devices, thereby avoiding human involvement, reducing maintenance costs, and limiting device downtime.

- **Rollback mechanisms:** Allow devices to revert to previous firmware version if an update fails or does not restore a prior level of stability.

Collaboration and Standardization

Green IoT systems leverage collaboration among manufacturers, researchers, and policymakers. Developing consistent security structures with standardization can help secure many devices and platforms:

- **Industry collaboration:** Create a collaborative environment for stakeholders by creating and implementing best practices for secure and Green IoT systems.
- **Comply with standards:** Use formal standards such as ISO/IEC 27001 and NIST guidelines when securing IoT devices and hosts.
- **Security audits and penetration testing:** Conduct regular assessments of your vulnerabilities and strategies for validating completed security efforts.

User Awareness and Training

The human element of Green IoT systems can also significantly affect security and the location of strategies for securing technology. You can reduce the risk of inadvertent harm or risk due to a lack of knowledge by training users and administrators in a number of ways:

- **Training:** Provide training on information systems regularly as part of a stakeholder education process on cybersecurity threats and mitigation.

- **Education as a component of awareness:** Encourage and reinforce security strategies such as changing passwords and recognizing phishing.
- **Security solutions considered with stakeholders:** Have security solutions in a user interface style that provides an advantage. This is done by minimizing potential for misconfigurations or mistaken actions.

Incident Response and Recovery Planning

Even when security threats are adequately contained, data breaches and cyberattacks may still occur. Existence of a well-defined incident response and recovery plan can limit the damage and enable the organization to use their extensions of Green IoT systems earlier.

- **Incident detection:** Use automated monitoring systems to identify potential security breaches in real time.
- **Response protocols:** Develop step-by-step procedures for containing and responding to security incidents, such as isolating affected devices and sandboxing analysis of attack vectors.
- **Data backup and recovery:** Backup important data on a regular basis and restore it quickly in the event of lost or corrupted data.
- **Incident analysis:** Sort through the incident to identify the cause and lessons learned, with the goal of improving overall security practices in the future.
- **Ongoing improvements:** Update response plans regularly as a result of changing threats and lessons learned from previous incidents.

Implementing these comprehensive mitigation strategies will allow Green IoTs to achieve additional security and privacy without compromising energy efficiency. Security and sustainability require multi-faceted solutions that take into account technology and people. Future research and innovation to develop secure and sustainable IoT solutions will be critical for developing sustainable ecosystems that help mitigate future threats and protect the environment

Future Directions

Future research in security and privacy within the Green IoT ecosystem will focus on integration of advanced technologies such as AI-driven threat detection, cryptographic techniques that are quantum-resistant, and resilient blockchain structures. The Green IoT ecosystem will likely be proactively addressed with advanced technologies and solutions to solve difficult, dynamic, and sophisticated security problems. Collaboratively, researchers, practitioners, and regulators must draft international standards and frameworks that will be operationalized and updated to account for evolving threats and threats based on novel technologies.

Advancements in AI-based anomaly detection with ML use algorithms to analyze behavior of people and things connected to the Internet. As a result, AI-based anomaly detectors can identify suspicious behavior patterns in real time and point to the possibility of a cyberattack. The anomaly detector learns about each entity with combinations of supervised learning and unsupervised methods (e.g., clustering, classification, regression). As a result, the algorithm can identify known and anticipated behaviors and likely anomalies. In the context of federated learning, the significant added benefit of privacy is ensured as raw data is never shared to conduct cooperative model training.

Another future consideration must be quantum resistant cryptography. Clearly there is a strong likelihood that quantum computing technologies will evolve quickly and thus pose a threat to interoperability in Green IoT environments when they can actualize the attacks on traditional cryptographic algorithms such as RSA or ECC. Being able to integrate cryptographic techniques that are quantum-resistant (i.e., lattice-based, hash-based, etc.) will be helpful to the longevity of security in Green IoT environments. Further, hybrid cryptographic frameworks that have both classical and quantum safe algorithms can converge in functionality as transitional security technologies as quantum matures.

Robust blockchain architectures are also essential to support data integrity and trust management in Green IoT systems. Future research should improve blockchain protocols' scalability and energy-efficiency to align with sustainability objectives in Green IoT. For example, using lightweight consensus mechanisms like Proof of Authority (PoA) or Directed Acyclic Graphs (DAGs) with less computational composite, and maintaining valid, reliable data. Further potential research opportunities related to ZKPs may look to other implications of ZKPs with regard to protecting confidentiality of data while also being able to demonstrate truthfulness in a transparent and accountable way, essentially combining accountability with preserving user data privacy.

Future investigations should work on allowing space for scalable, adaptive modes of operations based on 6G communications and quantum computing. As 6G provides ultra-low latency and large-scale connectivity, enabling a secure Green IoT system through dynamic network segmentation utilizing paradigms of network slicing and software defined networking (SDN) will be extremely important. Moreover, it will be beneficial to incorporate fog and edge computing into Green IoT architectures to reduce latencies and improve security and privacy aspects. This will keep the data closer to where it is generated, which is crucial in terms of environmental impact.

In addition, the field of Green IoT must also deal with serious global issues, such as data sovereignty, regulatory compliance, and cross-border data sharing. These must be addressed as security and privacy issues and in particular within the context of respective international efforts. Green IoT research should focus on developing innovative privacy-preserving data sharing frameworks that respect local and international regulations, including existing practical regulations such as the GDPR and others. Working farmers should also collaborate with multiple growers, policymakers, developers, and industry stakeholders to ensure wherever feasible that regulatory frameworks keep pace with technology changes.

In addition, future research should incorporate socio-technical aspects of Green IoT security such as user awareness and ethics, while taking into account the creation of user-friendly interfaces, secure configurations, and mechanisms that support best practices with the aim of reducing human error and security breaches. Indirectly, ethnographic and human-centric studies can highlight where user knowledge fails, and therefore pinpoint areas for design that support understanding and user-friendly security.

In summary, an interdisciplinary and broader approach to future research on Green IoT security and privacy must be taken. The challenge is to combine new and upcoming technologies with ethics and regulation. By taking action and focusing on the identifiable challenges we face with next-generation technologies, and creating data flows across borders for better information sharing, researchers and practitioners alike may be able to address new challenges and build resilient Green IoT ecosystems driven by sustainability, sociability, and security. All this while also being considerate and responsible to the environment.

Conclusion

Green IoT systems are an exciting opportunity for integrating ecological sustainability and advanced technology solutions. This evolving Green IoT space will ultimately depend on the security and privacy required to foster user trust and to sustain data integrity and longevity. The convergence of low-power communication protocols, low-power data processing, and other eco-friendly parameters provides a substantial opportunity for reducing carbon footprint with highly reliable connectivity. Developing context-based authentication mechanisms, privacy-preserving approaches for the data aggregation phase of Green IoT systems, and more lightweight cryptographic protocols, can greatly strengthen Green IoT security while enhancing sustainability.

The most critical aspect of Green IoT security is building resilient architectural designs that consume less energy but can withstand hostile attacks. This will require a shift from traditional security models to lightweight and adaptable frameworks. Providing context-aware authentication methods, privacy-preserving mechanisms for the data aggregation process, and lightweight cryptographic protocols can greatly enhance Green IoT security while maintaining sustainability.

In addition, cross-industry collaboration would be necessary to align security standards and security best practices. Stakeholders must implement a global policy so that there will be a set of common practices for securely storing data and implementing cybersecurity and environmental policy. Regulators, academia, organizations, and technologists should collectively develop a strategic plan to help balance security and sustainability, despite the difficulties imposed. This initiative is necessary to help clarify key issues related to data sovereignty, global data flows, and regulatory compliance, so that secure and interoperable Green IoT ecosystems can be developed.

Helping users incorporate security practices is also critical. Regular training sessions and awareness campaigns will help users adopt better practices and behavior and encourage them to take all the appropriate secure actions. Housing users in their own space, with friendly interfaces that maximize accessibility, will help them carry out security practices and in turn minimize human mistakes.

Ongoing research into next-generation technologies like quantum computing, AI ML-based security analytics, and blockchain enabled provenance will be important in framing the security design space for future Green IoTs. Quantum-resistant cryptographic systems and AI-enabled anomaly detection systems will help secure against sophisticated cyberthreats, and distributed model-based blockchain will provide users the means to trust the integrity and authenticity of the data. It is certain that with 6G networks and edge computing, adaptable security models must be adopted, with the importance of providing users optimal resources.

Moreover, sustainability and security cannot be seen as separate goals, but need to be pursued in parallel. Only then could the solutions be holistic to improve the environment and the digital space. Security protocols can be designed for energy efficiency, with intelligent power management and energy efficiency maintaining a secure Green IoT framework that is environmentally friendly.

Moreover, Green IoT infrastructures require continuous metrics and monitoring to ensure their efficiency. This could include risk assessment tools that completely automate adoption security guidelines and regular and specific penetration source tests to identify any vulnerabilities and provide the opportunity for security changes.

Moreover, predictive analytics could also be utilized to determine potential threats and allow organizations to start responding to threats before they occur. By addressing many of the major challenges originating from security, Green IoT can lead to a sustainable and secure connectivity. Continued research, sharing of best practices with industry stakeholders, and appropriate global policy frameworks will all be required to build sustainable Green IoT that resist threats and is robust and viable. Technology has never progressed so quickly in the digital landscape. Therefore, proactive thinking around security and privacy is required to positively engage in a future whereby Green IoT can sustain systems that positively contribute to environmental and societal well-being.

CHAPTER 12

Scalable Solutions for Large-Scale IoT Networks

There has been an exponential growth in the number of IoT devices inside IoT networks. This growth requires scalable, efficient, and resilient networks. These requirements are needed to manage the large volume of data, connectivity, and computational issues. This chapter presents a detailed analysis of scalable methods in IoT networks.

There are six scalable approaches in IoT networks—distributed computing architectures, low-power communication technologies, network virtualization, big data analytics, security frameworks, and energy-efficient designs. With the proper use of edge and fog computing, LPWANs, SDN/NFV, AI-driven data analytics, blockchain-based trust models, and sustainable energy strategies, IoT networks are delivering optimal performance, minimal latency, and high resilience. These scalable solutions are applicable across various application domains. The application areas of IoT include smart cities, transportation, healthcare, smart homes, agriculture, industry 4.0, and other critical infrastructure.

The studies in this chapter highlight the crucial role of coordination among infrastructure, protocols, and data intelligence in supporting the rapidly evolving IoT ecosystem while maintaining scalability, security, and

Dr. D. Sharma and Dr. B. Pandey, *Eco-Networking for IoT*,
https://doi.org/10.1007/979-8-8688-2317-6_12

sustainability. Including distributed computing architectures, low-power communication technologies, and network virtualization ions for large-scale IoT networks is crucial for handling the massive number of devices, high data throughput, diverse applications, and dynamic environments.

The key scalable solutions and technologies that support efficient deployment, management, and operation of large-scale IoT networks include edge and fog computing, hierarchical network architectures, low power wide area networks, software-defined networking, network function virtualization, scalable data management data lakes and distributed databases, and efficient communication protocols such as MQTT, CoAP, AMQP, AI/ML for network optimization. In addition, IoT networks utilize predictive maintenance, traffic forecasting, anomaly detection, use of blockchain for decentralized IoT security and trust use-cases, device and identity management platforms, scalable device provisioning, energy harvesting, and low-power designs.

Edge computing processes data closer to the source (sensor/device), reducing latency and offloading traffic from the cloud. Fog computing serves as an intermediary layer between the edge and the cloud, facilitating distributed processing and storage. It reduces bandwidth usage, enhances real-time processing, and scales better than cloud-only approaches.

In a hierarchical network architecture, cluster-based models group devices into clusters, with cluster heads handling local aggregation and communication. Multi-tier frameworks are very helpful in managing communication hierarchies and distributing workloads efficiently, such as in smart city applications, where clusters manage traffic lights, waste management, and surveillance. Low-power wide area network (LPWAN) technologies, such as LoRaWAN, NB-IoT, and Sigfox, offer several significant advantages. LPWANs are designed for low-power, long-range communication and support thousands of devices per gateway. The primary use-cases of low-power wide area networks include smart agriculture, utility metering, and asset tracking. Software defined networking (SDN) and its variant, Network Function Virtualization (NFV), provide centralized control over the network, enabling dynamic routing, load balancing, and policy enforcement. NFV virtualizes network services, enabling scalability without requiring changes to physical infrastructure. The major benefit of NFV is that it enhances flexibility, manageability, and scalability. The most popular examples of scalable data management solutions are Apache Hadoop, Apache Cassandra, and Amazon DynamoDB. Several stream-processing frameworks, including Apache Kafka, Apache Flink, and Spark Streaming, are primarily used for real-time analytics and decision-making.

Cloud-native storage automatically scales to accommodate the growing volume of IoT data. Efficient communication protocols, such as MQTT, CoAP, and AMQP, are lightweight protocols optimized for constrained devices and unreliable networks. HTTP/2 and QUIC enhance performance for resource-intensive applications. AI/ML is used for network optimization, predictive maintenance, traffic forecasting, and anomaly detection. AI improves network performance and resource allocation. Federated learning (FL) enables on-device model training, reducing data transfer and enhancing privacy. Blockchain is mainly used for decentralized IoT security and trust. Other use-cases of blockchain are device authentication, data integrity, and secure transactions. Other scalability solutions include layer-2 solutions (e.g., sidechains) and DAG-based blockchains, such as IOTA.

Device and identity management platforms have existing features for scalable device provisioning. They utilize platforms such as AWS IoT Core and Azure IoT Hub for secure onboarding and lifecycle management. Interoperability involves the adoption of open standards, such as oneM2M and OMA Lightweight M2M (LwM2M). Energy harvesting is possible with the help of low-power designs. This supports battery-less or long-life battery devices, which are crucial for scaling remote and massive IoT deployments. The most popular technologies related to energy harvesting are energy-efficient hardware, duty cycling, and adaptive transmission techniques. One group of researchers proposed a framework that integrates soft computing techniques for intrusion detection. Their research proposed a decentralized approach that shifted security to edge devices. These security approaches enable IoT networks to maintain efficient security without overutilizing resources.[1]

Researchers also provided a comprehensive review and design of a water supply system. They used Ethernet, Wi-Fi 802.11n, and Modbus. The integration of these communication protocol enabled scalable and flexible connectivity across diverse IoT devices deployed in an Italian cyber-range emulator. Their research highlights the importance of interoperability and scalability in IoT networks.[2] Pandey, B. K. (2019)[3] researchers focused on a scalable training environment for a water supply system within the Turin node of Italian cyber-ranges. Their emulator supports the testing and validation of a large-scale IoT water supply system. Their research emphasized the modularity and scalability of simulation environments to simulate real IoT network complexities.[3] Hasan, M. K., et al. (2021) [4] also introduced a smart IoT-based electricity monitoring system that utilizes IoT data to optimize power consumption. Their solution demonstrates scalable data-collection techniques that can handle different distributed sensors and actuators. Both large-scale data integration and real-time control were essential for a scalable IoT architecture in smart grid applications.[4] Hasan, M. K., et al. (2021)[5] explore lightweight cryptographic algorithms customized for complex IoT applications for guessing attacks. Their work contributes to scalable IoT network security by proposing computationally efficient cryptographic solutions. These cryptographic solutions are suitable for resource-constrained devices in IoT networks. Ensuring security without sacrificing scalability is a major requirement of large-scale IoT networks.[5]

Distributed Computing and Network Architectures

Edge and fog computing reduce both latency and bandwidth by processing data near the source. Hierarchical structures use either multi-tier or cluster-based models to manage communication in IoT networks. Researchers in Bittencourt, L., et al (2018)[6] introduced fog computing, which extends cloud capabilities to the edge to overcome latency and bandwidth constraints in IoT environments.[6] They also present a reference architecture spanning physical devices, fog nodes, and cloud data centers, enabling low-latency, geographically distributed services and highlighting key characteristics such as virtualization, mobility support, and proximity-aware processing. Dastjerdi, A. V., et al. (2016)[7] identify orchestration, resource management, task offloading, and heterogeneous quality of service expectations as core challenges in large-scale deployments. Prieto, J. (2018)[8] emphasizes the trade-offs between communication and computation, and the necessity of load balancing across edge devices. They discuss the limitations of fully centralized (cloud-only) models and advocate for distributed computing via fog/edge layers to reduce bandwidth, enforce latency constraints, and enable near-sensor analytics.[8] Thiruchadai Pandeeswari, S., et al. (2020)[9] explore auto-scaling, task offloading, and container-based deployment strategies in fog architectures to dynamically adapt to changing demand and resource availability. Hamdan, S., et al. (2020)[10] review data-placement strategies in fog/edge environments, such as IFogStorM, which partitions and places data replicas close to consumers to reduce latency. The comparative insights are shown in Table 12-1. These approaches reduce both latency and bandwidth by processing data closer to low-power communication technologies.

LoRaWAN, NB-IoT, and Sigfox are LPWAN technologies. These LPWAN technologies cover a wide area and provide low-power connectivity for large deployments. Lightweight protocols, such as MQTT, CoAP, and

AMQP, optimize communication for constrained devices. SDN and NFV enable the dynamic allocation and virtualization of network functions to ensure scalability. Device management guarantees secure onboarding and interoperability across either AWS IoT Core or Azure IoT Hub. Scalable and low-power communication technologies play a crucial role in enabling the efficient and widespread deployment of IoT networks. LPWAN offers energy-efficient long-range communication, making it ideal for IoT devices powered by batteries.[11] Scalability becomes a challenge when the number of connected devices increases significantly. The latest research has proposed dynamic spreading factor allocation, optimized channel usage, and collision avoidance mechanisms to enhance the capacity and performance of LoRaWAN.[12] Hybrid communication architectures are also emerging as promising solutions. This hybrid architecture is integrating long-range protocols such as LoRa with short-range ones. The hybrid approach provides power-efficient networks to improve scalability and energy efficiency.[13] These hybrid mesh structures intelligently distribute traffic, minimizing power consumption while maintaining reliable connectivity. Real-world deployments have validated the effectiveness of such designs in IoT networks. IoT networks are expanding. At the same time, scalable communication technologies are evolving to support millions of devices without compromising latency, energy consumption, or cost.

Scalable Data Handling and Analytics

To combine scalable data management and AI/ML for optimization, big data platforms use distributed databases and streaming tools like Apache Kafka and Spark for high-volume IoT data. AI/ML enable intelligent analytics, anomaly detection, and predictive maintenance for network optimization. Federated learning allows local model training, reducing communication overhead and preserving privacy. Scalable data architectures for IoT require robust pipelines that ingest, process, and analyze high-volume, heterogeneous sensor data.

Nuthalapati, A. (2023)[14] proposed a scalable data lake framework that utilizes Hadoop for distributed storage, Kafka for real-time ingestion, and Spark for data processing and deep learning. They proposed an architecture that enables CNN-LSTM and GRU models to give predictive accuracy while maintaining efficient storage and computation.[14]

Dang-Ha, T. H., et al. (2017)[15] introduced the Graph of Virtual Actors (GOVA) for IoT applications such as smart grids. GOVA addresses real-world “noninvariants” in IoT by organizing computation through a graph model. GOVA enables horizontal scaling in computation, caching, data storage, and programmability.[15]

Nguyen, D. C., et al. (2021)[16] explored federated learning for IoT analytics. They enabled AI training across distributed devices without centralizing raw data. Their approach supports scalability in large IoT networks and preserves privacy. Their novel approach is also applicable to various applications, including crowd-sensing, localization, and anomaly detection.[16]

Security, Privacy, and Trust

Blockchain guarantees integrity, decentralized authentication, and secure data sharing. The blockchain-based enhanced security models employ scalable encryption, access control, and trusted execution environments. The scaling in IoT networks introduces significant security, privacy, and trust issues. A zero-trust security framework tailored explicitly for 5G-enabled IoT emphasizes identity authentication, least-privilege access control, continuous device health monitoring, and dynamic policy enforcement to mitigate threats across millions of devices.[17]

Trust-based blockchain authorization leverages a decentralized attribute-based access control model integrated with a trust and reputation system. This enables flexible and dynamic authorization decisions, as well as scalable identity management without central bottlenecks.[18] For large-scale IoT deployments, Trust2Vec utilizes signed network embeddings and community detection to identify clusters of malicious nodes, thereby combating large-scale trust attacks, such as self-promotion and bad-mouthing, with up to 94% mitigation effectiveness in simulations.[19] Altogether, these approaches address device authentication, evolving trustworthiness, dynamic and decentralized policy enforcement, and scalable threat mitigation. They represent emerging paradigms that blend zero-trust, decentralized authorization, and graph-based trust analytics to secure large-scale IoT ecosystems.

Conclusion

IoT networks are expanding. Scalability is becoming a basic requirement for efficient network operation. The integration of edge and fog computing is reducing latency in IoT networks. Both hierarchical network structures and LPWAN technologies are becoming the backbone for efficient communication in IoT networks. SDN is adding flexibility and helping with dynamic resource allocation. This SDN feature supports diverse and growing device populations. When scalable data management is combined with AI and ML, the IoT network gains real-time insights and network optimization. Blockchain and decentralized trust models are increasing security and reliability across distributed nodes in IoT networks. At the same time, energy-efficient designs and energy harvesting ensure the long-term operability of devices in the IoT network. The proper use of all these solutions delivers a holistic path for addressing the technical and operational complexities of large-scale IoT networks.

Future Scope

The future of scalable IoT networks will be decided by the integration of AI, automation, security, and decentralized architectures. 6G and quantum communication will introduce ultra-reliable, low-latency connectivity in IoT networks. There is scope for integrating AI at the network edge to enable autonomous decision-making, adaptive routing, fault detection, and real-time optimization in IoT networks. Above all, federated learning and homomorphic encryption will be used for secure data handling in IoT networks. Self-sustaining sensors and biodegradable electronics will support large-scale IoT infrastructures in the future. Eventually, the emergence of digital twins and cyber-physical systems will transform the current architecture of IoT networks. These future developments will transform the current IoT networks into intelligent and self-managing ecosystems.

References

Chapter 1

[1] Farhan, L., Hameed, R. S., Ahmed, A. S., Fadel, A. H., Gheth, W., Alzubaidi, L., ... & Al-Amidie, M. (2021). Energy efficiency for green internet of things (IoT) networks: A survey. *Network, 1*(3), 279-314.

[2] Ashton, K. (2009). That 'Internet of Things' Thing. *RFID Journal*, 22(7), 97–114.

[3] Atzori, L., Iera, A., & Morabito, G. (2010). The Internet of Things: A Survey. *Computer Networks*, 54(15), 2787–2805.

[4] Baccarelli, E., Naranjo, P. G. V., Scarpiniti, M., Shojafar, M., & Abawajy, J. H. (2017). Fog of Everything: Energy-Efficient Networked Computing Architectures, Research Challenges, and a Case Study. *IEEE Access*, 5, 9882–9910.

[5] Cisco. (2020). Cisco Annual Internet Report (2018–2023) White Paper. Cisco Systems.

[6] Forbes, G. (2017). The IoT in Plain English. *Technopedia Journal*, 11(2), 75–82.

[7] Hu, Y., & Verma, A. (2021). Green Networking for IoT: A Survey. *IEEE Access*, 9, 11234–11249.

Dr. D. Sharma and Dr. B. Pandey, *Eco-Networking for IoT*,
https://doi.org/10.1007/979-8-8688-2317-6

[8] Moghaddam, M., Bourque, J. B., & Salois, M. (2022). Energy-Efficient Networking for IoT Systems. *Journal of Green Computing*, 23(4), 215–229.

[9] Zanella, A., Bui, N., Castellani, A., Vangelista, L., & Zorzi, M. (2014). Internet of Things for Smart Cities. *IEEE Internet of Things Journal*, 1(1), 22–32.

Chapter 2

[1] Meo, Michela, Esther Le Rouzic, Ruben Cuevas, and Carmen Guerrero. "Research challenges on energy-efficient networking design." Computer Communications 50 (2014): 187-195.

[2] Cao, Xianghui, et al. "Towards energy-efficient wireless networking in the big data era: A survey." IEEE Communications Surveys & Tutorials 20.1 (2017): 303-332.

[3] S. Bi, R. Zhang, Z. Ding, and S. Cui, "Wireless communications in the era of big data," IEEE Commun. Mag., vol. 53, no. 10, pp. 190–199, Oct. 2015.

[4] Fischer, M. T. Beck, H. De Meer, and X. Hesselbach, "Virtual network embedding: A survey," IEEE Commun. Surveys Tuts., vol. 15, no. 4, pp. 1888–1906, Oct.–Dec. 2013.

[5] Nonde, Leonard, Taisir EH El-Gorashi, and Jaafar MH Elmirghani. "Energy efficient virtual network embedding for cloud networks." Journal of Lightwave Technology 33.9 (2014): 18281849.

[6] Malik, U.M.; Javed, M.A.; Zeadally, S.; ul Islam, S. Energy-Efficient Fog Computing for 6GEnabled Massive IoT: Recent Trends and Future Opportunities. IEEE Internet Things J. 2022, 9, 14572- 14594.

[7] Ghiasi, M.; Wang, Z.; Mehrandezh, M.; Jalilian, S.; Ghadimi, N. Evolution of smart grids towards the Internet of energy: Concept and essential components for deep decarbonisation. IET Smart Grid 2023, 6, 86–102.

[8] Fernando, Xavier, and George Lăzăroiu. "Energy-efficient industrial internet of things in green 6G networks." Applied Sciences 14.18 (2024): 8558.

[9] R Mahmud, R Kotagiri, R. Buyya, Fog computing: a taxonomy, survey and future directions, in: Internet of Everything, Springer, Singapore, 2018, pp. 103–130.

[10] F Bonomi, R Milito, J Zhu, S. Addepalli, Fog computing and its role in the internet of things, in: Proceedings of the First Edition of the MCC Workshop on Mobile Cloud Computing, 2012 Aug 17, pp. 13–16.

[11] AV Dastjerdi, R. Buyya, Fog computing: helping the Internet of Things realize its potential, Computer 49 (8) (2016 Aug 15) 112–116.

[12] Kaur, Loveleen, and Rajbir Kaur. "A survey on energy efficient routing techniques in WSNs focusing IoT applications and enhancing fog computing paradigm." Global transitions proceedings 2.2 (2021): 520-529.

[13] Alsharif, Mohammed H., et al. "A comprehensive survey of energy-efficient computing to enable sustainable massive IoT networks." Alexandria Engineering Journal 91 (2024): 12-29.

Chapter 3

[1] Kaur, N., & Sood, S. K. (2015). An energy-efficient architecture for the Internet of Things (IoT). *IEEE Systems Journal, 11*(2), 796-805.

[2] Rana, B., Singh, Y., & Singh, P. K. (2021). A systematic survey on the internet of things: Energy efficiency and interoperability perspective. *Transactions on Emerging Telecommunications Technologies, 32*(8), e4166.

[3] Musavi, S. H. A., Chowdhry, B. S., Kumar, T., Pandey, B., & Kumar, W. (2015). IoTs enable active contour modeling based energy efficient and thermal aware object tracking on FPGA. *Wireless Personal Communications, 85*, 529-543.

[4] Sharma, R., Bhasin, N., Sharma, S., Sharma, V., Das, B., & Abdullah, M. F. L. (2015, September). Time analysis based IOTs (Internet of Things) enable TeraHertz RAM design on 40nm FPGA. In *2015 International Conference on Signal Processing, Computing and Control (ISPCC)* (pp. 312-315). IEEE.

[5] Khanna, A., Das, B., Pandey, B., & Jain, V. (2016). A discussion about upgrading the quick script platform to create natural language based IoT systems. *Indian Journal of Science and Technology, 9*(46).

[6] Pandey, B. K., Hussain, D. A., & Levy, J. (2020). AI and FPGA-Based IoT Architectures, Models, and Platforms for Smart City Application. In *IoT Architectures, Models, and Platforms for Smart City Applications* (pp. 94-106). IGI Global.

[7] Baker, Y. A., Somanshu, C., & Keshav, K. (2020). Soil moisture and environmental temperature and humidity sensor-based data breaches in IoT enable irrigation system design using Arduino and FPGA. *Gyancity Journal of Engineering and Technology, 6*(2), 1-12.

[8] Kumar, A., Sharma, S., Goyal, N., Singh, A., Cheng, X., & Singh, P. (2021). Secure and energy-efficient smart building architecture with emerging technology IoT. *Computer Communications, 176,* 207-217.

[9] Alharbi, H. A., & Aldossary, M. (2021). Energy-efficient edge-fog-cloud architecture for IoT-based smart agriculture environment. *Ieee Access, 9,* 110480-110492.

[10] Mao, W., Zhao, Z., Chang, Z., Min, G., & Gao, W. (2021). Energy-efficient industrial Internet of Things: Overview and open issues. *IEEE transactions on industrial informatics, 17*(11), 7225-7237.

[11] Yashwant, A., Kumar, K., Pandey, P., Aldasheva, L., Konyrkhanova, A. A., Bakar, W. A. W. A., & Pandey, B. (2024). IoT, Cloud and AI Enable Sensor Based Water Monitoring to Handle Water Crisis in Indian Cities. *International Journal of Geoinformatics, 20*(5), 4-53.

[12] Plastras, S., Tsoumatidis, D., Skoutas, D. N., Rouskas, A., Kormentzas, G., & Skianis, C. (2024). Non-Terrestrial Networks for Energy-Efficient Connectivity of Remote IoT Devices in the 6G Era: A Survey. *Sensors, 24*(4), 1227.

[13] Alsharif, M. H., Kelechi, A. H., Jahid, A., Kannadasan, R., Singla, M. K., Gupta, J., & Geem, Z. W. (2024). A comprehensive survey of energy-efficient computing to enable sustainable massive IoT networks. *Alexandria Engineering Journal, 91*, 12-29.

[14] Chakraborty, C., Othman, S. B., Almalki, F. A., & Sakli, H. (2024). FC-SEEDA: Fog computing-based secure and energy efficient data aggregation scheme for Internet of healthcare Things. *Neural Computing and Applications, 36*(1), 241-257.

[15] Siyanwal, R., Agarwal, A., & Srirama, S. N. (2025). An energy efficient fog-based internet of things framework to combat wildlife poaching. *Sustainable Computing: Informatics and Systems, 45*, 101070.

[16] Almudayni, Z., Soh, B., Samra, H., & Li, A. (2025). Energy Inefficiency in IoT Networks: Causes, Impact, and a Strategic Framework for Sustainable Optimisation. *Electronics, 14*(1), 159.

[17] Hakiri, A., Sellami, B., & Yahia, S. B. (2025). Joint energy efficiency and network optimization for integrated blockchain-SDN-based internet of things networks. *Future Generation Computer Systems, 163*, 107519.

[18] Lau, C. H., & Chan, S. (2025). Comparison on resilience and energy efficiency of authentication schemes in IoT networks. *Expert Systems, 42*(1), e13603.

Chapter 4

[1] Pandey, B., & Kumar, R. (2013, April). Low voltage DCI-based low power VLSI circuit implementation on FPGA. In *2013 IEEE Conference on Information & Communication Technologies* (pp. 128-131). IEEE.

[2] Verma, G., Moudgil, A., Garg, K., & Pandey, B. (2015, March). Thermal and power-aware Internet of Things enables RAM design on FPGA. In *2015 2nd International Conference on Computing for Sustainable Global Development (INDIACom)* (pp. 1537-1540). IEEE.

[3] Kumar, P. V., Kulkarni, A., Mendhe, D., Keshar, D. K., Babu, S. B. T., & Rajesh, N. (2024, April). AI-Optimized Hardware Design for Internet of Things (IoT) Devices. In 2024 5th International Conference on Recent Trends in Computer Science and Technology (ICRTCST) (pp. 21-26). IEEE.

[4] Bekasiewicz, A. (2023). Optimisation of the hardware layer for IoT systems using a trust-region method with adaptive forward finite differences. IEEE Internet of Things Journal, 10(11), 9498-9512.

[5] Dutta, L., & Bharali, S. (2021). Tinyml meets iot: A comprehensive survey—Internet of Things, 16, 100461.

[6] Raval, M., Bhardwaj, S., Aravelli, A., Dofe, J., & Gohel, H. (2021). Smart energy optimisation for massive IoT using artificial intelligence. Internet of Things, 13, 100354.

[7] Prakash, C., Singh, L. P., Gupta, A., & Lohan, S. K. (2023). Advancements in smart farming: A comprehensive review of IoT, wireless communication, sensors, and hardware for agricultural automation. Sensors and Actuators A: Physical, 362, 114605.

[8] Loo, M. H. W., Ramiah, H., Lei, K. M., Lim, C. C., Lai, N. S., Mak, P. I., & Martins, R. P. (2022). Fully-integrated timers for ultra-low-power Internet-of-Things nodes—Fundamentals and design techniques. IEEE Access, 10, 65936-65950.

[9] Alajlan, N. N., & Ibrahim, D. M. (2022). TinyML: Enabling of inference deep learning models on ultra-low-power IoT edge devices for AI applications. Micromachines, 13(6), 851.

[10] Raval, M., Bhardwaj, S., Aravelli, A., Dofe, J., & Gohel, H. (2021). Smart energy optimisation for massive IoT using artificial intelligence. Internet of Things, 13, 100354.

[11] Sathish Kumar, L., Ahmad, S., Routray, S., Prabu, A. V., Alharbi, A., Alouffi, B., & Rajasoundaran, S. (2022). Modern energy optimisation approach for efficient data communication in IoT-based wireless sensor networks. Wireless Communications and Mobile Computing, 2022(1), 7901587.

[12] Ugwuanyi, S., Paul, G., & Irvine, J. (2021). Survey of IoT for developing countries: Performance analysis of LoRaWAN and cellular NB-IoT networks. Electronics, 10(18), 2224.

[13] Pooyandeh, M., & Sohn, I. (2021). Edge network optimization based on AI techniques: A survey. Electronics, 10(22), 2830.

[14] Surianarayanan, C., Lawrence, J. J., Chelliah, P. R., Prakash, E., & Hewage, C. (2023). A survey on optimisation techniques for edge artificial intelligence (AI). Sensors, 23(3), 1279.

[15] Chang, Y. H., Boukhobza, J., & Han, S. (2022). Introduction to the special issue on memory and storage systems for embedded and IoT applications. ACM Transactions on Embedded Computing Systems (TECS), 21(1), 1-4.

[16] Reddy, B. V., Chaudhary, T., Singh, M., & Raj, B. (2024). Ferroelectric Random Access Memory (FeRAM). Integrated Devices for Artificial Intelligence and VLSI, 125-156.

[17] Xie, H., Zheng, J., He, T., Wei, S., & Hu, C. (2023). TEBDS: A trusted execution environment-and-blockchain-supported IoT data sharing system. Future Generation Computer Systems, 140, 321-330.

[18] Cabrera-Gutiérrez, A. J., Castillo, E., Escobar-Molero, A., Álvarez-Bermejo, J. A., Morales, D. P., & Parrilla, L. (2022). Integration of hardware security modules and permissioned blockchain in industrial IoT networks. IEEE Access, 10, 114331-114345.

[19] Al-Meer, A., & Al-Kuwari, S. (2023). Physical unclonable functions (PUF) for IoT devices. ACM Computing Surveys, 55(14s), 1-31.

[20] Desbiens, F. (2022). Operating Systems. In Building Enterprise IoT Solutions with Eclipse IoT Technologies: An Open Source Approach to Edge Computing (pp. 243-267). Berkeley, CA: Apress.

[21] B. Pandey, Home Automation Security, 2024, ISBN 979-8304580113, Kindle Academic Publisher, `https://www.amazon.in/Home-Automation-Security-Bishwajeet-Pandey/dp/B0DRGBS2Z7`

Chapter 5

[1] Bayılmış, Cüneyt, et al. "A survey on communication protocols and performance evaluations for Internet of Things." Digital Communications and Networks 8.6 (2022): 1094-1104.

[2] Sobral, José VV, et al. "Routing protocols for low power and lossy networks in internet of things applications." Sensors 19.9 (2019): 2144.

[3] Perera, C.; Zaslavsky, A.; Christen, P.; Georgakopoulos, D. Context aware computing for the internet of things: A survey. IEEE Commun. Surv. Tutor. 2014, 16, 414–454.

[4] Watteyne, T.; Winter, T.; Barthel, D.; Dohler, M. Routing Requirements for Urban Low-Power and Lossy Networks; RFC 5548; IETF Secretariat: Fremont, CA, USA, 2009

[5] Martocci, J.; Mil, P.; Riou, N.; Vermeylen, W. Building Automation Routing Requirements in Low-Power and Lossy Networks; RFC 5867; IETF Secretariat: Fremont, CA, USA, 2010

[6] Zarpelão, B.B.; Miani, R.S.; Kawakani, C.T.; de Alvarenga, S.C. A survey of intrusion detection in Internet of Things. J. Netw. Comput. Appl. 2017, 84, 25–37.

[7] Sobral, José VV, et al. "LOADng-IoT: An enhanced routing protocol for internet of things applications over low power networks." Sensors 19.1 (2019): 150.

[8] Depedri, Andrea, Alberto Zanella, and Roberto Verdone. "An energy efficient protocol for wireless sensor networks." Proc. AINS (2003): 1-6.

Chapter 6

[1] Kodi, D. (2023). A Pythonic Approach to API Information Management: Fetching, Processing, and Displaying Data for Business Intelligence. *International Journal of Emerging Research in Engineering and Technology*, *4*(2), 33-42.

[2] Hu, T., Yang, S., Wang, Y., Li, G., Wang, Y., Wang, G., & Yin, M. (2023). N-Accesses: a blockchain-based access control framework for secure Internet of Things information management. Sensors, 23(20), 8535.

[3] Al-Ali, A. R., Gupta, R., Zualkernan, I., & Das, S. K. (2024). Role of IoT technologies in big information management systems: A review and Smart Grid case study. Pervasive and Mobile Computing, 101905.

[4] Bramantyo, H. A., Utomo, B. S., & Khusna, E. M. (2022). Data processing for IoT in oil and gas refineries. Journal of Telecommunication Network (Jurnal Jaringan Telekomunikasi), 12(1), 48-54.

[5] Ferreira, C. M. S., Garrocho, C. T. B., Oliveira, R. A. R., Silva, J. S., & Cavalcanti, C. F. M. D. C. (2021). IoT registration and authentication in innovative city applications with blockchain. *Sensors, 21*(4), 1323.

[6] Naghib, A., Jafari Navimipour, N., Hosseinzadeh, M., & Sharifi, A. (2023). A comprehensive and systematic literature review on the big information management techniques in the Internet of Things. Wireless Networks, 29(3), 1085-1144.

[7] Maurya, R., Nambiar, K. A., Babbe, P., Kalokhe, J. P., Ingle, Y. S., & Shaikh, N. F. (2021). Application of RESTful APIs in IoT: A review. Int. J. Res. Appl. Sci. Eng. Technol, 9(10.22214).

[8] Mishra, B., & Kertesz, A. (2020). The use of MQTT in M2M and IoT systems: A survey. Ieee Access, 8, 201071-201086

[9] Joshva Devadas, T., Thayammal, S., & Ramprakash, A. (2019). IoT data management, data aggregation and dissemination. In Principles of Internet of Things (IoT) ecosystem: insight paradigm (pp. 385-411). Cham: Springer International Publishing.

[10] Giambona, R., Redondi, A. E., & Cesana, M. (2018, October). MQTT+ enhanced syntax and broker functionalities for data filtering, processing and aggregation, in Proceedings of the 14th ACM International Symposium on quality of service and Security for Wireless and Mobile Networks (pp. 77-84).

[11] Martikkala, A., Lobov, A., Lanz, M., & Ituarte, I. F. (2021). Towards the interoperability of IoT platforms: a case study for data collection and data storage. IFAC-PapersOnLine, 54(1), 1138-1143.

[12] Alonso, Á., Fernández, F., Marco, L., & Salvachúa, J. (2017). Iaacaas: IoT application-scoped access control as a service. Future Internet, 9(4), 64.

[13] Oh, S. R., Kim, Y. G., & Cho, S. (2019). An interoperable access control framework for diverse IoT platforms based on OAuth and role. Sensors, 19(8), 1884.

[14] Khan, R., & Noor Mian, A. (2020). Sustainable IoT sensing applications are developed through the GraphQL-based abstraction layer. Electronics, 9(4), 564.

[15] Koutsimpogiorgos, G. (2023). Comparative analysis of SQL queries performance on vehicle sensor data in RDBMS and Apache Spark (Master's thesis, Πανεπιστήμιο Πειραιώς).

[16] Escarda-Fernández, M., López-Riobóo-Botana, I., Barro-Tojeiro, S., Padrón-Cousillas, L., Gonzalez-Vázquez, S., Carreiro-Alonso, A., & Gómez-Area, P. (2024). LLMs on the Fly: Text-to-JSON for Custom API Calling. Proceedings of the SEPLN-CEDI.

[17] Morlandstø, M. K. (2022). Prototyping and evaluation of sensor data integration in cloud platforms (Master's thesis, The University of Bergen).

Chapter 7

[1] Reddy, K. S. S., Manohara, M., Shailaja, K., Revathy, P., Kumar, T. M., & Premalatha, G. (2022). Power management using AI-based IOT systems. *Measurement: Sensors, 24,* 100551.

[2] Rochd, A., Benazzouz, A., Ait Abdelmoula, I., Raihani, A., Ghennioui, A., Naimi, Z., & Ikken, B. (2021). Design and implementation of an AI-based & IoT-enabled Home Energy Management System: A case study in Benguerir—Morocco. *Energy Reports, 7,* 699-719.

[3] Khan, N., Khan, S. U., Ullah, F. U. M., Lee, M. Y., & Baik, S. W. (2023). An AI-assisted hybrid approach for energy management in IoT-based smart microgrid. *IEEE Internet of Things Journal, 10*(21), 18861-18875.

[4] Raju, M. P., Sagar, E. S., & Laxmi, A. J. (2022). AI-powered IoT-based home energy management system for DG integration. *Procedia Computer Science, 215*, 846-855.

[5] Prasad, A., & Chawda, P. (2018, March). Power management factors and techniques for IoT design devices. In *2018 19th International Symposium on Quality Electronic Design (ISQED)* (pp. 364-369). IEEE.

[6] Stecyk, A., & Miciuła, I. (2023). Harnessing the power of artificial intelligence for collaborative energy optimisation platforms. Energies, 16(13), 5210.

[7] Raval, M., Bhardwaj, S., Aravelli, A., Dofe, J., & Gohel, H. (2021). Intelligent energy optimisation for massive IoT using artificial intelligence. Internet of Things, 13, 100354.

[8] Ma, Y., Chen, X., Wang, L., & Yang, J. (2021). Study on smart home energy management system based on artificial intelligence. *Journal of Sensors, 2021*(1), 9101453.

[9] Kwon, K., Lee, S., & Kim, S. (2021). AI-based home energy management system considering energy efficiency and resident satisfaction. IEEE Internet of Things Journal, 9(2), 1608-1621.

[10] Dini, P., Diana, L., Elhanashi, A., & Saponara, S. (2024). Overview of AI models and tools in embedded IoT applications. Electronics, 13(12), 2322.

[11] Doshi, M., & Varghese, A. (2022). Smart agriculture using renewable energy and AI-powered IoT. In AI, edge and IoT-based smart agriculture (pp. 205-225). Academic Press.

[12] Kumar, A., Sharma, J., Goel, M., Kumar, M., & Chaudhary, V. (2024, November). The intelligent power optimisation for sensor-based wearable IoT devices using AI-based deep learning. In 2024 International Conference on IoT, Communication and Automation Technology (ICICAT) (pp. 17-22). IEEE.

Chapter 8

[1] Sanjuan, E. B., Cardiel, I. A., Cerrada, J. A., & Cerrada, C. (2020). Message queuing telemetry transport (MQTT) security: A cryptographic smart card approach. IEEE Access, 8, 115051-115062.

[2] Rafique, S. H., Abdallah, A., Alhosani, S. A., & Jamil, N. (2025). A Review of AMQP Protocol: Characteristics, Security Challenges and Proposed Enhancement. *JOIV: International Journal on Informatics Visualization*, 9(3), 1283-1297.

[3] Palmese, F., Redondi, A. E., & Cesana, M. (2022). Adaptive quality of service control for mqtt-sn. *Sensors, 22*(22), 8852.

[4] Lakshminarayana, S., Praseed, A., & Thilagam, P. S. (2024). Securing the IoT application layer from an MQTT protocol perspective: Challenges and research prospects. *IEEE Communications Surveys & Tutorials, 26*(4), 2510-2546.

[5] Syed, N. F. (2020). IoT-MQTT based denial of service attack modelling and detection. Thesis of Edith Cowan University, Australia

[6] Ester, A. (2025). *Implementace víceformátového mock serveru v jazyce Kotlin* (Master's thesis, České vysoké učení technické v Praze. Vypočetní a informační centrum.).

[7] bin Uzayr, S. (2022). *Kotlin: The Ultimate Guide*. CRC Press.

[8] Sobral, V. A. L., Saoda, N., Shah, R., Wang, W., & Campbell, B. (2022, October). RetroIoT: retrofitting internet of things deployments by hiding data in battery readings. In *Proceedings of the 28th Annual International Conference on Mobile Computing And Networking* (pp. 69-81).

[9] Ibaseta, D., García, A., Álvarez, M., Garzón, B., Díez, F., Coca, P., ... & Molleda, J. (2021). Monitoring and control of energy consumption in buildings using WoT: A novel approach for smart retrofit. *Sustainable Cities and Society, 65*, 102637.

[10] Durkop, L., Czybik, B., & Jasperneite, J. (2015, February). Performance evaluation of M2M protocols over cellular networks in a lab environment. In 2015 18th international conference on Intelligence in Next Generation Networks (pp. 70-75). IEEE.

[11] Bayılmış, C., Ebleme, M. A., Çavuşoğlu, Ü., Küçük, K., & Sevin, A. (2022). A survey on communication protocols and performance evaluations for Internet of Things. Digital Communications and Networks, 8(6), 1094-1104.

[12] Dizdarević, J., Carpio, F., Jukan, A., & Masip-Bruin, X. (2019). A survey of communication protocols for internet of things and related challenges of fog and cloud computing integration. ACM Computing Surveys (CSUR), 51(6), 1-29.

[13] Iqbal, F., Gohar, M., Karamti, H., Karamti, W., Koh, S. J., & Choi, J. G. (2023). Use of QUIC for AMQP in IoT networks. Computer Networks, 225, 109640.

[14] Alzahrani, A., Alshahrani, S., & Alotaibi, F. (2023). Performance Evaluation of QUIC-based Messaging for AMQP in IoT Networks. *Journal of King Saud University - Computer and Information Sciences.* `https://doi.org/10.1016/j.jksuci.2023.102253`

[15] C Cleland, G., Wu, D., Ullah, R., & Varghese, B. (2022, December). FedComm: Understanding communication protocols for edge-based federated learning. In 2022 IEEE/ACM 15th International Conference on Utility and Cloud Computing (UCC) (pp. 71-81). IEEE.

[16] Satamraju, V. (2023). *A Comparison of AMQP and MQTT Protocols for Internet of Things.* ResearchGate. https://www.researchgate.net/publication/339759697_A_comparison_of_AMQP_and_MQTT_protocols_for_Internet_of_Things

[17] Kotak, J., Shah, A., Shah, A., & Rajdev, P. (2019, March). A comparative analysis on security of MQTT brokers. In 2nd Smart Cities Symposium (SCS 2019) (pp. 1-5). IET.

[18] Longo, E., Redondi, A. E., Cesana, M., Arcia-Moret, A., & Manzoni, P. (2020, June). Mqtt-st: a spanning tree protocol for distributed mqtt brokers. In ICC 2020-2020 IEEE International Conference on Communications (ICC) (pp. 1-6). IEEE.

[19] G Giambona, R., Redondi, A. E., & Cesana, M. (2018, October). Mqtt+ enhanced syntax and broker functionalities for data filtering, processing and aggregation. In Proceedings of the 14th ACM International Symposium on QoS and Security for Wireless and Mobile Networks (pp. 77-84).

[20] Ali-Pour, M., & Gascon-Samson, J. (2025). *SDFLMQ: A Semi-Decentralized Federated Learning Framework Using MQTT for Edge-Clustered IoT Systems.* arXiv preprint arXiv:2503.13624. https://arxiv.org/abs/2503.13624

[21] Pandey, B., Farulla, G. A., Indaco, M., Iovino, L., & Prinetto, P. (2019). Design and review of water management system using ethernet, Wi-Fi 802.11n, modbus, and other communication standards. *Wireless Personal Communications, 106*(4), 1677-1699. https://doi.org/10.1007/s11277-018-5380-7

[22] Pandey, B. K. (2019). *Design of training environment: An emulator of water supply system in Turin node of Italian Cyber Ranges* (Doctoral dissertation, Gran Sasso Science Institute, Italy). https://iris.gssi.it/handle/20.500.12571/9724

[23] Khanna, A., Das, B., Pandey, B., Hussain, D. M. A., & Jain, V. (2016). A discussion about upgrading the quick script platform to create natural language based IoT systems. *Indian Journal of Science and Technology, 9*(46), Article 106917. https://indjst.org/articles/a-discussion-about-upgrading-the-quick-script-platform-to-create-natural-language-based-iot-systems

Chapter 9

[1] Albreem, Mahmoud A., et al. "Green Internet of Things (GIoT): applications, practices, awareness, and challenges." IEEE Access 9 (2021): 38833-38858.

[2] Alsharif, Mohammed H., et al. "Green IoT: A review and future research directions." Symmetry 15.3 (2023): 757.

[3] Sukjaimuk, Rungrot, Quang Ngoc Nguyen, and Takuro Sato. "A smart congestion control mechanism for the green IoT sensor-enabled information-centric networking." Sensors 18.9 (2018): 2889.

[4] Suarez, Luis, Loutfi Nuaymi, and Jean-Marie Bonnin. "An overview and classification of research approaches in green wireless networks." Eurasip journal on wireless communications and networking 2012 (2012): 1-18.

[5] Alsharif, Mohammed H. "Techno-economic evaluation of a stand-alone power system based on solar/battery for a base station of global system mobile communication." Energies 10.3 (2017): 392.

[6] Yang, Zhai, et al. "Green internet of things and big data application in smart cities development." Complexity 2021.1 (2021): 4922697.

[7] Memić, Belma, Adisa Hasković Džubur, and Elma Avdagić-Golub. "Green IoT: sustainability environment and technologies." Science, Engineering and Technology 2.1 (2022): 24-29.

[8] Dalal, Sandeep. "Futuristic investigative study of IoT/Green IoT as a driving force for sustainable development." Indian J. Sci. Technol 14.8 (2021): 738-751.

[9] Fraga-Lamas, Paula, Sérgio Ivan Lopes, and Tiago M. Fernández-Caramés. "Green IoT and edge AI as key technological enablers for a sustainable digital transition towards a smart circular economy: An industry 5.0 use case." Sensors 21.17 (2021): 5745.

[10] Almalki, Faris A., et al. "Green IoT for eco-friendly and sustainable smart cities: future directions and opportunities." Mobile Networks and Applications 28.1 (2023): 178-202.

[11] Saini, Lalit Mohan, et al. "KubeEdge for Scalable IoT Applications." 2024 7th International Conference on Contemporary Computing and Informatics (IC3I). Vol. 7. IEEE, 2024.

[12] Aggarwal, Vaishali, et al. "CleanComm: A Hybrid ACO-WOA-MOA Model for Sustainable Communication." 2024 IEEE 4th International Conference on ICT in Business Industry & Government (ICTBIG). IEEE, 2024.

[13] Ajmani, Prerna, et al. "Patient behaviour analysis and social health predictions through IoMT." 2022 10th international conference on reliability, infocom technologies and optimization (trends and future directions)(ICRITO). IEEE, 2022.

[14] Wang, Dayu, Daojun Zhong, and Alireza Souri. "Energy management solutions in the Internet of Things applications: Technical analysis and new research directions." Cognitive Systems Research 67 (2021): 33-49.

[15] Heidari, Arash, et al. "A green, secure, and deep intelligent method for dynamic IoT-edge-cloud offloading scenarios." Sustainable Computing: Informatics and Systems 38 (2023): 100859.

[16] Popli, Sakshi, Rakesh Kumar Jha, and Sanjeev Jain. "Green IoT: A short survey on technical evolution & techniques." Wireless Personal Communications (2022): 1-29.

[17] Singh, Ramanjeet, and Amit Jain. "A study of various energy efficiency techniques in green IoT." 2021 3rd International Conference on Advances in Computing, Communication Control and Networking (ICAC3N). IEEE, 2021.

[18] Zhu, Sha, Kaoru Ota, and Mianxiong Dong. "Green AI for IIoT: Energy efficient intelligent edge computing for industrial internet of things." IEEE Transactions on Green Communications and Networking 6.1 (2021): 79-88.

[19] Narsimhulu, Pallati, et al. "An intelligent fl-based vehicle route optimization protocol for green and sustainable iot connected iov." Internet of Things 27 (2024): 101240.

[20] Sinha, Mudita, et al. "Energy-Efficient smart cities with green Internet of things." Green technological innovation for sustainable smart societies: post pandemic Era (2021): 345-361.

[21] Ajmani, Prerna, Neeta Singh, and Poonam Verma. "Internet of vehicles taxonomy and evaluation: architectures, protocols, and issues." 2022 5th International Conference on Contemporary Computing and Informatics (IC3I). IEEE, 2022.

[22] Sharma, Vandana, Prerna Ajmani, and Celestine Iwendi. "Blockchain Application with Specific Reference to Smart Contracts in the Insurance Sector." The Application of Emerging Technology and Blockchain in the Insurance Industry. River Publishers, 2024. 179-208.

Chapter 10

[1] Usama, Muhammad, and Melike Erol-Kantarci. "A survey on recent trends and open issues in energy efficiency of 5G." Sensors 19.14 (2019): 3126.

[2] Behera, Trupti Mayee, et al. "Energy-efficient routing protocols for wireless sensor networks: Architectures, strategies, and performance." Electronics 11.15 (2022): 2282.

[3] Al-Obaidi, Karam M., et al. "A review of using IoT for energy efficient buildings and cities: A built environment perspective." Energies 15.16 (2022): 5991.

[4] Miraz, Mahdi H., et al. "Internet of nano-things, things and everything: future growth trends." Future Internet 10.8 (2018): 68.

[5] Almuhaya, Mukarram AM, et al. "A survey on Lorawan technology: Recent trends, opportunities, simulation tools and future directions." Electronics 11.1 (2022): 164.

[6] Malik, Usman Mahmood, et al. "Energy-efficient fog computing for 6G-enabled massive IoT: Recent trends and future opportunities." IEEE Internet of Things Journal 9.16 (2021): 14572-14594.

[7] Mahmood, Aamir, et al. "Industrial IoT in 5G-and-beyond networks: Vision, architecture, and design trends." IEEE Transactions on Industrial Informatics 18.6 (2021): 4122-4137.

[8] Alahi, Md Eshrat E., et al. "Integration of IoT-enabled technologies and artificial intelligence (AI) for smart city scenario: recent advancements and future trends." Sensors 23.11 (2023): 5206.

[9] Almuhaya, Mukarram AM, et al. "A survey on Lorawan technology: Recent trends, opportunities, simulation tools and future directions." Electronics 11.1 (2022): 164.

[10] Li, Shan, Muddesar Iqbal, and Neetesh Saxena. "Future industry internet of things with zero-trust security." Information Systems Frontiers 26.5 (2024): 1653-1666.

[11] Quy, Vu Khanh, et al. "IoT-enabled smart agriculture: architecture, applications, and challenges." Applied Sciences 12.7 (2022): 3396.

[12] Qadir, Zakria, et al. "Towards 6G Internet of Things: Recent advances, use cases, and open challenges." ICT express 9.3 (2023): 296-312.

[13] Maraveas, Chrysanthos, et al. "Applications of IoT for optimized greenhouse environment and resources management." Computers and Electronics in Agriculture 198 (2022): 106993.

[14] Osama, Manar, et al. "Internet of medical things and healthcare 4.0: Trends, requirements, challenges, and research directions." Sensors 23.17 (2023): 7435.

[15] Kashani, Mostafa Haghi, et al. "A systematic review of IoT in healthcare: Applications, techniques, and trends." Journal of Network and Computer Applications 192 (2021): 103164.

[16] Sanislav, Teodora, et al. "Energy harvesting techniques for internet of things (IoT)." IEEE access 9 (2021): 39530-39549.

[17] Albreem, Mahmoud A., et al. "Green Internet of Things (GIoT): applications, practices, awareness, and challenges." IEEE Access 9 (2021): 38833-38858.

[18] Guo, Fengxian, et al. "Enabling massive IoT toward 6G: A comprehensive survey." IEEE Internet of Things Journal 8.15 (2021): 11891-11915.

[19] Li, Wei, et al. "A comprehensive survey on machine learning-based big data analytics for IoT-enabled smart healthcare system." Mobile networks and applications 26 (2021): 234-252.

[20] Zhang, Tuo, et al. "Federated learning for the internet of things: Applications, challenges, and opportunities." IEEE Internet of Things Magazine 5.1 (2022): 24-29.

[21] Ajmani, Prerna, Neeta Singh, and Poonam Verma. "Internet of vehicles taxonomy and evaluation: architectures, protocols, and issues." 2022 5th International Conference on Contemporary Computing and Informatics (IC3I). IEEE, 2022.

[22] Sharma, Vandana, et al., eds. Wireless Communication Technologies: Roles, Responsibilities, and Impact of IoT, 6G, and Blockchain Practices. CRC Press, 2024.

[23] Chadha, Anmol, et al. "Adoption as a Population Stabilization Strategy in India: A Predictive Modeling Approach." 2024 IEEE 4th International Conference on ICT in Business Industry & Government (ICTBIG). IEEE, 2024.

[24] Aggarwal, Vaishali, et al. "CleanComm: A Hybrid ACO-WOA-MOA Model for Sustainable Communication." 2024 IEEE 4th International Conference on ICT in Business Industry & Government (ICTBIG). IEEE, 2024.

[25] Sharma, Vandana, Prerna Ajmani, and Celestine Iwendi. "Blockchain Application with Specific Reference to Smart Contracts in the Insurance Sector." The Application of Emerging Technology and Blockchain in the Insurance Industry. River Publishers, 2024. 179-208.

[26] Garg, Sheena, et al. "An extensive review and comparison of different machine learning algorithms for customer behaviour pattern analysis." 2023 10th IEEE Uttar Pradesh Section International Conference on Electrical, Electronics and Computer Engineering (UPCON). Vol. 10. IEEE, 2023.

[27] Gupta, Kartavya, et al. "Integrating LLM with CNN-RNN for Optimizing Crop Production." 2024 International Conference on Intelligent & Innovative Practices in Engineering & Management (IIPEM). IEEE, 2024.

[28] Saini, Lalit Mohan, et al. "KubeEdge for Scalable IoT Applications." 2024 7th International Conference on Contemporary Computing and Informatics (IC3I). Vol. 7. IEEE, 2024.

Chapter 11

[1] Kaur, Manjit, et al. "Secure and energy efficient-based E-health care framework for green internet of things." IEEE Transactions on Green Communications and Networking 5.3 (2021): 1223-1231.

[2] Li, Xingwang, et al. "Physical layer security of cognitive ambient backscatter communications for green Internet-of-Things." IEEE Transactions on Green Communications and Networking 5.3 (2021): 1066-1076.

[3] Ahmed, Imran, et al. "A blockchain-and artificial intelligence-enabled smart IoT framework for sustainable city." International Journal of Intelligent Systems 37.9 (2022): 6493-6507.

[4] Zikria, Yousaf Bin, et al. "Next-generation internet of things (iot): Opportunities, challenges, and solutions." Sensors 21.4 (2021): 1174.

[5] Singh, Prashant, et al. "Internet of Things for sustainable railway transportation: Past, present, and future." Cleaner Logistics and Supply Chain 4 (2022): 100065.

[6] Shahid, Jahanzeb, et al. "Data protection and privacy of the internet of healthcare things (IoHTs)." Applied Sciences 12.4 (2022): 1927.

[7] Saxena, Shivam, Bharat Bhushan, and Mohd Abdul Ahad. "Blockchain based solutions to secure IoT: Background, integration trends and a way forward." Journal of Network and Computer Applications 181 (2021): 103050.

[8] Ferrag, Mohamed Amine, and Lei Shu. "The performance evaluation of blockchain-based security and privacy systems for the Internet of Things: A tutorial." IEEE Internet of Things Journal 8.24 (2021): 17236-17260.

[9] Gerodimos, Apostolos, et al. "IoT: Communication protocols and security threats." Internet of Things and Cyber-Physical Systems 3 (2023): 1-13.

[10] Abdulmalek, Suliman, et al. "IoT-based healthcare-monitoring system towards improving quality of life: A review." Healthcare. Vol. 10. No. 10. MDPI, 2022.

[11] Thabit, Fursan, et al. "Cryptography algorithms for enhancing IoT security." Internet of Things 22 (2023): 100759.

[12] Mao, Bomin, et al. "Security and privacy on 6G network edge: A survey." IEEE communications surveys & tutorials 25.2 (2023): 1095-1127.

[13] Porambage, Pawani, et al. "The roadmap to 6G security and privacy." IEEE Open Journal of the Communications Society 2 (2021): 1094-1122.

[14] Hireche, Rachida, Houssem Mansouri, and Al-Sakib Khan Pathan. "Security and privacy management in Internet of Medical Things (IoMT): A synthesis." Journal of cybersecurity and privacy 2.3 (2022): 640-661.

[15] Ruan, Zhengping. "Blockchain technology for security issues and challenges in IoT." 2023 International Conference on Computer Simulation and Modeling, Information Security (CSMIS). IEEE, 2023.

[16] Ajmani, Prerna, et al. "Machine learning and deep learning techniques for breast cancer detection using ultrasound imaging." Computational Intelligence and Modelling Techniques for Disease Detection in Mammogram Images. Academic Press, 2024. 235-257.

[17] Sharma, Vandana, Prerna Ajmani, and Celestine Iwendi. "Blockchain Application with Specific Reference to Smart Contracts in the Insurance Sector." The Application of Emerging Technology and Blockchain in the Insurance Industry. River Publishers, 2024. 179-208.

[18] Garg, Sheena, et al. "An extensive review and comparison of different machine learning algorithms for customer behaviour pattern analysis." 2023 10th IEEE Uttar Pradesh Section International

Conference on Electrical, Electronics and Computer Engineering (UPCON). Vol. 10. IEEE, 2023.

[19] Gupta, Kartavya, et al. "Integrating LLM with CNN-RNN for Optimizing Crop Production." 2024 International Conference on Intelligent & Innovative Practices in Engineering & Management (IIPEM). IEEE, 2024.

[20] Saini, Lalit Mohan, et al. "KubeEdge for Scalable IoT Applications." 2024 7th International Conference on Contemporary Computing and Informatics (IC3I). Vol. 7. IEEE, 2024.

Chapter 12

[1] Pandey, B., et al. (2023). Evaluation of soft computing in intrusion detection for secure social Internet of Things based on collaborative edge computing. *Soft Computing*. `https://doi.org/10.1007/s00500-023-08397-1`

[2] Pandey, B., Farulla, G. A., Indaco, M., Iovino, L., & Prinetto, P. (2019). Design and review of a water management system utilizing Ethernet, Wi-Fi 802.11n, Modbus, and other communication standards. *Wireless Personal Communications, 106*(7), 1677–1699. `https://doi.org/10.1007/s11277-018-5380-7`

[3] Pandey, B. K. (2019). *Design of Training Environment: An Emulator of Water Supply System in Turin Node of Italian Cyber Ranges* (PhD thesis). Gran Sasso Science Institute. https://iris.gssi.it/handle/20.500.12571/9724

[4] Hasan, M. K., Pandey, B., & Gohel, H. (2021). Internet of Things-based smart electricity monitoring and control system using usage data. *Wireless Communications and Mobile Computing.* https://doi.org/10.1155/2021/6544649

[5] Hasan, M. K., Shafiq, M., Islam, S., Pandey, B., El-Ebiary, Y. A. B., Nafi, N. S., Rodriguez, C., & Vargas, D. E. (2021). Lightweight cryptographic algorithms for guessing attack protection in complex Internet of Things applications. *Complexity.* https://doi.org/10.1155/2021/5540296

[6] Bittencourt, L., Immich, R., Sakellariou, R., Fonseca, N., Madeira, E., Curado, M., ... & Rana, O. (2018). The Internet of Things, Fog, and Cloud Continuum: Integration and Challenges. *Internet of Things, 3,* 134-155.

[7] Dastjerdi, A. V., Gupta, H., Calheiros, R. N., Ghosh, S. K., & Buyya, R. (2016). Fog computing: Principles, architectures, and applications. In *Internet of Things* (pp. 61-75). Morgan Kaufmann.

[8] Prieto, J. (2018). *IoT Approaches for Distributed Computing. Wireless Communications and Mobile Computing,* 2018, Article 9741053.

[9] Thiruchadai Pandeeswari, S., Padmavathi, S., & Hemamalini, N. (2020). *Engineering Full Stack IoT Systems with Distributed Processing Architecture—Software Engineering Challenges, Architectures and Tools*. In *A Journey Towards Bio-inspired Techniques in Software Engineering* (Vol. 185, pp. 71–87). Springer.

[10] Hamdan, S., Ayyash, M., & Almajali, S. (2020). *Edge-computing architectures for Internet of Things applications: A survey. Sensors, 20(22), 6441.*

[11] Boulogeorgos, A. A. A., Diamantoulakis, P. D., & Karagiannidis, G. K. (2016). Low power wide area networks (LPWANs) for Internet of Things (IoT) applications: Research challenges and future trends. *arXiv preprint arXiv:1611.07449.*

[12] Jouhari, M., Saeed, N., Alouini, M. S., & Amhoud, E. M. (2023). A survey on scalable LoRaWAN for massive IoT: Recent advances, potentials, and challenges. *IEEE Communications Surveys & Tutorials, 25*(3), 1841-1876.

[13] Jiang, X., Zhang, H., Yi, E. A. B., Raghunathan, N., Mousoulis, C., Chaterji, S., ... & Bagchi, S. (2020). Hybrid low-power wide-area mesh network for IoT applications. *IEEE Internet of Things Journal, 8*(2), 901-915.

[14] Nuthalapati, A. (2023). *Building scalable data lakes for Internet of Things (IoT) data management. Educational Administration: Theory and Practice, 29*(1), 412–424.

[15] Dang-Ha, T. H., Roverso, D., & Olsson, R. (2017, February). Graph of virtual actors (gova): A big data analytics architecture for IoT. In *2017 IEEE International Conference on Big Data and Smart Computing (BigComp)* (pp. 162-169). IEEE.

[16] Nguyen, D. C., Ding, M., Pathirana, P. N., Seneviratne, A., Li, J., & Poor, H. V. (2021). Federated learning for Internet of Things: A comprehensive survey. *IEEE Communications Surveys & Tutorials, 23*(3), 1622-1658.

[17] Liu, C., Tan, R., Wu, Y., Feng, Y., Jin, Z., Zhang, F., ... & Liu, Q. (2024). Dissecting Zero Trust: Research Landscape and Its Implementation in IoT. *Cybersecurity, 7*(1), 20.

[18] Putra, G. D., Dedeoglu, V., Kanhere, S. S., Jurdak, R., & Ignjatovic, A. (2021). Trust-based blockchain authorization for IoT. *IEEE Transactions on Network and Service Management, 18*(2), 1646-1658.

[19] Dhelim, S., Aung, N., Kechadi, M. T., Ning, H., Chen, L., & Lakas, A. (2022). Trust2Vec: Large-scale IoT trust management system based on signed network embeddings. *IEEE Internet of Things Journal, 10*(1), 553-562.

Index

A

Access control, 155
Active contour model (ACM), 69, 70
Actuating and processing units (APUs), 81
Actuator nodes, 103
Adaptive AI, 17, 18
Adaptive authentication mechanisms, 369, 370
Adaptive routing techniques, 34
Adaptive security frameworks, 342
Adaptive transmission, 48
Ad hoc networks, 106
Advanced IoT network design
    AMQP, 184, 185
    applications, 177
    benefits, 182
    features, 179
    future enhancements, 188
    integration, 188
    layer, 183
    MQTT, 178, 186, 187
    retrofitting, 178
    tech stack suggestion, 182, 183
    water supply system and NLP-based device control, 187
Advanced message queuing protocol (AMQP), 177, 178, 184–186
African wildlife conservation project, 15
AI-based energy-management systems, 17
AI-based HEMS (AI-HEMS), 174
AI-driven energy optimization, 45, 51
AI-driven power management, 279, 280
Anonymization, 369
Ant colony optimization (ACO), 272
Application layer, 157
Artificial intelligence (AI), 267
Artificial neural network (ANN), 170
Associativity layer, 156
Attribute-based access control (ABAC), 350
Autoencoder (AE) model, 170

B

Backscatter communications, 270
Big data, 27, 192

Dr. D. Sharma and Dr. B. Pandey, *Eco-Networking for IoT*,
https://doi.org/10.1007/979-8-8688-2317-6

Biodegradable electronics, 389
Blockchain-based authentication models (BasIoT), 269
Blockchain-based food supply chain, 241
Blockchain technology, 8, 284–286, 302, 322, 341, 351, 363
Bluetooth low energy (BLE), 15, 117–119
Building automation LLN (BA-LLN), 105
Building management system (BMS), 105

C

California Consumer Privacy Act (CCPA), 357, 365
Carbon dioxide (CO_2) emissions, 200, 201
Carbon footprint, 200
Cellular networks, 269
Climate change, 201, 336
Cloud computing, 100, 210, 211, 270, 321
Cloud layer, 80
Cluster-based communication *vs.* traditional routing, 106, 107
Cluster heads (CHs), 107
Cognitive ambient backscatter communication (C-AmBC), 321
Cognitive radio-based routing, 44
Cognitive radio networks (CRNs), 44, 50, 270
Collaboration/process layer, 157
Collaborative learning, 295
Communication methodologies, 181
Communication protocols, 62, 153
Compressed sensing methods, 369
Compression techniques, 107
Confidentiality, 155
Constrained application protocol (CoAP), 74
Contemporary networking, 64
Context-based authentication mechanisms, 378
Corporate social responsibility (CSR), 203
COVID-19 pandemic, 271
Cryptographic algorithms, 323, 351, 384
Cryptographic methods, 367
Cyber-physical systems (CPS), 94, 187, 389
Cyberthreats, 318

D

Data abstraction layer, 157
Data accumulation layer, 156–157
Data aggregation techniques, 353
Data fusion, 107
Data management
  access control and security, 160
  APIs, 156–157

BI systems, 154
domains, 164
filtering and aggregation, 158, 159
interoperability and integration, 161, 162
querying and analytics, 160, 161
smart grids, 155
storage, 159
techniques, 153
Data-placement strategies, 385
Data privacy, 345, 365
Decentralization, 363
Decentralized ledger system, 284
Decentralized security models, 370, 371
Decentralized systems, 65
Deep learning (DL), 88, 167, 323
Deep reinforcement learning (DRL), 175
Device-to-device (D2D) communication, 50
Dielectric permittivity, 75
Differential privacy, 362, 369
Digital twins, 8, 389
Directed acyclic graphs (DAGs), 376
Disaster management, 313
case studies, 247–250
definition, 244
future trends, 250–252
role of, 245–247
Disruptive IoT applications, 271
Distributed computing, 385, 386
Distributed ledger technology (DLT), 351, 370
Distributed systems, 58
Duty cycling mechanisms, 281, 282
Dynamic frequency scaling (DVFS), 88
Dynamic network adaptation, 39
Dynamic resource allocation, 25
Dynamic voltage scaling, 88

E

Earthquake early warning system, 249, 250
Edge computing, 47, 66, 91, 93, 167, 192, 210, 211, 263, 277–279, 302, 379, 382, 385
Edge (fog) computing layer, 156
Electronic waste (e-waste), 212
challenges, 211
environmental and health impacts, 199
green IoT strategies, 200
scale, 199
strategies, 212
Elliptic curve cryptography (ECC), 368
Energy-aware geographic routing (EAGR), 42
Energy-aware link mapping, 38
Energy-aware routing, 49
Energy consumption
environment impact, 198
green IoT solutions, 198
IoT networks, 198

Energy distribution systems, 219, 220, 243
Energy efficiency
  definition, 205
  medical systems, 215, 216
  principles, 205
  techniques, 206
Energy-efficient communication protocols, 282, 284, 316
Energy-efficient ethernet (EEE), 56
Energy-efficient IOT networking
  adoption, 316
  advantages, 296
    automated energy distribution and predictive maintenance, 294
    data processing, 295
    decentralized method, 295
    environmental impact, 298
    extended device lifespan, 296, 297
    improved network efficiency, 297
    reliability and stability, 298
    remote and harsh environments, 299
    resource utilization, 300
    scalability, 299
    security and low-power communication, 300, 301
    solar and thermal energy, 294
  applications, 266, 267
    environmental monitoring and disaster management, 313
    healthcare and remote patient monitoring, 310, 311
    home automation and smart buildings, 314
    smart agriculture and precision farming, 311
    smart cities, 310
    smart energy management and power grids, 312
    smart manufacturing and industrial automation, 311
    smart transportation and logistics, 313
    water management and smart irrigation, 315, 316
    wearable technology and personal IoT, 314
  blockchain, 284–286
  challenges, 288
    data transmission and processing overhead, 290, 291
    data transmission efficiency, 287
    environmental impact and sustainable energy sources, 292, 293
    large-scale deployments, 286
    latency and real-time processing, 293, 294

power consumption and battery life, 288, 289
scalability and network management, 289, 290
standardization and interoperability, 291, 292
sustainable energy, 287
disadvantages, 303, 304
balancing computational demands, 302
data transmission and processing capabilities, 304
device reliability, 301
energy harvesting, 307
high initial deployment costs, 305
large-scale deployments, 306, 307
low-power constraints, 306
network management and maintenance, 305
standardization and compatibility issues, 308
literature review, 267–272
methods, 266
routing protocols, 267
and sustainability (*see* Sustainable IoT solutions)
usage, 309
Energy-efficient networking
challenges and opportunities
battery constraints, 54, 55
computational and data processing, 57, 58
IoT network proliferation, 54
network infrastructure requirements, 56, 57
sustainable system design, 58–60
communication protocols, 65
concepts, 22
future of, 61–63
networking research, 23–26
pillars of, 65
principles, 66
smart industrial and urban environments, 51–53
stability and dependability, 26–28
strategies, 45–51
VNE, 36–40
workload distribution, 63
Energy-efficient routing techniques, 41–45
Energy harvesting, 97, 383
Energy-harvesting methods, 16
Energy-harvesting technologies, 65, 267, 270, 276, 277, 307, 342
Energy-LEACH (E-LEACH), 114
Energy monitoring reports, 326
Energy-saving techniques, 267
Environmental monitoring systems, 192
Environmental stewardship, 20
Environmental sustainability, 280
Ethos-U55, 86
European stakeholders, 23

Extended producer responsibility (EPR), 203
Extensible access control markup Language (XACML), 160
Extensible Markup Language (XML), 156

F

Fairphone, 235, 236
Federated learning (FL), 8, 92, 167, 176, 271, 295, 303, 341, 363, 375, 383
Ferroelectric random-access memory (FRAM), 94
Field programmable gate arrays (FPGAs), 71
Firmware, 347
Flood management systems, 247, 248
Fog computing, 35, 63, 66, 268, 382, 385
  characteristics
    context awareness, 31
    data security and privacy, 31
    energy efficiency, 32
    interoperability and flexibility, 33
    latency-critical applications, 33, 34
    localized data processing, 30
    low latency, 29
    mobility, 32
    reduced network bandwidth, 31
    scalability, 30
  definition, 28
  idleness-based services, 29
Foundation layer, 156
FreeRTOS, 95

G

Gateway, 182, 184
General Data Protection Regulation (GDPR), 342, 357, 365
Genetic algorithm-based hardware optimization, 97
Google's Project Ara, 236, 237
Graph of virtual actors (GOVA), 387
GraphQL, 160, 161
Green cloud computing, 50
Greenhouse effect, 201
Green IoT (GIoT), 271
  adoption, 322
  advantages, 227–230
  applications, 213, 328
    agricultural sector, 326
    data-driven insights, 327
    energy-efficient smart homes, 330–332
    healthcare, 215, 216
    healthcare solutions, 332–334
    industrial automation and manufacturing, 218, 219

intelligent transportation systems, 327, 334–335
renewable energy management and smart grids, 219, 220
smart agriculture, 214, 215
smart cities, 213, 214
smart grids, 325, 328–330
smart homes, 216, 217
telemedicine, 326
transportation systems, 217, 218
case studies, 336–340, 354
challenges, 221–224, 244
cloud and edge computing, 210, 211
CO_2 emissions, 200, 201
cyberattacks and data breaches, 320
data stewardship practices, 319
disadvantages, 230–235
disaster management, 244–252
energy consumption, 189, 317
energy efficiency, 205, 206
e-waste, 199, 200, 211, 212
finite natural resources and raw material depletion, 201, 202
future research, 354, 375–377
future trends, 224–226, 244
goal, 190
high-energy consumption, 198–199
importance, 197
large-scale deployment, 317
limitations, 318
literature review, 191–192, 321–324
low-power communication protocols, 210
mitigation, 367–375
modular and recyclable IoT devices, 235–239
opportunities
biodegradable electronics, 261
circular economy, 261
edge computing, 263
energy harvesting, 260
energy optimization, 260
low-power communication protocols, 262
sustainable urban development, 262
principles, 189
privacy, 318, 323
applications, 363, 364
challenges, 356, 358–360, 366
constant data flow, 356
data protection and energy-efficiency, 357
future research, 365, 366
innovative services, 356
preserving techniques, 362, 363
regulation compliance, 364, 365
requirements, 360–362

Green IoT (GIoT) (*cont.*)
- privacy considerations, 320
- problems, 317
- quantum computing, 252–260
- renewable energy integration, 208, 209
- research opportunities, 340–343
- resource efficiency, 324
- security, 320, 323
  - challenges, 344–347, 355–356
  - requirements, 348–350
  - solutions, 350–353
- smart energy management, 209
- supply chains, 239–244
- sustainable development, 203, 204
- sustainable IoT hardware, 207, 208
- sustainable materials, 319

Green networking, 3
- *See also* Internet of Things (IoT)

Green resource allocation, 38

Green wireless networks, 191

H

Hardware optimization
- adoption and scalability, 96
- definition, 83
- edge computing, 91, 93
- future of, 96
- IoT middleware and OS, 95
- memory and storage, 93
- power communication modules, 90, 91
- RAM design, 85
- resources, 84–88
- security, 94, 95
- sensor, network, service and application layer, 87
- strategies, 83
- techniques, 86
- traditional RAM architectures, 97
- ultra low power controllers, 88, 89

Hardware security modules (HSMs), 94

Healthcare 4.0, 270

Healthcare IoT (HIoT), 270

Heterogeneous systems, 164

Holographic beamforming, 270

Home energy management system (HEMS), 169, 173

Homomorphic encryption, 362, 368

Hybrid communication architectures, 386

Hyperparameter tuning, 93

I

IKEA's TRÅDFRI smart lighting, 238, 239

Industrial IoT (IIoT), 6, 15, 76, 77, 174, 187, 269

Information-centric networking (ICN), 190

Intelligent sleep modes, 18, 19

Intelligent transportation systems (ITS), 52
Internet of Agricultural Things (IoAT), 78
Internet of Arctic Things (IoAT), 78
Internet of Battle Things (IoBT), 78
Internet of Energy cyber-physical systems, 28
Internet of Everything (IoE), 266, 268, 270
Internet of Healthcare Things (IoHT), 79, 80, 322
Internet of Maritime Things (IoMT), 78
Internet of Medical Things (IoMT), 323
Internet of Nano-Things (IoNT), 266, 268
Internet of Remote Things (IoRT), 78
Internet of Satellite/Space Things (IoST), 78
Internet of Things (IoT), 99
  algorithms, 8
  applications, 4
  case studies, 14, 15
  challenges, 11–12
  components, 5, 6
  development, 268
  energy-aware routing protocols, 3
  energy efficiency, 2
  examples, 7
  hardware, 153
  importance, 9
  information management techniques, 154
  layers, 156, 157
  networking technologies, 13–14
  overview, 5–6
  protocols, 12–13
  role of, 10–11
  transformative concept, 2
Internet of Underground Things (IoUT), 78
Internet of Underwater Things (IoUwT), 78
Internet of Vehicles (IoV), 271
Intrusion detection, 384
Intrusion detection and prevention systems (IDPS), 352
IoT energy efficient techniques
  ACM, 69, 70
  agriculture, 75, 76
  components, 67
  emerging technologies, 82
  Fog-cloud computing, 79, 81
  IIoT, 76
  issues, 81
  networks, 81, 82
  object-tracking mechanism, 69
  parameters, 76
  power consumption, 71
  RAM memory design, 71, 72
  6G era, 78, 79
  smart cities, 72–75
  topology, 67
  user interface, 68
Irrigation system, 75

J

JSON schema, 162

K

Key-value pair, 162
Kinetic energy harvesting, 276
Knowledge distillation, 92
Ktor, 177–180
KubeEdge, 272, 324

L

Land Transport Authority, 14
Large-scale IoT networks
  cluster-based models, 382
  communication protocols, 383
  coordination, 381
  device and identity management platforms, 383
  distributed computing and network architectures, 385, 386
  scalable approaches, 381
  scalable data handling and analytics, 386, 387
  security, privacy and trust, 387, 388
LEACH-centralized (LEACH-C), 114
LEACH-fixed (LEACH-F), 114
License management, 155
Lightweight block ciphers, 368
Load-balanced energy routing (LBER), 43
Long range (LoRa), 127–129
Long-range low-power protocols, 126–137
Long-range wide-area network (LoRaWAN), 266, 268
LoRaWAN, 14
Low-energy adaptive clustering hierarchy (LEACH)
  advantages, 109–111
  applications, 115
  cluster-based communication *vs.* traditional routing, 106, 107
  definition, 106
  limitations, 111–114
  variants, 114, 115
  working mechanism, 107, 108
Lower-power communication protocols
  advantages, 143–146
  applications, 140–143
  developments, 99
  disadvantages, 147–150
  evaluation, 151
  factors, 152
  importance, 147
  issues, 100
  LEACH protocol, 106–115
  routing efficiency, 152
  routing requirements, 100–106

types, 116
long-range, 126–137
medium-range, 137–139
short-range, 117–126
Low-power and lossy networks (LLNs), 105
Low-power communication protocols, 210
Low-power communication technologies, 267
Low-power hardware, 25
Low-power wide-area networks (LPWANs), 266, 269, 275, 276, 382
Low-power wireless personal area network (LoWPAN), 99
LTE-M (LTE Cat-M1), 135–137

M

Machine learning (ML), 17, 18, 45, 167, 267, 323
Magneto resistive random access memory (MRAM), 94
Medium-range low-power protocols, 137–139
Message authentication codes (MACs), 349
Message queuing telemetry transport (MQTT), 75, 156, 177, 178, 186, 187
Microsensors, 106
Microservices, 179
Middleware layer, 184
Minimum energy routing (MER), 42
Mitigation strategies, 367
adaptive authentication mechanisms, 369, 370
automated firmware updates, 372, 373
collaboration and standardization, 373
cryptography, 367
data aggregation, 368, 369
decentralized security models, 370, 371
description, 367
dynamic risk assessment, 372
incident response and recovery planning, 374, 375
security by design, 371
user awareness and training, 373, 374
ML4IoT framework, 155
Mobile ad hoc networks (MANETs), 42
Mobile networks, 190
Model optimization methods, 93
Moth flame optimization (MFO), 272
Motion sensing units (MSUs), 81
Multi-factor authentication (MFA), 349
Multipath energy-efficient routing, 44
Multi-tier frameworks, 382

N

Name-value pair, 162
Narrowband IoT (NB-IoT), 132–134, 181
Network architectures, 385, 386
Network function virtualization (NFV), 39, 40, 383
Networking research, 23–26
Network integration, 302
Network layer, 154, 183
Network modeling, 268
Network slicing, 376
Network virtualization, 48
Network vulnerabilities, 346
NLP-based device control, 187
Node-based IoT region, 90
Noninvariants, 387
Non-terrestrial networks (NTNs), 62, 79
Non-volatile memories (NVMs), 93

O

Online trip planning, 26
Opportunistic routing (OR), 43
Over-the-air technology (OTA), 32

P

Perception layer, 154, 183
Personal area networks (PANs), 181
Personally identifiable information (PII), 320
Phase-change random access memory (PRAM), 94
Physical hardware/controllers layer, 156
Physically unclonable functions (PUFs), 94
Physical threats, 346, 347
Policy administration point (PAP), 160
Policy decision point (PDP), 160
Policy enforcement points (PEPs), 160
Power-aware node mapping, 38
Power-aware routing (PAR), 42
Power dissipation, 68
Power generation (PG), 169
Power management
    battery-powered and remote applications, 167
    dual-layer adaptive control mechanism, 168
    energy optimization, 172, 173
    energy units and terminology, 172, 173
    factors, 170, 171
    implementation
        conventional methods, 175
        IIoT, 174
        smart agriculture, 174
        smart homes, 173, 174
        wearables, 175
    intelligent irrigation sensor network, 168
    methodology, 169, 171

optimization techniques, 169
sectors, 168
sensors, 170
Power optimization strategies, 34
Power-saving techniques, 210
Practical Byzantine fault tolerance (PBFT), 285
Predictive analytics, 61, 379
Privacy impact assessments (PIAs), 342
Privacy violations, 318
Probability theory, 90
Proof of authority (PoA), 376
Proof-of-stake (PoS), 285
Proof-of-work (PoW), 285
Pseudonymization, 369

Q

Quality of service (QoS), 179, 180
Quality of service 1 (QoS 1), 180
Quality of service 2 (QoS 2), 180
Quantum computing, 340, 376
applications, 254–256
challenges, 257, 258
future trends, 258, 259
integration, 252
role of, 253, 254
Quantum resistant cryptography, 376
Quantum-resistant encryption algorithms, 340
Quick script integrated development environment (QS IDE), 72, 73

R

Railway systems, 322
Rare earth metals, 202
Reinforcement learning (RL), 167
Renewable energy, 208, 209, 338–340
Representational State Transfer (REST), 156
Resilient distributed dataset (RDD), 161
Resistive random access memory (ReRAM), 94
Resource allocation, 34, 63
Resource-constrained IoT devices, 295
Resource constraints, 344, 345
Retrofit, 177–179, 181, 184
Role based access control (RBAC), 349
Routers, 103, 104
Routing schemes, 19, 20

S

Secure multi-party computation (SMPC), 363, 369
Secure routing protocols, 352
Security by design, 371
Self-healing systems, 165

Self-sustaining energy, 16
Self-sustaining sensors, 389
Sensing layer, 154, 183
Sensor nodes, 102, 106, 113
Short-range low-power protocols, 117–126
Siemens' sustainable sensors, 237
Sigfox, 129, 131, 132
Simple Object Access Protocol (SOAP), 156
Sixth-generation (6G) networks, 28, 51–53, 379
Sleep and wake mechanisms, 49
Sleep mode techniques, 281, 282
Sleep-wake scheduling-based routing, 43
Small and medium-sized businesses (SMEs), 301
Smart adaptive power management (SmartAPM), 175
Smart agriculture, 174, 275
Smart city lighting systems, 336–338
Smart contracts
  energy-efficient, 241–243
  energy waste, 240, 241
Smart energy management, 192, 209
Smart grid integration, 316
Smart homes, 173, 174
Smart routing schemes, 19
Smart traffic management, 14
Smart wildfire detection, 248, 249
Software-defined networking (SDN), 25, 39, 40, 376, 382–383, 388
Software vulnerabilities, 347
Soil moisture sensor, 75
Solar energy harvesting, 276
Spatial aggregation, 158
Static power-management techniques, 170
STMicroelectronics, 88
Storage management, 159, 164
Suicide devices, 318
Supervised learning, 375
Sustainability, 68, 191, 324
Sustainable development, 192, 203, 204
Sustainable IoT hardware, 207, 208
Sustainable IoT solutions
  AI-driven power management, 279, 280
  edge computing, 277–279
  energy-efficient communication protocols, 273, 282, 284
  energy-harvesting techniques, 276, 277
  LPWAN, 275, 276
  next-generation networks, 274
  power consumption, 273
  sectors, 272
  sleep mode and duty cycling mechanisms, 281, 282
Sustainable networked systems, 4
Sustainable networking ecosystem, 26

T

Task offloading, 52
Techno-economic analysis, 191
Telecommunication systems, 266
Temperature compensation (TC), 88
Temporal aggregation, 158
Thread, 124–126
Time division multiple access (TDMA), 108
TinyML, 8, 86
TinyOS, 95
TradeLens, 242, 243
Traditional cryptography, 95
Traffic-aware routing, 24
Traffic management systems, 327
Transportation systems, 217, 218
Trust-based blockchain authorization, 387
Trusted execution environment and blockchain-supported data sharing (TEBDS) architecture, 94
Trusted execution environments (TEE), 94

U

United Nation Sustainable Development Goals (UN SDG), 82
Unmanned Aerial Vehicles (UAVs), 80
Unsupervised learning, 375
Urban environments, 213
Urban LLN (U-LLN)
  applications, 101
  considerations, 104, 106
  device types, 101
    actuator nodes, 103
    routers, 103, 104
    sensor nodes, 102
  routing specifications, 101

V

Vice cluster head LEACH (V-LEACH), 114
Virtualization technologies, 24, 46
Virtual network embedding (VNE), 36–40
Virtual network resources (VNRs), 38

W, X, Y

Water supply system, 187, 384
Wearables, 175
Whale optimization algorithm (WOA), 272
Wi-Fi HaLow (IEEE 802.11ah), 138, 139
Wildlife trafficking, 80
Wireless charging, 18
Wireless communication, 27, 34
Wireless sensor networks (WSNs), 35, 42, 99, 100, 152, 266, 267, 270
Wireless technology, 271

Z

Zephyr, 95
Zero energy, 16, 17
Zero-trust security architectures, 269
Zero-trust security
framework, 387
Zigbee, 119–121, 181
Z-wave, 122–124